Medieval Dress and Fashion

MEDIEVAL
Dress & Fashion

Margaret Scott

The British Library

In memoriam Mariae, felis optimae, a.d. vii Id. Feb. MMIII

Acknowledgements

It is a pleasure to acknowledge here the debts I owe to many people. First of all, I have to thank the staff of the British Library – my endlessly patient editors Lara Speicher and Trish Burgess, and their associates Kathy Houghton, Kate Hampson and Charlotte Lochhead, as well as the people who tirelessly produced actual manuscripts in the Manuscripts Room at the British Library. Various others helped in an assortment of ways, which they may not realise that they did. These include my former students Francesca Middleton, Helen Miles, Domniki Papadimitriou, Anoushka Der Sarkissian, Lara Rayburn and Miren Arzalluz, and my former colleagues Georgia Clarke, John Lowden, Janet Nelson, and especially Aileen Ribeiro. Robert Gibbs, Thomas Kren, Scot McKendrick, Catherine Reynolds and Timothy Wilson helped with specifically manuscript-related problems. Outside the academic world I have to thank my late parents, Jean and Charles Scott, for never questioning my decision to study dead languages; my mother-in-law, Marjorie Avery, for taking charge of the cats; my friend Moira Knox for providing years of unfailing hospitality in London; and my husband Jeff Avery for his unceasing efforts to ensure that my life runs smoothly.

Contents

Introduction

THE ILLUMINATED MANUSCRIPT IS AN INCOMPARABLE RESOURCE
for studying the dress of the Middle Ages, since it encompasses people of all classes,
in all sorts of situation, and from all sorts of angle. With so little clothing surviving
from the period, the illuminated manuscript becomes even more important as a
means of showing us not just what people wore, but how they wanted to look in
their clothing (which can be two very different things). But illuminated manuscripts
are not just a store of information on the past – they are also extraordinary works of
art with their own conventions, and these conventions have to be understood before
the works can be fully appreciated. One of the main aims of this book is to show the
reader how, with care, manuscripts can be 'read' through dress.

    Until around 1100 the copying of existing images was common practice;
therefore images may contain distortions or misunderstandings of the dress of
earlier periods. Before the fourteenth century elaborate textile patterns were
frequently excluded from western European illuminations when clothing was being
depicted, and patterns tended to act as backgrounds to scenes. Perhaps the size of
the images made it difficult to depict with reasonable accuracy the details of
patterned textiles on various parts of garments. To understand as fully as possible
what was actually being worn, one has also to work with contemporary documents.
Of the documents, the most objective are the seemingly humdrum records kept by
the clerks responsible for recording the spending on fabrics by great households.
The least objective are probably diatribes by moralists, who had a professional
interest in ensuring that the 'problems' of fashion were talked of in the most lurid
terms possible.

Today, dress and fashion are often synonymous. With items of working-class or functional clothing, such as workmen's jeans or sportswear, finding their way into the wardrobes of those who use neither garment for its original purpose, and with haute couture designs rapidly being translated into affordable versions for the mass market, there is often little idea that there could be a difference in meaning between the terms. In the Middle Ages, however, when dress did evolve into something approaching the modern idea of fashion, a quest for the new and sometimes outrageous in clothing, it was the preserve, by cost and by law, of the upper classes. 'Novelty' is the term first and most frequently used in the twelfth century to describe what was being sought; 'fashion' is, strictly speaking, a word taken from the sixteenth-century phrase 'of the new fashion', used to describe the way in which something was made. Although some access to 'fashion' was granted to the favoured among the merchant and professional classes, for everyone else there were just clothes – that is, dress as opposed to fashion. This book looks mostly at the garments of the upper classes, where 'fashion' evolved; but it considers, too, the dress of the rest of society.

In many of the images looked at in this book, dress, fashionable or not, is used to help narrate stories or to indicate moral or social standing. Evidence survives in a few cases to demonstrate that artists were issued with clear instructions by scribes or authors about the contents of the scenes they were to paint, with the clothing sometimes being included in the instructions. Sometimes there were clothing conventions to be followed with particular people, such as biblical figures. More often there is no indication why the artist proceeded as he (usually he) did. The quest for information on fashionable dress is on safest ground when it reaches images of those who commissioned the manuscripts.

The words 'medieval' and 'illuminated' are often used together when manuscripts are being talked of. This book covers the period c.840 to c.1570; this is not everyone's definition of the medieval period, but it is the period in which illuminated manuscripts can be used as crucial sources for information on dress. The definition of the term 'medieval', like that of so many terms, is fraught with difficulties, as boundaries that ought to define are fluid. Art historians have argued that the medieval period starts in AD 800, with the revival of the title of 'emperor in western Europe' for Charlemagne. The same people would see the fifteenth century in Italy as being definitely Renaissance because of the interest in the literature and architecture of antiquity. For fifteenth-century Italians 'medieval' meant everything between themselves and the collapse of the old Roman Empire in the West in AD 476. Italian manuscripts from the fifteenth century find a place in this book because in that period Italian towns were very busy legislating about the wearing of clothing and textiles, making exceptions to the laws for persons of power or wealth and their families. This hierarchical view of society is basically medieval, as is the mechanism used to sustain it, the sumptuary law. The illuminated manuscript, along with great cathedrals and castles, is so much part of today's image of the Middle Ages that I feel justified in including sixteenth-century examples in this book – I do not feel any more constrained by terminology than do people in other fields.

Clothing styles can rarely be equated sensibly with the architectural styles against which they were worn – clothing changes faster than buildings, and it is quite impossible to see any link between solid Romanesque churches and the clothing worn during the period of their construction (c.1050–c.1200). The division of the book by centuries, either alone or in groups, does not reflect the sequences of changes in fashion, or the length of time a particular fashion existed; but as clothing styles have no convenient names, such as 'Gothic', division by century is as neat and convenient a method as any. The first and last chapters of this book are shorter than the others because there is less material to discuss; in a way they are prologue and epilogue to the main body of evidence that can be garnered from illuminated manuscripts.

Recently, it has become fashionable to look at dress through the often separate lenses of theories on gender, the body and material culture. Remarkably, many of those practising these theories have shown little interest in what dress actually looked like, and they have tended to dismiss any attempt to discuss visual material as old-fashioned and concerned only with rising and falling hemlines. The 'archaeological' approach, of looking at objects, has gone out of fashion, in favour of neo-puritanical abstractions. But dress is an inescapably material object that has to be looked at in conjunction with the documentary sources with which many theorists feel more comfortable. It takes time and effort to understand not just the structure of dress in visual sources, but what it meant to contemporaries who saw clothing depicted. With something as glorious as the illuminated manuscript to use as a textbook, the effort can be immensely pleasurable.

I

Dressing the Great and the Good
c.840–c.1100

I OPPOSITE
Clothing was first invented in the
Garden of Eden, as soon as man
lost his innocence, and it
remained a worry for
ecclesiastical and civil authorities
thereafter. On the less elevated
level of the dress historian,
translations of dress terms can
be problematic. The Bible, in
Latin, uses the Greek word
perizomata for the garments
Adam and Eve made for
themselves; God made them
tunicas (a Latin word). The *King
James Bible* calls them respectively
'aprons' and 'coats'. Today the
first term would be translated as
'loincloths' or 'belts', and the
second as 'tunics'.
(*Moutier-Grandval Bible*, Tours,
834–43: British Library, Add. MS
10546, f. 5v)

THIS INTRODUCTORY CHAPTER DEALS WITH DRESS IN THE PERIOD
between the middle of the ninth century and the end of the eleventh century. At the
start of this period valuable visual and documentary information began to appear in
western Europe; this coincided with a return to the creation of sacred imagery, after
over a century of prohibition of such works, in the eastern part of Christendom. The
production of illuminated manuscripts was chiefly dedicated to sacred texts, for both
ecclesiastical and lay patrons. Much of what can be learned about dress from these
visual sources, and from contemporary documentary sources, almost inevitably
concerns those who were great, good, and sometimes both.

Politically, the period saw the existence of two rival empires, both claiming
to be the Roman Empire. The heirs to the eastern half of the ancient Roman Empire,
reduced to little more than the Balkans and present-day Turkey, had their seat in the
former Greek city of Byzantium, later named Constantinople (and even later
Istanbul). Today their culture is called Byzantine; although they called themselves
Romans, they spoke Greek and their culture was Christian. Their dress was an
amalgam of survivals from ancient Greek and Roman times, with a steadily
increasing admixture of garments and textile designs from their non-Christian
Middle Eastern neighbours.

At the start of this period the only 'barbarians' for whom the Byzantines
had any respect were the Franks, who controlled much of western Europe; their
rulers, since the coronation of Charlemagne by the pope in 800, had also been
alled Roman emperors. (The Franks of this period are usually described today as
Carolingians.) The language of the educated elite was Latin, and the clothing of

the Franks was an amalgam of the simple clothing shapes of ancient Rome, such as sleeved, T-shaped tunics, and leg-coverings and furs that came from their own 'barbarian' past.

Family squabbles over who ruled where were frequent and detrimental to the Carolingian Empire, and invading Norsemen were able to sack Paris in 861. The control of southern Italy was often contested with the Byzantines. In 911 Norsemen settled in what became Normandy, bringing to an end Viking raids. In the years of disorder the power base of the western empire had been gradually slipping towards Germany. With it went the *Codex Aureus of St Emmeram* showing Charles the Bald (fig. 3), and visions of imperial majesty (compare fig. 6). The German king Otto was crowned Holy Roman emperor in Rome by the pope in 962. Otto and his successors oversaw a revival of classical learning, often from Carolingian sources, which lent prestige to images of the latest family of western emperors. Rome itself remained of paramount importance to the German emperors, with their coronations usually taking place there. The books illuminated within the German Empire, and the clothing they illustrate, are the most lavish of their time in western Europe.

Anglo-Saxon England also produced manuscripts of some merit, but the artists' style, depending more on drawing than on painting, offered less scope for colour and interesting details of dress and textiles. England suffered a series of invasions, from peoples of Scandinavian origin, and in 1066 the Anglo-Saxon royal line was swept away by the Norman William the Conqueror. Although the Normans were impressed by the embroidery skills of their new subjects, they displayed little interest in encouraging their production of illuminated manuscripts, and little of note was produced in England for the rest of the eleventh century. In the meantime, other Normans had invaded Sicily, in 1061; they completed their conquest of the island in 1091.

Documentary sources for the whole period are rare in comparison with later centuries. A few wealthy people mentioned their clothing in wills, but not often in sufficient detail to help with identifying garments in the visual sources; women seem to have been more likely than men to receive or leave clothing and textiles within the family. Often there is most to be learned about secular clothing from the strictures against it emanating from the Church.

For most people clothing derived from two fibres – linen for under-clothing (shirts for both sexes, underpants for men) and wool for outer clothing, much of it made at home. Quality and colour of material, and social class were linked. The very rich could import silks, through the agency of Italian merchants, from the Byzantine Empire, or from Islamic areas of the Mediterranean, which included southern Spain and Sicily. Possibly less luxurious silks were woven in Greece from the eleventh century onwards; it was from Greece that the Sicilian Normans abducted silk workers in 1147. Silk slowly worked its way down the social ladder, stopping short, by law and by economic reality, of the working classes. The warming of the climate in Europe between the ninth and twelfth centuries perhaps helped fuel a demand for lighter fabrics, such as some of the silks, and possibly also led to a change in the type of lining used in clothing. Fur is rarely seen in this early period, though documentary sources from late tenth-century France and from eleventh-century Italy indicate that by then even some churchmen were refusing to wear sheepskins and lambskins, preferring instead to wear extremely expensive imported, and less bulky, furs, such as sable, marten and fox.

This study of dress through medieval illuminated manuscripts begins at what the Middle Ages believed was the beginning of human existence, and of clothing, in the Garden of Eden (fig. 1). According to the Bible, God himself created the first outer clothes, from animal skins, for Adam and Eve when they were driven from Eden. Clothes were part of the proof of man's (and especially woman's) fallen state. The Bible says nothing about what God and his angels wore in Eden, but the artist of this great Carolingian bible, made 834–43 at Tours, dressed them in clothing derived from that worn by the early Christians. Biblical figures are often shown dressed as they are here, following a well-established tradition. God's white tunic, with its vertical stripes from shoulder to hem, derived from the tunics of the late Roman world, of which many examples are still to be found in archaeological museums. The rectangular cloak, wrapped diagonally across the front of the body, was also part of the tradition. It derived from the Greek cloak, called the *himation* by its original Greek wearers, and the *pallium* by those Romans who took to wearing it. The latter adopted it either because they found it relatively easy to wear in comparison with the much more complex *toga* of the Roman citizen, or because, as Christians, they disdained to wear the distinguishing garment of the Roman, pagan oppressor. Because Carolingian artists often relied on late antique images as sources for their own work, they could quite successfully re-create dress that was no longer worn; but later artists, copying what were themselves copies (the copying of

2 LEFT TOP

Moses expounds the Law to the Israelites, watched by Joshua. Joshua wears Carolingian dress; the Israelites wear 'biblical' dress, with Carolingian sock-like garments; and Moses wears full 'biblical' dress, complete with sandals.
(*The Moutier-Grandval Bible*, Tours, 834–43: British Library, Add. MS 10546, f. 25v, detail)

3 LEFT BOTTOM

Charles the Bald wears one of the less lavishly bejewelled outfits seen on Carolingian rulers. The cover of this manuscript is also bejewelled. The limited means available to cut gemstones make them seem, to modern eyes, crude and heavy, but they create an undeniably lavish appearance.
(*Codex Aureus of St Emmeram*, West Francia, c.870: Munich, Bayerische Staatsbibliothek, Clm. 14000, f. 5v, detail)

4 OPPOSITE

Charles the Bald and his wife (Irmintrude, d. 869?, or Richildis, m. 870?). Carolingian women seem to have worn long veils-cum-mantles; two tunics, the outer one with loose sleeves; and, as jewellery, bracelets and earrings.
(*Bible of San Paolo fuori le Mura*, or *San Callisto Bible*, West Francia, Reims?, 866–75: Rome, Church of San Paolo fuori le Mura, f. 1r. © Istituto Poligrafico e Zecca dello Stato)

existing manuscripts was important in the period c.600–c.1100), often failed to understand the layers and construction, and turned these garments into unconvincing exercises in pattern and colour (as in figs 7 and 11).

It would be an oversimplification to claim that a link across time would have been forged for a Carolingian viewer who saw his remote ancestors, Adam and Eve, wearing the kind of tunic that he himself habitually wore. The gold edging to these tunics is totally inappropriate to the life of hardship that the guilty couple is about to embark on: according to Thegan, writing his *Life* of the emperor Louis the Pious in 836, even Louis wore gold-decorated clothing only on important occasions. The presence of the edging here is part of the desire to make the book impressive and glorious, not part of a desire to produce a 'realistic' image. Real Carolingian male dress had two strands to it (see figs 3 and 4): sleeved tunics and loose cloaks, requiring relatively little tailoring; and long leg-coverings, requiring rather more tailoring. The outfit of rectangular cloak, short T-shaped tunic and leg-coverings formed the basis of male dress in western Europe until around 1100.

Much effort was expended by the Carolingians in portraying themselves not just as the legitimate political and cultural successors of the late Roman (Christian) Empire, but also as the Chosen People of their day, with their kings being equated to Old Testament kings. The reign of Charlemagne's son Louis (814–40) saw the concentration of efforts to create imperial images, which involved the production of bibles, psalters and prayer books. These books offer the earliest surviving royal portraits (apart from coin images) after Roman times, in otherwise sacred texts, among or in images that stress the Franks' perception of themselves as the new Chosen People and as the successors of (Christian) Rome. The rulers, as far as can be determined, wore rich versions of contemporary dress. Charles the Bald (king of the western Franks 840–77 and emperor 875–7) appears in bejewelled clothing in a variety of sacred texts (for instance, figs 3 and 4).

Ostentation was the privilege, and the duty, of princes; and the aristocracy did what they could to emulate them, as is shown by the will of Charles the Bald's sister Gisela and her husband Eberhard, Count of Friuli, drawn up in 863 or 864. They left to their eldest son, Unroch, a mantle decorated with gold, with a golden brooch (*fibula*), and a garment of some kind (a *vestitum*) decorated with gold, and to their next son, Berengar, another *vestitum*, also decorated with gold. This kind of bequest may also suggest that clothing styles were not expected to change so rapidly as to make the clothing unfashionable when it eventually passed from one generation to the next.

Charles the Bald and one of his wives appear in the *San Paolo Bible* (also known as the *San Callisto Bible*), which seems to have been taken to Rome by Charles at the time of his imperial coronation there in 875 (fig. 4). Clothing was a woman's special province. Instructions for the management of the estates of Charles's grandfather, Charlemagne, show that the women who lived on them had been expected to produce linen and woollen cloth, and even to dye the wool. Even Carolingian queens were not exempt from the duty of providing clothing. According to John Scottus Eriugena (c.810–77), Charles's wife Irmintrude (cr. 866, d. 869) made her husband's clothes shine with gold threads (presumably in embroidery), and she covered them with jewels. (Charles's half-brother, the Emperor Lothar (r. 840–55). appears in jewel-covered clothing in the *Lothar Psalter*, BL Add. MS 37768, f. 4.) As embroidery tends to be reserved for one-off types of decoration, the repeated pattern on Charles's tunic and on his wife's veil suggests a woven silk fabric, which was almost certainly imported from the Byzantine Empire.

Despite the difference in fabrics, Charles and his bodyguards are united in wearing clothing cut in the Frankish style. Indeed the tenor of other images in this bible reinforces the idea of Frankishness, and the widely held belief that the Franks were the new Chosen People. The scene of Moses expounding the Law to the Israelites shares the same composition as the corresponding scene in the *Moutier-Grandval Bible* (fig. 2), but whereas in that manuscript the Israelites wear 'biblical' dress, in the *San Paolo Bible* they wear Frankish dress.

The hostile chronicler of the *Annales Fuldenses* (*Annals of Fulda*, composed at Fulda Abbey and recording events in the eastern kingdom of the Franks) talks of changes in Charles's behaviour after his return to Francia following his coronation in Rome. Charles now despised the ways of Frankish kings and thought Greek (that is, Byzantine) glories the best. The first of the changes that the annalist mentions is to do with clothing – and this would have been the most immediately obvious sign. Charles would go to church on Sundays and feast days (sometimes even hearing Mass according to the Greek rite) with his head wrapped in a silk veil on top of which he placed a diadem, and in an ankle-length dalmatic with a belt on top hanging to his feet. The dalmatic was a church vestment; perhaps Charles was wearing it in recognition of the declaration by Pope Paul I (757–67) that the Franks

5 ABOVE

St Helena, mother of Constantine the Great (sole emperor 324–37) is dressed much as the empress Irene was at the end of her coronation in 768, to judge by an account written by the emperor Constantine VII. The bodyguards (centre) wear typical Byzantine tunics, with decorated shoulders and hems.

(*Homilies of Gregory of Nazianzos*, 'The Paris Gregory', Constantinople?, 879–83: Paris, Bibliothèque Nationale, MS gr. 510, f. 440r, detail)

6 OPPOSITE

An Ottonian emperor receives tribute from four provinces, personified as four women. Both the eastern and western emperors styled themselves 'kings of the Romans'; Otto II and Otto III promoted themselves as rivals to, and replacements for, the Byzantine emperors. As a result, the western emperor has abandoned the short tunic of the previous century, and adopted a longer tunic, resembling the grand Byzantine imperial tunic (the *divetesion*). The cloak, however, has the rectangular shape of western cloaks, not the curved lower edge of the Byzantine *chlamys*.

(Fragment of *Registrum Gregorii*, Trier, Master of the *Registrum Gregorii*, c.983: Chantilly, France, Musée Condé, MS 14 bis. © Photo RMN-Ojeda)

were a holy tribe and a royal priesthood. The veil, however, was almost certainly an emulation of Byzantine practice, not otherwise adopted in the West. When two dogs were taken from the King of Italy in 927 to Constantinople as a gift for the Byzantine emperor Romanos I, they had to be prevented from biting their new owner because of his strange clothes and covered face. The long belt could have been an attempt to emulate the Byzantine imperial garment called a *loros* (see fig. 13). The importance of the link between western Christianity and Frankish dress would seem to be stressed by Notker the Stammerer's account of the annual baptisms of northern pagans at the court of Charles's father, Louis the Pious – after baptism they would receive white clothes to symbolize their rebirth, and precious clothes, and weapons, in the Frankish manner.

Notker saw Charles the Bald's nephew Charles the Fat (emperor 881–7) in 883, and has left a description of that emperor's appearance that is difficult to make sense of; and no textual emendations have been suggested that would clarify the matter. Notker describes Charles the Fat as gleaming, with two golden-petalled flowers coming out of his thighs. The first flower was as tall as Charles himself, and the second grew gradually upwards, decorating the top of his body, and protecting him as he walked along. In fig. 3, from a manuscript made for Charles the Bald around 870, flowers sprout from cornucopias held by the personifications of the regions of Francia and Gotica. The origins of these two female figures lie in the fourth century, in a register of the officials of the late Roman Empire known as the *Notitia Dignitatum*. It included personifications of Roman provinces – crowned women carrying the tribute of their provinces. Perhaps the cornucopias were what Charles the Fat was trying to re-create on his own person. This second Charles, however, was almost totally ineffectual as a ruler; and, as has been said above, such western imperial power as was left shifted into the eastern part of the empire, Germania, which adopted and adapted Carolingian ruler imagery and Byzantine dress (figs 6 and 10).

The Byzantine Empire had, for the court circle, an extremely elaborate set of clothing rules concerning who wore what and when. The garments of the courtiers formed blocks of colour around the emperor, according to the status of their wearers and the events of the ceremonial year. Quite a lot can be learned about how dress operated as a marker of rank at the Byzantine court from a work called the *Kletorologion* (*Treatise on Invitations to Banquets*), finished in 899 by Philotheos, and based on his experience in arranging the seating at imperial banquets according to precedence, which clothing would have indicated.

In fig. 5 the beardless attendants of St Helena (the mother of Constantine the Great, the first Christian emperor), in short white tunics, are probably eunuch bodyguards. Of the eight ranks of eunuchs mentioned in the *Kletorologion*, a group called the protospatharians (first sword-bearers) ranked sixth. One of their garments was a white, gold-worked *chiton* (an ancient Greek word for a tunic-like garment). An important survival from antiquity was the Greek *chlamys*, a cloak with a curved lower edge. It was particularly important as part of the emperor's coronation regalia, when it seems to have been purple, with a gold *tablion* (a decorative panel) set at about chest height on its side edges both front and back (compare fig. 14). The empress might wear a *chlamys*, because she too could wield considerable power, but it was essentially a male garment.

Clothing could form part of the salaries of high Byzantine officials, and silks were even part of a diplomatic row. In Constantinople in 950 Liutprand of Cremona, on a diplomatic mission for the Regent of Italy, witnessed Constantine VII distributing to his senior officials and courtiers tunics called *skaramangia*, which were woven and sewn in the palace's silk workshop. (The *skaramangion* seems to have been originally a Persian garment.) On his second visit to the city, towards 970, seeking the hand of a Byzantine bride for the heir of the emperor Otto I, Liutprand was granted imperial permission to buy fabrics for church use. They, and items given to him, later became part of a diplomatic wrangle when he said that the proposed marriage would not take place. Possibly to justify their actions, court eunuchs told him that the emperor could never have imagined that he would presume to buy such expensive materials, and confiscated five pieces of very costly *purpuras* that he had bought, and even what he had been given. (*Purpura* seems to have been high-quality silk cloth, possibly shiny, and not necessarily purple in colour.) Perhaps he had unwittingly broken the silk industry's extremely complex regulations on the buying and selling of silk between natives and foreigners, contained in *The Book of the Eparch* (drawn up in 911 or 912). The matter of these fabrics and the differences between western and Byzantine dress loomed large in Liutprand's subsequent anger.

Liutprand disliked the long sleeves and the ankle-length tunics worn by the Greeks, as well as their long hair, their brooches and their head-coverings. He told the eunuchs who had confiscated his silks that the fabrics they thought so highly of

7 OPPOSITE

King Edgar presents a charter to Christ, watched by the Virgin and St Peter. The king wears a typical, short Anglo-Saxon tunic, with wrinkled lower sleeves, a gold-edged mantle and bandage-like wrappings over his leggings. Christ and the angels wear traditional, but illogically constructed, 'biblical' dress. St Peter, with book and key, is also traditionally clad. The Virgin Mary is dressed as an Anglo-Saxon woman.
(*New Minster Charter*, Winchester, 966–84: British Library, Cotton Vespasian MS A VIII, f. 2v)

8 LEFT

King Cnut and Queen Aelfgyfu receive heavenly sanction for their rule. Cnut seems to have jewelled garters. There is a hint of a jewelled circlet beneath the queen's veil, though the angel appears to be trying to cover her with another veil, to complement Cnut's crown. The Virgin Mary (top left) is more fashionably dressed than the queen because the Virgin's outer sleeves are wider than the queen's.
(*Liber Vitae*, Winchester, c.1020–30: British Library, Stowe MS 944, f. 6r)

were worn in the West by prostitutes and conjurors. This was most unlikely to have been the truth, as in Liutprand's own lifetime gold-embellished silks formed part of the trousseau of the sister of Duke William I of Normandy, thus indicating the social group that did wear such fabrics in the West. Byzantine fabrics were also imported to the West for use in churches as vestments and relic-covers; even secular garments made of silks were sometimes donated to churches to be made into ecclesiastical vestments and ornaments. As a result, most surviving Byzantine silks are to be found not in the eastern Mediterranean, where silks were used in secular clothing and therefore wore out, but in western Europe, preserved in church treasuries.

Finally, Theophano, a granddaughter of Constantine VII, was sent to the West to marry Otto I's son in Rome in 972, with the marriage contract being written against a background mimicking Byzantine textile designs. Carolingian ruler imagery, late antique art as filtered through Carolingian culture, and Byzantine court dress can be seen, in manuscripts, to have added to the image of the Ottonian rulers. Charles the Bald initiated compositional aspects of this imperial portraiture, but we have no visual record of his adoption of Byzantine dress forms. In fig. 6 we have, around 983, a later western emperor, Otto II (d. 983) or Otto III (the husband or son of Theophano), whose tunic, with its decoration of gold bands and side split at the hem, is clearly indebted to Byzantine dress (compare fig. 5). The cloak's lower edge, however, seems to be straight, in the western style, rather than curved in the Byzantine style. Approaching Otto are four personifications of the western empire (reworked from the women in fig. 3), representing (from left to right) Germania, Francia, Italia and Alamania. Despite their supposedly different origins, their clothing is basically identical – and obviously German because of the decorative bands on the outer tunics and the very long veils (compare figs 10 and 11).

After the opulent dress found in German manuscripts, the dress shown in Anglo-Saxon manuscripts seems much less interesting, since the rulers are depicted in much simpler and probably more everyday dress. The more linear quality of Anglo-Saxon images perhaps helped militate against the depiction of elaborate textiles, whose presence could have overburdened, and possibly destroyed, the composition of a figure. Anglo-Saxon women were famed across western Europe for their embroidery skills, and it is therefore extremely frustrating that the style of illumination chosen for Anglo-Saxon manuscripts leaves little or no room for depictions of this beyond a hint in gold edgings to garments. Well before the

9

Ostentation throws off her finery as she prepares to flee from the Virtues. Relying too heavily on an image as a precise reflection of its time can be problematic because texts and pictures can fail to match up. The text with this image calls for wreaths and gold at the figure's head and neck. None of these is depicted. (Prudentius, *Psychomachia*, southern England, late 900s: British Library, Add. MS 24199, f. 21v, detail)

Norman Conquest in 1066 Anglo-Saxons across a wide social range were documented as wearing rich clothing.

The relatively plain-looking clothing worn in figs 7 and 8 by King Edgar (r. 959–75) and by King Cnut (r. 1016–35 in England) fails to convey the splendour indicated in documentary evidence. Edgar, for instance, is known to have donated to the church at Ely, where it was made into a vestment, a *purpura* cloak into which so much gold had been woven that the cloak looked like armour. The kings here are identified as kings only by the presence of their crowns. Anglo-Saxon men seem to have dressed very much in the way that the Carolingians had dressed, except for the crinkling of their lower sleeves and their hose. Some men seem to wear a form of bandaging over their leg-coverings, like extended garters. The gold band around Edgar's upper arm may be one of the armlets that William of Malmesbury (who began writing shortly before 1118) says Anglo-Saxon men had worn, or else decoration vaguely reminiscent of that seen in fig. 6.

Anglo-Saxon women were more or less shrouded in their clothes, with a large veil, or even a kind of hood, around the head, and two tunics (an outer one, apparently called a *cyrtel*, and an under one, the name of which is not known). The under-tunic's sleeves often seem to be too long and, as a result, are corrugated (perhaps semi-permanently pleated, as with modern cheesecloth) on the forearm. Documents from pre-Conquest England refer to jewellery, such as brooches and necklaces, which cannot be seen on Anglo-Saxon women in manuscripts, where their appearances must be classified as public, and therefore requiring their almost total swathing. The Church could invoke the instruction of St Paul to women to cover their heads; but St Paul was simply reflecting an ideal that had existed long before his day.

The British Library has a number of manuscripts of Prudentius's *Psychomachia* (battle for the soul between the Vices and the Virtues), a text written in the second half of the fourth century AD. Scenes representing vices (as in fig. 51) are often able to indicate what was considered questionable about then-current clothing practices; and one would hope that the personification of Ostentation (*Pompa*) in fig. 9 would fall into that useful category. However, Prudentius's text, written in a world in which women wore and displayed expensive jewellery, seems all but impossible for an illuminator – used to swathed Anglo-Saxon women – to illustrate in the late 900s. The text tells us that, as she is attacked by the Virtues, 'Ostentation, the displayer of

10 OPPOSITE

The emperor Henry III and the empress Agnes are crowned by Christ. Henry's clothing for his coronation in Rome in 1046 was probably even more elaborate than that shown here: according to an anonymous work, written around 1030 and known as the *Book of the Golden City of Rome*, the emperor should have in his regalia golden footwear decorated with lions, dragons and eagles made of jewels. He was also to have a flame-coloured (*diarodina*) dalmatic decorated with eagles of gold and pearls at the back and the front, and 365 little bells of gold. In Exodus the clothing prescribed for the priest Aaron includes bells as decoration. The Latin–German 'dictionary' known as the *Summarium Heinrici*, of *c.*1007–32, says the dalmatic was a priestly garment. The contemporary Investiture Controversy dealt with the extent to which the emperor could involve himself in ecclesiastical affairs. Putting on the already Christian priestly dalmatic, with bells to give it connotations of Old Testament priesthood, was presumably a way of declaring that the emperor saw himself as fully qualified to be as involved as he wished.
(*Uppsala Gospels* [*Codex Caesareus*], Echternach, 1043–50: Uppsala University Library, MS C 93, f. 3v)

11 ABOVE

The Archangel Gabriel announces to the Virgin Mary that she will give birth to Christ. The archangel's *pallium* has degenerated into an incomprehensible muddle of folds. For the continuing breakdown in understanding of the *pallium* in the next century, see fig. 25. The veil worn by the Virgin suggests that, at this date, unmarried women in Germany were expected to cover their heads, just as married women were. Later artists would dress her in much plainer tunics than the quasi-Byzantine one here.
(*Gospel Book*, Germany, Echternach, mid-1000s: British Library, Harley MS 2821, f. 22r)

12
The depiction of Judith of
Flanders, Countess of
Northumberland, devoutly
embracing the foot of Christ's
cross, shows how the slim fit of
the middle of the eleventh
century was almost certainly
being achieved by gathering
some of the outer garment into
a band at the side of the waist,
either by drawing the fabric into
a band applied to the surface,
or by cutting holes at the side
through which a belt could pass
from inside to hold the excess
fabric in gathers.
(*Gospel Book of Countess Judith of
Flanders*, southern England,
c.1052–65: New York, Pierpont
Morgan Library, MS M.709, f. 1v,
detail)

empty splendour, divests herself, denuded of her vain
peplum (usually 'veil'); the torn wreaths of her beauty are
trailing and the gold on her head and neck is loosened.'

It is difficult to accept the figure of Ostentation
here as particularly ostentatious since she is swathed as
effectively as any other Anglo-Saxon woman, in a veil,
a shawl-like garment, and a tunic. All that she is clearly
removing is a strip of patterned material, with wedge-
shaped tabs at the end – hardly torn, trailing wreaths.
The tabs resemble those at the end of the streamers worn
by Queen Aelfgyfu in fig. 8; but they are most like the so-
called small maniple of St Cuthbert, one of a number of
surviving Anglo-Saxon embroideries probably donated to
the shrine of St Cuthbert in Durham around 934 by King
Athelstan. (A maniple is a strip of fabric hung on the
priest's left arm during the celebration of the Eucharist.)
It is thought that this 'small maniple' was originally a belt, about 53 inches long by
about 1 inch wide (137 x 2.5 cm). However this item held by Ostentation is to be
interpreted – as an Anglo-Saxon headband, called a *binde*, and apparently worn under
the head-covering, or as a belt – it does not particularly help with an interpretation
of the text, nor clarify how the illuminator understood ostentation.

As for the colours of the clothes, plant-based dyes (red from madder, blue
from woad, yellow from weld, purple from lichens and green from woad plus weld,
dyed in two different stages) were all available in England at this period and they all,
except for purple, appear in the Bayeux Tapestry (probably made before 1082). By the
tenth century Muslim Spain was famous for the varieties of red it produced from the
dried-insect dye called kermes, which could account for over sixty per cent of the
cost of the fabrics in which it was used. Strong colour in dress was perhaps
becoming more desirable to more people: writing in the 990s, the French monk
Richer of Saint-Remi noted that in 972 the abbot had complained about the monks,
who were unduly concerned with their clothing, refusing to wear naturally black
wool, and insisting on wool dyed black.

With the end of the worst of the Norse raids, northern France was able to
enjoy a growth in trade and productivity. In the early 1000s improvements in the

weaving and finishing processes of woollen cloths produced a much finer quality cloth, known as scarlet (apparently meaning 'shorn cloth'). It could be treated so that all traces of the weaving process would be lost under the fine felting of its surface, and in wear it had a far superior draping quality. This high-quality cloth, dyed with kermes to produce a variety of colours, including what we today call scarlet, was to become the most sought-after woollen cloth in the following centuries. Unfortunately, the styles of the manuscript illuminators do not allow us to see any difference between the older, coarser cloths and the new ones. In addition, it can be difficult to distinguish between wool and silk in illuminations, unless the textile involved has a pattern or is in a rare colour, such as purple, in which cases it is likely to be silk. The new semi-industrial production of cloth also changed weaving from being women's work, done at home, to men's work carried out in the growing towns of north-eastern France and Flanders in particular. However, the full implications of these changes would not show themselves until the twelfth century.

As with the concerns of the Abbot of Saint-Remi in the tenth century, most complaints in the eleventh century seem to be directed against men's appearance. Criticisms could involve the presence or absence of beards and the length of men's hair. According to the chronicler Rodulf Glaber, in the early years of the century the Abbot of Saint-Bénigne in Dijon was outraged by the short hair and clean-shaven cheeks, like those of actors, of the men of Aquitaine who had come to central France in the wake of the new queen. Indeed, little seems to have been said about women's appearance, though it was changing more rapidly than men's. In the 1020s the Virgin and the English queen Aelfgyfu (fig. 8) are both shown in slightly narrower garments than had been worn by the Virgin in fig. 7; and somewhat surprisingly, given the reluctance of later centuries to associate her with anything as questionable as fashion, the Virgin has the more novel sleeves, with wide flaring cuffs. By about 1050 narrower outer tunics with extremely wide, trailing over-sleeves had become quite usual in Germany and England (figs 10, 11 and 12). When Anglo-Saxon manuscripts are compared with German manuscripts, the lack of splendour in the former is exasperating: according to Guillaume de Poitiers, William the Conqueror displayed gold-encrusted Anglo-Saxon garments in Normandy after his conquest of England, and left spectators convinced they had never seen anything so precious.

Gold and purple make suitably rich clothing for the emperor Henry III (r. 1039–56; cr. 1046) in fig. 10. The portrayal of the empress Agnes, whom he

ΚΡΙΜΑΤΑΟΛΗΘΕΑCΟΠΟΙΗCΑCΚΑΤΑ
ΤΑΤΑΑΑΒΟΝΓΑΥΤΟΗΙΜΡΙΕΑΙΒΟΙΤΗΝ
ΤΟΜΕΡΤΗΝΑΝΓΑΤΗΝΤΟΥΟΑΡΡΩΜΟΟ
ΙΕΡΟΥCΑΛΗΜ :·

ΘΕΝΔΑΒΑΛΛΩΝΑΥΤΟΥCΕΙCΤΟΝ
ΝΑΒΟΥΧΟΔΟΝΟCΟΡΤΟΝΕC ΤΙΓΕ·

ΟΙ ΑΓΓΟΙ
ΟΥ ΠΑΥ

Ο ΑΓΓ ΚΥ

ΟΙ ΠΑΑ ΔΕ ΕΚ
ΤΗ ΚΑΜΙΝΩ

13 OPPOSITE

In the Book of Daniel, King Nebuchadnezzar (seated top and bottom left, and, like his courtier, wearing a *chlamys* fastened on his shoulder) acknowledges the God of Daniel as a God of gods and a Lord of kings. He later makes a huge golden image that he requires everyone to worship, along with his other gods. Although the Bible does not specify that the golden image is meant to represent the Jewish God, the artist here suggests that it is, as he has dressed the great image, 'pinned' at the top right of the page, as a ruler, complete with a jewelled *loros*. The companions of Daniel (shown together in the probably more everyday outfit of short tunics and front-fastening cloaks) are thrown into a furnace (bottom right) for refusing to worship this idol, but are protected by the angel shown between it and them.

(*Theodore Psalter*, Constantinople?, 1066: British Library, Add. MS 19352, f. 202r)

14 ABOVE

The Byzantine emperor Niketas Botaniates (1078–81), whose face has been painted over that of Michael VII (1071–8), sits among four court officials and is guarded by Truth and Justice. Their short-sleeved tunics hark back to the dress of antiquity. The fabrics visible on the forearm of the emperor suggest that he is wearing a purplish-red tunic below a blue one. On top he has a deeper blue *chlamys*, which is worn in what is now an old-fashioned (and probably therefore more dignified) way. Three of his officials wear the *chlamys* in the new way, with the opening at the centre front and both *tablia* meeting there. This style seems to have been introduced between the mid-tenth and mid-eleventh centuries.

(*Homilies of St John Chrysostom*, Constantinople?, 1072? and 1078–81?: Paris, Bibliothèque Nationale, MS Coislin 79, f. 2r)

married in 1043, shows that in Germany women continued to wear Byzantine-inspired tunics, and very long veils that fell to around ankle level. Despite the competition for space round the face that the veils must have created, some women wore pendant earrings. Earrings seem to have been common among aristocratic women in central Europe in the eleventh century: they are among the gifts made for the hero's bride in the German epic *Ruodlieb* (c.1025–50). In real life, Richeza, Queen of Poland, but in exile in her native Germany, gave all her finery, including her earrings, to a monastery when she was overwhelmed by grief at the death of her brother in 1047.

Around 1000 there were two types of silk in production – monochrome silks, sometimes in mid-tones, such as olive-green, and vivid polychrome, patterned silks. Thanks to a technical improvement introduced in the eastern Mediterranean world around this time, patterned silks could be woven with less effort. Textile historians call these new fabrics 'lampas silks'. The German Gospel book known as the *Codex Aureus Epternacensis*, of c.1025–40, now in the Germanisches Nationalmuseum in Nuremberg, contains pages decorated with bands of the animals and birds that feature in contemporary Byzantine silks. The empress Agnes gave what must have been Byzantine silks, including one with elephants, to the great Italian abbey of Monte Cassino. In 1054 irreconcilable differences led to the division of the Christian Church into Greek Orthodox, based at Constantinople, and Roman Catholic, based at Rome. However, this split seems to have had no effect on the prestige enjoyed in the West by Byzantine silks.

The British Library's *Theodore Psalter*, completed in 1066, offers a complex image in fig. 13. An idol dressed as a ruler in a *loros* is the cause of an attempt to kill three Jews who refuse to worship it; yet the *loros* was also a symbol, as they were, of Christ's triumph over death. The *loros* was a vestigial survival of the ancient Roman garment par excellence, the *toga*, in the form of a decorative band of jewels wound around the body of the wearer in a complex manner, which can be reconstructed from the fourteenth-century *loros* still to be seen in the Schatzkammer in Vienna. When the *loros* was worn by the Byzantine emperor and twelve high-ranking courtiers at Easter, it seems to have been highly charged with symbolism: the *Kletorologion* of 899 saw the *loros* as symbolizing Christ's winding-sheet and his eventual victory over death. The image of Daniel's companions being thrown into the fiery furnace, from which they escape, is a common prefiguration of the rising of

Christ from the tomb. Thus here the costume of the idol is not only that of a ruler –
it is an entirely appropriate accompaniment to a tale of triumph over death.

In the famous Byzantine manuscript of the *Homilies of St John Chrysostom*,
datable to the 1070s, the emperor appears a number of times, in a very rich, full-
length tunic. In fig. 14 his gold-embellished clothing is enriched by the application
of pearls (the white dots on his neckline, cuff, hem, shoes and *chlamys*). The dislike
of the empress Zoë (r. 1028–50) for the clothing of her rank attracted contemporary
comment, but her attitude is understandable – the Arab visitor Ibrahim b. Ali al-
Kafartabi saw the emperor Romanos IV (r. 1068–71) in a garment that he could not
carry properly, nor sit in, because of its weight. It was decorated with 30,000 pearls.

Three of the men with the emperor in fig. 14, dressed alike in red and gold
over blue, are identified by inscriptions as *proedroi*, members of the civilian, as
opposed to military, aristocracy. These men all share the same rank, and therefore
wear the same garment – the *chlamys*, worn in a new way, which makes them look
like beetles with folded wings. The red hats with tassels were possibly those
introduced by imperial decree by Michael VI (r. 1056–7).

The courtier second from the viewer's left is a eunuch. He is a *protoproedros*
(higher ranking than a mere *proedros*) and *protovestiarios* (originally the eunuch keeper
of the emperor's private wardrobe and private treasury, but by this time an official
with powers that ranged from the military to the diplomatic). His clothing is a
sleeved garment with a centre-front opening, like a modern overcoat. This opening,
not seen in Byzantine garments deriving from the ancient world or in contemporary
western clothing, suggests that the 'overcoat' here is one of the Middle Eastern
garments that found their way into the Byzantine wardrobe. The use of such front
openings may also explain why, in some cases, the cloak was swung around to open
at the centre front instead of at the side.

In some ways the Byzantine world, despite the seeming inflexibility at its
administrative and ritual core, was more open to novelty and change, at least in
textiles and dress, than western Europe seems to have been in the same period.
Western Europe was shortly to start voicing growing outrage at changes in dress,
which must have come as a considerable shock to a culture where basic clothing
had remained very similar for centuries. The changes were happily adopted by the
young among the great, but, as will be seen, the Church was clear that they were
definitely not good.

Sanctissimi Ecclesiæ Doctoris Gregorii Papæ
ad Leandrum Episcopum Hispalensem Epistola
in expositionem libri Iob.

INCIPIT PROEMIUM

EVE
RENTIS
SIMO
ET SCissimo
FRI LEANDRO
CO EPO
GREGORI

SERVVS

SERVORV DI;

II

The Start of Fashion
c.1100–c.1300

FASHION AS IT IS UNDERSTOOD TODAY, A CONSTANT SERIES OF
changes in clothing that has nothing to do with anything more than a desire for
novelty, is often said to have started in the fourteenth century; but there are clear
signs two hundred years before that novelty was a driving force in many aspects of
dress. Tailors sought new ways to make clothes fit better; new types of textile were
introduced; new garments appeared; new guilds were established to control the
manufacturing of textiles and clothing; and novelty came to be valued for its own
sake. Money, sometimes a lot of it, was to be made from providing elaborate
clothing. And the clergy had more to complain about.

The sum total of changes and inventions led the historian of technology
Lynn White to describe the late thirteenth century as seeing 'the invention of
invention'. These changes happened against a background in which trade was
expanding, causing money, and accounting for it, to become more important.
Although the survival of documentary evidence from before the thirteenth century is
not consistently spread across western Europe, the accounting systems adopted in
royal, and then in aristocratic, households provide increasingly detailed insight into
the purchasing of fabrics and furs, and the making of individual garments. These
accounts throw into question the 'evidence' of dress in the popular chivalric
romances, where the characters routinely wear fabrics that in life would have been
reserved for special occasions.

By the end of the twelfth century six great annual fairs held in Champagne in
northern France were attended by merchants from all over the western world, some
selling silks from the Middle East and, latterly, from Italy, and buying the woollen

15 OPPOSITE
A highly fashionable knight,
without the benefit of armour,
fights dragons with the aid of
his rather more sensibly dressed
squire. Both men, however, wear
very long-toed shoes. Ordericus
Vitalis attributed the invention
of such shoes to Fulk, Count of
Anjou, who wanted to hide his
bunions. He said they became
fashionable because they
appealed to people's love
of novelty.
(St Gregory the Great, *Moralia in
Job*, Cîteaux, c.1111–15: Dijon,
Bibliothèque Municipale, MS 168,
f. 4v)

cloths woven just north of Champagne, in Flanders. In the 1250s Henry III of England's agents were buying fabrics for the king in Champagne; and English kings' tailors were in the habit of visiting similar fairs in England. Italian coastal cities, such as Genoa and Venice, were trading in silks with the Middle East and Muslim Spain. Although the Tuscan city of Lucca was weaving its own silks from the mid-twelfth century, the weaving of silk in Italy is documented chiefly from the thirteenth century. In the second half of that century Lucchese silk merchants established themselves in north-western Europe. The width of Italian silks began to narrow from the mid-thirteenth century, when they were almost 75 inches (1.9 metres) wide, to about 24 inches (60 cm) wide by the end of the fifteenth century. It is thought that narrower fabrics allowed more economical cutting of the panels and gores that increasingly featured in clothing construction.

In the late 1200s the term 'velvet', in various forms, first appeared in Europe. The fabric is thought to have been invented in Europe, probably in Italy, and it was extremely expensive. Also valued at that time were fabrics known as Tartar cloths, which were silks that sometimes had small patterns in gold. Some cities owed their rapid growth to the textile industries practised within them, and in Flemish cloth-making towns over half the population could be weavers. The growing demand for wool for weaving in turn stimulated the production of wool in the British Isles, especially in England, which owed its prosperity chiefly to the wool trade.

References from the beginning of the twelfth century to people specializing as cutters or sewers of clothing in the regions of northern France and the lower Rhine suggest that what we would regard as tailoring was beginning to be established. Refinements of cut became increasingly important, and in German romances of the later twelfth century clothing cut in the French manner was synonymous with what would today be called 'style'. For the first time in centuries radical changes were wrought in the appearance of clothing, which required increasingly to be made outside the domestic sphere.

Attacks by the clergy on the clothing of the laity were more likely to be directed against women's clothing, which seems to have occupied more and more of women's thoughts now that some of them had less to occupy their time. Women seem also to have enlisted attractive clothing in the quest to find a husband, a quest that was becoming more difficult, for at least three reasons. First, the female element in the population seems to have grown by the twelfth century, perhaps partly because of a reduction in female infanticide. The Church was also reducing the supply of husbands, in two other ways – partly through calls for Crusaders from the end of the eleventh century, and partly because in the eleventh and twelfth centuries it was taking very seriously the imposition of celibacy (in its correct sense, the unmarried state) on the clergy. This led also to growing efforts to separate the clergy from secular clothing styles by a regular series of edicts, most notably in the years 1187 to 1220. In 1215 the fourth Lateran Council made confession compulsory for all, and there followed a number of texts to help priests hear confession. This penitential literature saw the main sinners as men, who could be snared for the Devil by women. Women's chief sins lay in their obsession with clothes. Clerical misogyny coexisted with a devotion to the Virgin Mary, and in secular society, in the world of courtly love, with the supposed elevation of (noble) women to the status of beings adored from afar.

In the twelfth century the majority of illuminated manuscripts were still religious works, produced sometimes by religious houses themselves, and sometimes by itinerant lay craftsmen. From around 1200, however, the production of manuscripts seems to have been taken over by laymen (and some laywomen), often working in cities where universities would require basic texts, and rich lay patrons would want illuminated copies of the increasingly popular secular texts, in the vernacular, whether chivalric romances or works on health. New image types had to be created for these books, and the copying of earlier images therefore became rarer. Full-page miniatures are still rare at this point, and the smaller images to be found in initial letters or at the foot of pages often limit the scope for detailed depictions of dress. Many of the best manuscripts were made in France and Flanders.

In France and the Low Countries, when lay people wanted religious works they often wanted private prayer books, known as books of hours; in England they wanted psalters. The psalter was fashionable from the late 1100s, the book of hours from the mid-1200s. Both contain calendars with the labours of the months of the year, which can illustrate clothing suitable for the seasons and for the activities that go with them. Towards the end of the thirteenth century the margins of the pages were often decorated, sometimes humorously, and such images can provide insight into how clothing was constructed (fig. 36). The thirteenth century saw a rapid increase in the production of illuminated manuscripts in France, though, unfortunately, it is seldom possible at this period to establish who owned any of

16 OPPOSITE
A fashionable young man out hawking. The long, split tunic is said to have been introduced into the Anglo-Norman world by Robert Curthose, Duke of Normandy, after a visit to Sicily. (St Gregory the Great, *Moralia in Job*, Cîteaux, *c*.1111–15: Dijon, Bibliothèque Municipale, MS 173, f. 174r, detail)

17 ABOVE
This calendar scene for May, showing a young man hawking while on horseback, can be explained by reference to Bartholomaeus Anglicus (d. 1240): 'May is a time of solace and of liking, therefore he is painted as a youth, riding and bearing a fowl on his hand.' The unusual garment is probably a *pellison* or *pliçon*, or a variant thereof (*pel* being the French word for 'skin' or 'fur'). (*Shaftesbury Psalter*, West of England, Entangled Figures Master?, *c*.1135: British Library, Lansdowne MS 383, f. 5r, detail)

these books, as heraldic decoration and marks of ownership are rare. Most of the manuscripts discussed in this chapter were produced in England or France, but others were made in Germany, Spain and the Holy Land. There is also discussion of some surviving secular clothing.

In looking at the history of dress through illuminated manuscripts, it can often be a challenge to interpret the intentions of the artist in depicting a particular type of clothing. When the clothing is looked at in conjunction with contemporary documentary evidence, if it is not of the purely objective kind provided by wardrobe accounts, the possible motivation of the artist(s) and writer(s) has to be considered. A prime example lies in the complaints made about the appearance of young men in England and northern France that begin just before the end of the eleventh century, and the early twelfth-century French manuscripts that are often looked at as representations of that appearance.

Initially, the main complaint seems to have been that young men were growing their hair long. Eadmer, a monk at Canterbury, says in his *History of New Things in England* that at the court of William Rufus in 1094 young men were growing their hair like women and combing it every day, nodding irreligiously as they looked around them (really just tossing their hair out of their eyes?), and walking with delicate steps. Eadmer's friend Anselm, the archbishop of Canterbury, preached a sermon that year, attacking men's long hair. But it has to be remembered that these events happened shortly before William Rufus refused Anselm's request that a council be convened to examine the question of sodomy, a vice that later ecclesiastical historians were happy to hint that Rufus was guilty of. Eadmer's account was expanded by later English historians with a growing list of clothing sins, some from their own day, 'proving' that men had become effeminate; but only Eadmer was writing from his own contemporary notes. Manuscripts do not show new looks for men until early in the twelfth century (figs 15 and 16). The chroniclers are, by and large, careless about the dates when major changes in men's garments were introduced, and which show, in their extreme forms, the hallmarks of fashion – inconvenience for the wearer, and time consumed in the maintenance of a fashionable appearance.

Eadmer's words were picked up and built upon some years later by William of Malmesbury (writing in an abbey in England from about 1118 to 1125, and revising his work in the 1130s), and Ordericus Vitalis (writing in an abbey in Normandy from

1109 until the 1140s). To disentangle the layers of accretion requires care, as these two later writers are not always talking of clothing at the end of the previous century – they start there, slide into discussions of the problems of their own time, and then slide back to the late eleventh century. The sequence of changes seems to be: long hair definitely by 1094, and perhaps beards; long hair so common in 1109 that Eadmer says anyone who wasn't long-haired would be branded a priest or a country bumpkin; and long hair persisting till around 1130, when there was a brief fashion for cutting it short after a knight dreamt he was being strangled by his own long hair.

    William talks of clothing that left men's sides naked (compare fig. 21). He saw the rot as starting with a relaxation of military discipline in the reign of William Rufus; but in fact that reign was marked by a series of campaigns to gain control over Normandy and pacify the borders with Wales and Scotland. Ordericus, in a section of his *Ecclesiastical History* written and revised in the mid to late 1130s, talks of shirts and tunics that were too long and too tight, and long, wide sleeves (compare figs 15 and 16). This clothing made men incapable of walking quickly or doing anything useful. William and Ordericus also talk of shoes with pointed and curled toes. Ordericus, anxious to attack the pointed shoes of his own day, said that in the past shoes had always been round and fitted the foot – but neither King Edgar's shoes nor those of King Cnut (figs 7 and 8) look particularly round.

    The attacks on the new clothing styles for men equated them with effeminacy, but not as a manifestation of homosexuality – indeed, they were a means of making men more attractive to women. Perhaps women had had enough of uncouth he-men who thought washing and cleanliness were disgusting, and preferred men with a modicum of refinement, such as was to be displayed in the cult of courtly love. Men in the previous century had been criticized for shaving and having short hair; now they were being criticized for having long hair and beards. The most convincing explanation of the complaints takes account of the hierarchical nature of the society making the complaints. Clean-shaven men with short hair were adopting an appearance that was the prerogative of churchmen, which they were not; by wearing long hair and simpering about like women, men were acting like women, which they weren't. Complaints arose whenever boundaries were crossed – from lay to cleric; male to female; and later, bourgeois to aristocrat. The one reason knights had for existing was warfare, and these young knights with their awkward clothes and effeminate ways were undermining that.

18 LEFT
The poor receiving alms from King Edmund have been prettified and cleaned up, as sometimes happens, perhaps because rich owners of manuscripts could not bear to have the reality of the great unwashed appear in their books. Blue was often the colour of working-class dress.
(*Life, Passion and Miracles of St Edmund, King and Martyr*, Bury St Edmunds, Alexis Master and shop, *c*.1130: New York, Pierpont Morgan Library, MS M.736, f. 9r)

19 OPPOSITE
A stupendously elongated, 'Gothic' figure of Philosophy visits Boethius in prison. Beside Boethius stand his other consolations – two of the muses, blowing trumpets.
(Boethius, *De consolatione philosophiae*, West of England, Entangled Figures Master, *c*.1130–40: Oxford, Bodleian Library, MS Auct. F.6.5, f. 1v)

It is usual to look at the images in the manuscripts produced soon after 1109 at the new abbey of Cîteaux in connection with the complaints about men's dress, but the images do not all bear out the common contention that the clothing was being criticized in these manuscripts. Many monks came from aristocratic backgrounds, where the military ethos predominated; and the texts of these manuscripts need to be looked at in conjunction with the images. Fig. 15 shows a knight who should not be able to function as a knight, with his long hair and beard, trailing outer sleeves, long, side-split tunic, and curling pointed shoes. Still, supported by a man in a much shorter split tunic, he is able to consider fighting a pair of dragons. It is difficult to be sure that there is outright criticism of this figure, even if it is his supporter who is wounding one of the monsters. The manuscript deals with the trials of Job and how he overcame them. This figure has been explained as an aristocratic spiritual warrior, a knight of God, whose zeal and faith mean that he does not require armour to face danger and overcome it.

The text ends with Job's spiritual and material restoration. The fashionable young huntsman in fig. 16, his cloak lined with the squirrel fur known as miniver, has been seen as a representation of this restoration. But there may be a note of criticism here – a couple of years after the manuscript was completed, the future great Cistercian preacher, Bernard of Clairvaux, arrived at Cîteaux. Between 1128 and 1136 Bernard would praise the Knights Templar for hating hunting and taking no pleasure in 'the stupid cruelty of falconry' (as well as not bothering with the appearance of their hair). Whatever the reasons for the creation of the youth in fig. 16, within a few decades fashionable young men out hawking on horseback became quite common figures on the pages for May in calendars (fig. 17).

The criticisms made by William of Malmesbury and Ordericus Vitalis seem to belong with those made by Bernard of Clairvaux when, having praised the Templars, he criticized young secular knights. He described them as 'not military, but malicious'. They could not function as soldiers because they had hair so long, like women's, that it fell into their eyes; as they walked they tangled themselves in their long, spreading shirts; and they buried their delicate hands in their wide sleeves that flowed round them. Inconveniently long clothing clearly continued to be worn by men until at least the middle of the twelfth century. And long clothing, split for movement, was still considered to be fit for the Devil (fig. 21). In time, however, such inconvenience would become an accepted hallmark of aristocratic clothing.

Short tunics clearly still existed in the male wardrobe, but the increasing availability of rich fabrics, allied to growing tailoring skills, must have accentuated class differences even more, though to achieve the tight fit of the tunic sleeve on the lower arm it had to be sewn closed every day. In fig. 18 King Edmund's clothing, for all that it is being worn by a future saint, has finally brought the English monarchy up to the levels of their German and Byzantine counterparts in terms of elaboration of fabric. The poor receiving alms are most unlikely to have worn such colourful clothing in real life. Blue underpants are even more unlikely, as underwear was made of linen, which was very difficult to dye, even though blue was one of the easiest colours to produce, from woad. (The dye seems to have stained the hands of cloth workers, who were sometimes nicknamed 'blue nails'.) Pink-dyed sheepskin cloaks are equally unlikely – what we have here is an exercise in very pretty colour schemes.

Around 1140 the attenuated building style now called Gothic started to appear, being first really noticeable at Saint-Denis, then outside Paris, in the rebuilding of the abbey church by Abbot Suger. Clothing styles also showed a growing preoccupation with attenuation, and some artists used the style to great effect. The English artist known to art historians as the Entangled Figures Master responded magnificently, if not entirely accurately, to the demands of the text with the opportunities offered by contemporary dress when he depicted (in fig. 19) Philosophy and the Muses of poetry visiting the philosopher Boethius in prison while he was awaiting execution in 524 or 525 on suspicion of treason. Boethius described Philosophy as sometimes seeming to strike the sky with the top of her head. The fashion for wide-cuffed sleeves played into the hands of the artist, who added to them a long veil and a long mantle to enhance her verticality.

Yet the artist has not been entirely true to Boethius, for Boethius also says that on the lower edge of Philosophy's clothing was woven the Greek letter pi (standing for the practice of virtue), and at the top edge the Greek letter theta (standing for the theory, or contemplation, of truth) with steps, like a ladder or staircase, between them. Her clothes had been torn by violent hands, and parts had been removed. Either these elements of the description proved too much for the artist, or they were not brought to his attention in the first place.

Philosophy described the Muses as 'theatrical little tarts' (*scenicas meretriculas*). The artist may be hinting at their lack of virtue by leaving their hair less modestly covered than Philosophy's, and by not giving them mantles to wear (in 1158

ICI VIENENT LI TREI REI A HERODE:

20 OPPOSITE
One of the Magi (bottom centre) gestures towards Herod, his hand lost inside a sleeve that makes his arm resemble an elephant's trunk. The etiquette of the period, by which an attendant of any rank removed his cloak on entering the presence of his master – possibly to show he was not carrying weapons – would indicate that the cloak-clad visitors are Herod's equals.
(*Psalter of Henry of Blois*, Winchester, *c.*1145–55?, or 1160s?: British Library, Cotton Nero MS C IV, f. 11r)

21 RIGHT TOP
The Devil, offering the world to Christ, wears a grotesque summary of worldly styles as worn by men (on the viewer's left) and as worn by women (on the viewer's right).
(*Psalter of Henry of Blois*, Winchester, *c.*1145–55, or 1160s?: British Library, Cotton Nero MS C IV, f. 18r, detail)

22 RIGHT BOTTOM
Virgo, the figure for August in the calendar in the *York Psalter*, has slung one sleeve around her neck, rather like a scarf. In another example of fashionable elongation, another woman in the manuscript has plaits that reach the ground.
(*York Psalter*, England, *c.*1150–75: Glasgow University Library, Special Collections MS U.3.2 [229], f. 4v, detail)

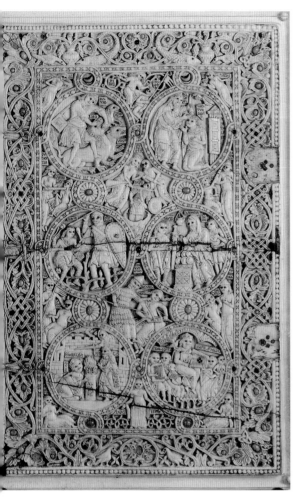

prostitutes in Paris were forbidden to wear mantles). Prohibitions like this, which seem, surprisingly, to have encouraged open display of sinful attractions, were sometimes enacted to discourage respectable women from dressing in ways that the authorities deemed undesirable.

It is not only inside illuminated books that information about dress can be found – in the case of the *Psalter of Queen Melisande of Jerusalem*, there is far more to be learned from the book's cover than from its contents (figs 23 and 24). Melisande was, in her own right, Queen of the Latin kingdom of Jerusalem, one of the Crusader states; her psalter is thought to date from the years of her joint rule with her husband, the Frenchman Fulk of Anjou (1131–43). The book, like the culture of the kingdom, is a hybrid – it is aware of the culture of the Byzantine Empire to the north, but is not a product of it or of its form of worship. The ruling class in the kingdom (probably never more than two to three thousand adults) remained resolutely French in their language and their laws. Although new arrivals from Europe were frequently appalled that the Franks (as they were called) seemed to have 'gone native' in many respects, they never accused them of wearing 'native' dress. In fact, to ensure that the conquered did not ape the conqueror, in 1120 the Council of Nablus forbade Muslims of both sexes to wear Frankish dress.

The settlers imported woollen cloths from northern Europe, as is shown by the cargo list of the *Saint Esprit*, sailing from Marseilles to Syria in 1248; but failure to adapt to local conditions was often fatal, and lightweight fabrics were widely available locally. Silks were made in Antioch and Tripoli, cottons were made in Beirut, and there were also silk-and-cotton mixtures woven in response to Koranic disapproval of pure silks for men's dress. The export of these fabrics was in the hands of Italian merchant colonies. Dress itself, whatever its fabric, seems to have retained the forms of western Europe, and the European-style freedom of the Frankish women appalled Muslim men. In 1184 at a wedding in Tyre, famous for its white silks, the bride was noted by Ibn Jobaïr, a Spanish Muslim en route to Mecca, as wearing a trailing outfit of silk, in the Christian style. He found her, with her tiny footsteps and cloud-like way of drifting, so overwhelming that he prayed to be protected from such a seductive sight. In walking so, she might have been

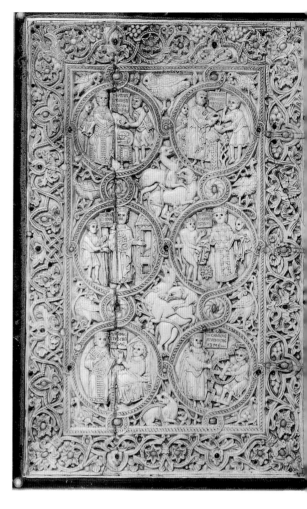

In the roundels are scenes from
the life of King David; outside the
David scenes are figures of the
Vices and Virtues, some of whom
are engaged in battle. The
personifications share with the
humble young David the
keyhole-shaped neck opening
on their tunics; as fashionable
figures, they wear tight sleeves
with long cuffs, and garments
that are gathered at the hips,
presumably as gored panels. The
Kaiserchronik (*Imperial Chronicle*) of
c.1150 attributes to Charlemagne
a law that really reflects the
clothing concerns of the twelfth
century – the lower orders were
allowed gores only at the sides
of their clothes, and could be
punished if they had gores at
the front or back.
(*Psalter of Queen Melisande of
Jerusalem*, Jerusalem?, 1131–43:
British Library, Egerton MS 1139,
front cover)

24 RIGHT

Zigzagging from top left, one can
see two forms of the *loros* – the
familiar belt-like one and the
other hanging from a jewelled
collar. The other outer garment is
the *chlamys*, with the middle one
on the left worn so as to display
its *tablion* in the centre front.
According to John of Ibelin,
writing in the 1260s, the kings
of Jerusalem wore a dalmatic
at their coronations. This aligns
them with French practice.
(*Psalter of Queen Melisande of
Jerusalem*, Jerusalem?, 1131–43:
British Library, Egerton MS 1139,
back cover)

complying with the advice given by the
late twelfth-century troubadour Garin lo
Brun – a lady should walk slowly, with
small steps, and not tire herself. But
perhaps she was walking in the only
way possible without tripping over her
trailing clothes.

In fig. 23 the Vices and Virtues
are fashionably dressed. Had only 'bad'
personifications looked fashionable, the
book's owner, who presumably dressed
this way, might have been offended.
The more accommodating of the clergy
accepted that higher social status called
for greater expenditure on clothing, as
befitting the wearer's rank, and they
were also prepared to argue that
wearing poor clothes could in itself be
a form of pride and ostentation.

Fig. 24 shows a bearded ruler performing the Six Works of Mercy in a variety
of garments that echo the imperial dress of the Byzantine Empire. As a number of
visual sources, such as coins and seals, depict rulers of the kingdom of Jerusalem
in clothing like that of Byzantine emperors, it is sometimes said that the kings of
Jerusalem did dress in such clothing. But images had a prestige of their own, which
can render suspect their literal accuracy; and the art of Jerusalem is shot through
with references to that of the great power to the north. Really imitating the dress
of the Byzantine emperor so close to his own territory would probably have been
unwise. Byzantine-style imperial clothing, complete with *loros*, also appears in
images of the Norman King of Sicily, Roger II (r. 1130–54); but he imported
Byzantine craftsmen to his kingdom to make them. Roger is perhaps most famous
today for the splendid semi-circular crimson mantle of samite with gold embroidery
and jewels made for him in Palermo in 1133/4 (fig. 27). An indubitable instance of a
westerner wearing a *loros* in the Middle East occurred when the Crusaders captured
Constantinople in 1204, drove out the Byzantine emperor and crowned one of their

25 OPPOSITE

The Presentation of Christ in the Temple, and the prophets Moses and Malachi below. In the upper register, underneath her stiff, richly patterned over-tunic (*Rock* in German), the Virgin's attendant wears a more fluid white under-garment, which is perhaps the German equivalent of the garment called a *chainse* in French romances. In the lower register the 'biblical' dress of Moses and Malachi has been painted by an artist who has lost sight of the original construction of this clothing, and used two different colours in each mantle. (*Psalter of Henry the Lion, Duke of Saxony*, Helmarshausen Abbey, Saxony, 1168–89: British Library, Lansdowne MS 381, f. 8r)

26 ABOVE

Henry the Lion, Duke of Saxony, rolls out the highest-ranking people in the family to witness his coronation by God. On Henry's side are his parents, Duke Henry the Proud and Duchess Gertrude, and his maternal grandparents, the emperor Lothar III and the empress Richenza. On the side of Henry the Lion's wife Matilda are her father, Henry II of England, and his mother Matilda, once married to the emperor Henry V, with an unidentified female.
(*Gospels of Henry the Lion, Duke of Saxony*, Helmarshausen Abbey, Saxony, c.1185–8: Wolfenbüttel, Herzog August Bibliothek, MS Guelph 105 Noviss. 20, f. 171v)

own, Count Baudouin of Flanders, in Hagia Sophia. Robert of Clari's account, written around 1216, describes Baudouin as tying the imperial mantle around himself because it was so long at the back, and then throwing it over his left arm, like a priest's maniple (compare fig. 13).

The so-called *Winchester Psalter* or *Psalter of Henry of Blois* (younger brother of King Stephen of England and Bishop of Winchester 1129–71) is interesting in both accepting the flowing, inconvenient dress of western Europe, as well as criticizing one of the oddest features of fashion, the display of the sides of the body, naked, behind the side-lacing of garments (figs 20 and 21). Extremely long cuffs are accepted as a part of women's dress – even the Virgin wears them – and rather narrower, but still flared cuffs are part of the dress of high-ranking figures, such as Herod and the Magi, who are all shown in fig. 20 as kings with crowns. Even the shepherd hiding his face inside his hood wears very slightly flared sleeves, so usual are they in the artist's world. But otherwise the shepherds' clothing shows how marked the division was between the highest and the lowest in society – they wear the short tunic of the active man, short hooded cloaks (one of sheepskin), and boots and leggings. How inconvenienced by their dress the Magi and Herod seem by contrast!

Some of the most fashionable (male) figures in the manuscript are also those portrayed as the most grotesque, including the tormentors of Christ (on f. 21r), in delicate shoes fastened across the front of the ankle, and tunics so long that they have to be hoisted up or else split at the sides to allow them to move – but instead they seem to be in danger of wrapping themselves around the legs in the manner of the clothing worn by Bernard of Clairvaux's secular knights. In his *De consideratione* (*On Consideration*) of 1149–52 Bernard criticized the exaggerated splits in garments for exposing the most intimate parts of the body. The most extreme of the fashionable figures in this manuscript is the famous figure of the Devil, tempting Christ with the kingdoms of the world (fig. 21). This particular devil first came to prominence in the nineteenth century, when the side-lacing on his bodice was added to documentary references to a garment called a 'corset', and the result was interpreted in nineteenth-century terms (when the corset was a laced under-garment, designed to shape women's bodies). This 'proved' that the corset had been worn in the Middle Ages. The corset of the Middle Ages has since been shown to be a garment requiring a considerable quantity of fabric, and was most probably a type of cloak! In fact, the Devil's outfit would appear to amalgamate the most extreme

27
The mantle of Roger II of Sicily
is one of the rare survivals of
clothing from this period,
preserved as part of the
Habsburg coronation regalia
because it was later believed to
have belonged to Charlemagne.
It is made of red samite, possibly
of Byzantine origin, and was
embroidered in the royal
workshops in Palermo in Sicily,
with an Arabic inscription that
dates it to the equivalent of
AD 1133/4. The layout of the
design suggests that it would
have looked most effective when
worn like a *chlamys*, with one
animal in front and one behind,
though by the sixteenth century
it was worn with the opening at
the front.
(Mantle of Roger II of Sicily,
Constantinople? and Palermo,
1133/4: Vienna, Schatzkammer,
Kunsthistorisches Museum)

elements of male and female dress of the period. The side-split overskirt, so long that it has to be knotted to keep it under partial control, comes from men's clothing, as may the sleeve on his left arm. His right sleeve, so long that it too has been knotted, probably comes from women's dress.

Both sexes wore garments that fitted tightly to the torso by means of lacing, but lacing was, to judge by the literature of the period, far more common in women's dress. Some heroines of chivalric romances, as in *Ipomedon* (c.1175–90), allow their flesh to be seen between the laces – in fig. 21 the Devil's shaggy torso can be seen. This hermaphrodite devil may coincide with the turning of the tide of clerical censure of dress, from men's to women's.

The great trailing sleeves could be extremely inconvenient, and more than once those who wished to wash their hands and faces are said to have had their sleeves held up for them. It would seem that sometimes these sleeves were simply slung out of the way, as an everyday way of wearing them (fig. 22). Yet they could also be made to serve a purpose, as bags (fig. 25). This upper scene, of the Virgin presenting Christ in the Temple, presumably reflects the sartorial tastes (or aspirations) of the very grand, as it was made for the German prince Henry the Lion (1129–95), one of the most powerful men in Europe. The Virgin's attendant wears a patterned *Rock*, the German equivalent of the French *bliaut*, which is often, in the romances, made from Islamic silks from Almeria in southern Spain, or from silks patterned with gold stars or coloured birds. (Lucca in Tuscany was already making silks by the 1160s, but the romances prefer silks from farther afield.)

The desirability of rich fabrics, and the care with which they would be treated, are clear from Heinrich von Veldeke's *Servatius* of c.1170, in which a countess was so enamoured of a rich silk in the treasury of the church of St Servatius in Maastricht that she stole it, and then had it carefully cut into a garment that was sewn together with gold thread (a reversal of the usual practice of giving silk clothing to be remade into vestments). In fig. 25 the richness of the attendant's over-tunic links her to the altar-cloth and to the backgrounds of her own scene and that below, where the roundels and the eagles that confront each other make references to contemporary patterned silks (probably those known as *samita rotata*).

Henry the Lion and his wife Matilda make an appearance in this manuscript, but they are far more spectacular (fig. 26) in the manuscript known as the *Gospels of*

28

These men of the court of King
Herod offer good examples of the
fashion for slashing hems, and
for *mi-parti* clothing (see page
57), with the fashion extending
even to their stockings. In 1187
Pope Gregory VII forbade the
clergy to wear red or green
cloaks, presumably because the
colours were popular in secular
dress.
(*John the Baptist Roll*, Alsace, late
1100s: British Library, Add. MS
42497, detail)

29

The second-century martyrs
St Felicity and her seven sons,
as imagined in Germany in the
late twelfth century. German
romances suggest that good legs
on men were much admired by
women – the legs here cannot be
ignored. Perhaps the hose are
slashed, as in Wolfram von
Eschenbach's *Parzival* of

*c.*1200–10. Elsewhere in this
manuscript are stockings that
look like a stylized rendering of
some kind of small-scale miniver,
but in red and yellow.
(*Ottobeuren Collectar*, Ottobeuren,
Swabia, late 1100s: British
Library, Yates Thompson MS 2,
f. 103r, detail)

Henry the Lion, which he gave to Brunswick Cathedral in 1188, the year before Matilda's death. This second manuscript is thought to have been made shortly after their return to Germany in 1185 from a three-year exile in Normandy, at the court of Matilda's father, Henry II of England. The richly patterned clothing of the main figures reflects their ranks, as well as being as close as one is likely to get to the rich clothing imagined for the heroes and heroines of romance. Perhaps not surprisingly, Henry the Lion was an active promoter of translations of French romances. The manuscript states that gold is used to show Henry's imperial connections; clothing that includes gold therefore helps relay this message. King Henry II (behind Matilda) and Henry the Lion's father both wear red stockings with long-toed gold shoes. The duke himself appears to be wearing no shoes, or else stockings with integral soles, so that nothing interrupts the view of his splendid gold- and pearl-trimmed red stockings. Henry the Lion visited Constantinople in the early 1170s, on a journey to the Holy Land, and received so many samite cloths from the Byzantine empress, Maria of Antioch, that he was able to dress all his knights in samite. Perhaps they felt like the hero of Chrétien de Troyes' romance *Erec et Enide*, of c.1170, who is dressed in a *cote* of 'noble *diapre* which was made in Constantinople'.

Much of the duchess's clothing is hidden by her miniver-lined cloak, but it does not hide her very long sleeves, far longer than those of her paternal grandmother, also called Matilda. By describing the younger Matilda's father as always dressed in precious fabrics, 'as was correct', the English writer Walter Map implied that he wore silks; but the wardrobe accounts show that most of the fabrics Henry II bought were woollens, even if they were the costliest woollens, scarlets.

After the fall of Jerusalem to Saladin in 1187, ecclesiastical representatives from the Crusader states came to western Europe seeking aid. According to the Englishman Radulfus Niger, their splendour could not be matched by any prince in the West. He was so appalled by them that he felt God had judged them by depriving them of Jerusalem. But westerners could put on great shows too. In 1191, while on the Third Crusade, Duchess Matilda's brother, Richard the Lionheart, met the self-styled Emperor of Cyprus. Richard, according to a work sometimes attributed to another Richard, Prior of Holy Trinity, London, wore a tunic of rose-coloured samite and a cloak with bands of half-moons, shining in solid silver, and orbs glittering like suns. His hat of scarlet had been skilfully embroidered in gold with birds or animals. The same work attacked the French crusaders for their descent into luxury and idleness in 1192, wearing sleeves closed up by multiple laces, and, apparently, developing a short-lived fashion in which they wore their cloaks back to front and gathered between their arms, so that the closure of their clothing could be seen more clearly.

In Europe a Parisian theologian, Master Pierre the Chanter, who died in 1197, launched a comprehensive attack on clothing practices. In addition to attacking the wearing of worms' excrement (silk) and gold-embroidered edges, he criticized the excessive variety of colour in clothing – red, green, yellow, violet, mixed and confused; the way in which colours divided clothing up as bi-partite (or mi-parti), tri-partite, quadripartite and even multi-partite (like a chequerboard?); and the way in which the clothing was cut, torn, sewn up, tied up, opened up and tailed. Red and green (the first two colours Master Pierre names) were probably the most fashionable colours around 1200. In the *John the Baptist Roll* (fig. 28) the male figures wearing fashionable dress split (mi-parti) into green and red are associated with the court of the wicked King Herod.

In fig. 29 there are several instances of what Master Pierre the Chanter was complaining about – and worn by martyrs, the seven sons of the second-century St Felicity. One of the youths has a garment fashionably cut at its hem; another has a side-split, revealing a patterned under-tunic. There are several cloaks lined in stylized versions of miniver, while another cloak has a brown and cream miniver-type pattern (probably strandling, the autumn fur of the squirrel). And the patterns on the legs cannot be ignored. This manuscript puts a great deal of emphasis on figures' having a very smooth outline, which literary sources suggest was the aim of clothing at this period, even though across parts of the body the clothing crinkles with the effort of fitting closely.

At one point clothing had been made to fit closely, not by particularly skilful cutting, but by tight lacing. Now all this cutting and sewing up again would suggest that another stage had been reached in the craft of tailoring, a recognition that clothing could be made up of many pieces, and quite obviously so, to the extent that its lower edges could be deliberately slashed just for the sake of extending the idea of cutting cloth up.

Alexander Neckam, in his *On the Nature of Things* of the late 1100s, regretted that no one was considered to be a courtier unless he dressed like an actor (that is, gaudily), and that new clothes now had to have an air of novelty about them so that,

30 RIGHT TOP

St Martin, out hawking with friends, cuts his cloak to share it with a beggar. When outdoors, women tended to cover their head to protect their skin and to retain their modesty. The monk, chronicler and illuminator Matthew Paris says that the English princess Isabella, entering Cologne in 1235 on her way to marry the emperor Frederick II, realized that the crowds wanted to see her, and removed her hat and veil (*capellum...cum peplo*) so that they could do so. For this gesture she earned herself much praise. (*Theological Tracts*, Tournai, c.1200: British Library, Add. MS 15219, ff. 11v–12r)

31 RIGHT

An English view of the Irish shows the latter as bearded, badly dressed and eating horsemeat while their king bathes – unfashionable barbarians on the doorstep of England. (Gerald of Wales, *Topographia Hibernica*, England, by 1220?: British Library, Royal MS 13 B VIII, f. 28v, detail)

32 OPPOSITE

The story of King David and his love for the married woman Bathsheba, with comments on improper and proper love in the two bottom scenes. Among the many clothing 'messages' here, some Old Testament Jews are assimilated into Christian tradition through current western clothing, and others are excluded by their being shown in pointed hats and beards. In 1221 the emperor Frederick II compelled the Jews of Sicily to wear beards. (*Bible moralisée*, Paris, c.1220: Vienna, Österreichische Nationalbibliothek, Cod. 2554, f. 45v)

Liuient
Dauid z
mande vr
rie lebato
Berfabee z lidit
qeil rescauec
qeil se fame z
qeil se repouse
z vrie respont
qeil naca nac
anz soffern
la mescaue en la
bataille.

Eqe dauid
mandavrieqe
li dit qeil sere
poulast auec q
sa fame z al not
eure sene sture
siurist q dist
ascretien qil
aillenz a la sainte
eglise z fist la con
fesse z tel respon
dent a lui en sest
plis digne amz
z en orpenie te
z maitre de los
ores.

Liuient
Joab z
prent vrie
z le met
en la ba
taille entel
leu qeil fu
ocis.

Eqe Joab
murst vrie
en la bataille
entel leu ouil
fu ocis senesie
le deable qi
met lom en
tel estat z la
monest a faire
tel pech emor
teil par qon lle
destruiz z dap
ner z trabuch
ez en enfers.

Liuient
Dauid si
baille avrie
leun ellectz
z li oumina
de qeil lel port
a Joab son sene
schulen la ba
taille. z cil si
fert.

Eqe dauid bail
la avrie lellet
trel zillespota
par qoil fu dest
z mor senesie le
siurist q baille
esqi cui l'aune zlos
z li uel en tendiit
prie noue secem te
cesu par qoil
fu en trorsur
tourb z ladum
ni z prinement
z cors. z ame

Liuient la
nouelle a
Berfabee q
sest barons
vrie est mor
z le eplore z fet
grant duel z dl
mentali z la
conforte z l'ec
poule z prent
a fame

Eqe Berfa
bee plora z
mena duel de la
mort de son baro
z la conforta z
la prist a fame. se
niefie sainte eglise
qi plore z ferz duel
de la mort z peche
oz z relieurist
uint a sainte e
glise z la confor
ta z la prist a
espouse.

through the novelty, they might declare that they were new. The next stage in tailoring would seem, logically, to have been to experiment further with the cutting up and reassembling of cloth implied in the bi-partite clothing and its variants; but it was not to be at this period.

One of Neckam's novelties might have been a sleeveless over-garment, denounced in 1184 in Johannes de Hauvilla's *Architrenius* as hiding fat bellies because it flared out from the fitted upper body. It is probably this garment that was referred to in French as a *surcot(e)/sorcot(e)* and in Latin as a *supertunica*. A *surcote* appears in the last romance by Chrétien de Troyes, *Perceval (Conte du Graal)*, unfinished at his death around 1191. Jean Renart's poem *L'Escoufle* of 1200–2 shows that by then the armhole was deep – the heroine Aelis was able to embrace the wearer of a *surcote* by putting her arm in through the opening. The new garment was worn by men and women alike, as can be seen in fig. 30 – the two *surcote*-clad figures on the extreme left with covered heads are women, while the bare-headed figure in front of them is a man in a *surcote*.

Even under-tunics had plenty of fabric in them, with sleeves sometimes set in as low as the waistline and fitting tightly only at the wrists. The beggar with whom St Martin is sharing his cloak wears the typically baggy, calf-length underpants of the period. All clothing is loose. Yet if literary sources are correctly dated, some of them seem to continue talking of extremely tight clothing until 1200 and beyond. This may mean that in the later romances tightly fitting clothing was now little more than a convention of the genre. This may be particularly true in Germany, where closely fitting clothing, in the French style, in literature inspired by French models, was for a long time equated with hero or heroine status.

The accounts for the wardrobe of King Philip Augustus of France and his family for the year 1202–3 show that red and green, the first colours listed by Master Pierre, were the favourite colours for clothes, and that, despite what the writers of romances would have liked their audiences to believe about the clothing of kings and queens, most of it was still made of woollen fabrics, not of silks. The romances are in many ways like modern soap operas, where characters live extraordinary lives and can be far more beautiful and more stylishly dressed than most people can ever hope to be. Even the immense quantity of booty that is said to have been taken when the Fourth Crusade sacked Constantinople in 1204 – including samite and miniver and grey squirrel fur – cannot have had very much effect overall in western Europe, as silks clearly remained a rarity even in the French royal wardrobe. However, the new century did eventually witness an increase in luxury fabrics, including satins and Tartar cloths, the latter dominating the papal inventory of 1295, and in the number of garments being made. Not surprisingly, legislation concerned with clothing also increased.

Fig. 30 shows that clothing was becoming more shapeless and, probably to the relief of those who could remember the tight styles, more comfortable. But closer consideration reveals that the shapelessness is contrived, the clothing being made of a fine fabric that falls easily into folds, and that it is therefore a product of 'civilization'. Comparison of this shapeless clothing with that worn in fig. 31 by the horse-eating Irishmen in the *Topographia Hibernica* (*Topography of Ireland*), probably illuminated by 1220, shows just how sophisticated it is. The *Topographia* was written for Henry II of England by his chaplain, Giraldus Cambrensis (Gerald of Wales), who went to Ireland in 1185, some fourteen years after Henry's papally approved invasion of the island. The Irish, who did not accept English rule and customs, tended to be referred to as the 'wild Irish', and this scene uses appearance as much as behaviour to justify this appellation. All the men have long hair and beards (Englishmen's hair was just long enough to cover their ears, and their beards were short at this time), and the Irish stockings fit badly. Gerald says that the Irish were as barbarian in their beards (in Latin, a pun of the type beloved of the period) as they were in their clothing. They wore woollen breeches-with-shoes or shoes-with-breeches (presumably the baggy garments seen here). He contrasted their appearance unfavourably with contemporary novelties – this was as near as he could get to expressing the idea that as well as being barbarous, they were also hopelessly unfashionable.

They were clearly desperately in need of the advice proffered in Guillaume de Lorris's section of the *Roman de la rose* (*Romance of the Rose*), written around 1230. There the god of love says that in order to be successful in love, a man had to be what would today be described as elegant. He was to entrust the making of his clothes to a good tailor who understood how to do sleeves, and make the common people wonder how he got into and out of his clothes. He was to wear laced shoes and small boots, which he was to replace frequently. He was to keep himself clean and comb his hair, but not to use make-up. The passage suggests that a great deal of care could be expended on men's appearance, and that the skill of the tailor was

33 LEFT
A youth, possibly a servant in a
great household, holds outsize
plants in a calendar scene for the
month of April. Royal households
issued cloth, or the money to buy
it, to their staff three or four
times a year. At the English court
apparently only those occupying
the humble rank of valet were
issued with *mi-parti* for Christmas
1236. Formally issued clothing for
great households seems, at this
stage, to have been used to
identify ranks within the
household at specific times of
the year rather than to indicate
membership of a particular
household.
(*Psalter*, Paris, for a nun in Nantes,
mid-1200s: British Library, Royal
MS 2 B II, f. 2v, detail)

34 OPPOSITE
Comparison of these images of
jewels from St Albans Abbey with
surviving jewels of the period has
shown Matthew Paris's drawings
to be remarkably accurate. Above
the cameo (bottom right) is a
ring with a sapphire set in gold
and surrounded by pearls and
garnets, the gift of Henry of
Blois, Bishop of Winchester, the
supposed owner of the psalter in
figs 20 and 21.
(*Lives of the Two Offas...*, Matthew
Paris, St Albans Abbey, mid-
1200s: British Library, Cotton
Nero MS D I, f. 146v)

prior de Walingeford deo 7 ecce sci Albani
Casto aut continens eande gema i non 7
ipse lapis ad maiore cancelam 7 secita
tem eiidam aureo cculo cue cingitur
prout in capite huii capituli figurat.
Ponderat au Ser denar. De Saphiro

Hunc lapide precosum dui Rich.
videlicet saphiru fere rotudu
et coloris remissi dedit domin
Nicholaus aurifab de sco alba
no oriundus deo 7 ecce s alb. H gema
esceq fuit bi Admundi cant archiepi.
Postea uero Sci Robti fris ei. Postea i
memorati dui Nicholai. In libo siside
castonis stilissime litie iscripuntur
nigellate. et crux cu crucifixo figurat.
Ponderat au Ser den. De anulo archidi

Hunc anulu cotinete aconi Johis.
unu Saphiru orientale intensi
coloris dedit huic ecce dui Johis
de Wundha hui ecce Archidiac
Que de dono dui Rogi ecce h poris
optinuerat. In una 7 parte anuli ad
memoria h nois Johis perpetuandam
isculpit 7 nigellat h litia .j. ex alia uero
o. Pondat au noue den 7 ob. d anulo Ric

Hunc anulu cotinentem animal.
Saphiru orientale coloris itensi
dedit dui Ric cognometo animal
deo 7 hui ecce. Que de dono cui
dam regine Alienore optinuerat
cuia discolaues i sua iuuentute excita
et sodales. fuerat au gema antea ipsi
regine A. In una 7 pte anuli isculpi
tiu R. In alia. A. R. pro Ric. A. pa al.
Pondat au dece den. de anulo epi Johis

Hunc anulu dedit deo cu magno
et hui ecce dui Johis Saphir o.
epe quidam andfertensis. In cui
castone otinet saphir ciid orien
tal pulchiiu murec; magnitudis
quatuor tenacul cue uulgarit petoi
dicunt ceusceptis. Qui dico saphir per
ceiuor angulos i una crusurgit i medio
sumitate. Deputatur ppuis festui
tatibz. Inscribiturcz hoc nome Johis.
Ponderat autem rvui den.

Hunc lapide precosum de peridoto
cui uulgarit di peridoc. Qui et
subuiridis coloris est. et in cui me
dio saphir mure pulchitudis colloca
tur. 7i nome Johis inuealit isculp
tur: dedit dui Johis epe ciida ardfitus
deo 7hui ecce. pforatur au. et uicui
hi spasmu potuit refrenandi. hi uticz
formia fere clipeale. Et pondat vi den.

Hunc lapide precosu De Saphiro ei
videl; saphiru orientale dem epi
dedit deo 7hui ecce pie recordacc
iuis memorac dui Johis epe ciida
arditius. In cui castone oblongo
et fere tangulari des saphir cotmetur
In longu vi eius sumitate pforatur.
Casto au hac notula signatur
Pondat au Ser den. Hec 7 alia mlta
bona cotulit dis epe huic ecce. q aliibi
diligens perscetatoi iueire poit anno

Hunc anulu De magno anulo
nobilissimu rotudo 7 gema
maria 7 ope precosu. In cui
medio saphir remissi colo
ris ie iui. aureos floseulos
collocac 7i ccuitu ei octo gem
ge. ceiuor. s. perle. 7 ceiuor guate: dedit
dui Henr epe Wintoii fr dui Angl regi
deo 7hui ecce ad memoria sui 7 eade
ppetuanda. Ipsius e nome iiebit ecu
lo anuli. Assignat au ornatui abbis
peipuis festuitatibz. Podata rrvui S.

Hunc lapide pre
ciosum ci videl;
costat ex sar
donice cal
cedonio et
onic pe
hoc qd in
tisec la
tec uerii
ipse totii
uulgarit
kaadman
applla ded
dit deo ecce

35

In this scene of the Flagellation, Christ is shown in baggy underpants gathered in at the knees, which may actually have been fashionable. A sermon preached before English nobles in December 1229 by the Dominican Jordan of Saxony suggests that men were rather proud of pleated underpants. In the background a fashionably clad woman accuses the traditionally dressed St Peter of being associated with Christ. (*De Brailes Hours*, Oxford, mid-1200s: British Library, Add. MS 49999, f. 1r, detail)

crucial to this. In order to understand the names for many of the new garments that appear about this time, one would have to spend a lifetime trawling through texts such as the *Roman de la rose*, and even then not expect to find all the answers. Only a few of the new garments to be seen in the visual sources can be matched with any certainty to those mentioned in documentary sources.

A number of new items of clothing appear in the story of King David and Bathsheba, the wife of Uriah the Hittite, in a *Bible Moralisée* of *c*.1220 (fig. 32). The clothes also help to identify the characters and tell the story in pairs from the two at the top to the third pair down. Interspersed are scenes of comments, linking the events to the teachings of Christianity. At the top left, Bathsheba, who is coveted by David after he has seen her bathing, first appears in what may be her white undershirt: thus the artist conveys the impropriety of the source of the king's infatuation. Her headdress is that of a married woman, a band with a fluted edge that encircles her head, and another band of fabric under her chin. (It is in marked contrast to the uncovered hair of the girl tempting a tonsured monk over a Hell-mouth at the bottom left.) This new form of headdress recurs until the end of the century. Evidence from the French poem *Flamenca* and the German poem *Parzival* suggests that women could neither hear nor move their mouths very easily when they were wearing it. Although these headdresses are usually shown as white, an anonymous French poem on the wares of a merchant, and criticism from the great German Franciscan preacher Berthold von Regensburg (*c*.1210–72), both make it clear that the chin bands (*guimples, gebende*) were often dyed yellow with saffron, which Berthold said took more work than a white one (though perhaps it was easier in the long run to dye them yellow than to try to keep white ones white).

David is introduced at the top as a king in a crown, a tunic and a long mantle; later (third scene down on the right) he dons a sleeveless *surcote* to go and comfort the widowed Bathsheba. Before this happens, David gives Uriah written instructions to the seneschal Joab (top right), which will lead to Uriah's death under the eyes of Joab (third scene down on the left). Uriah appears in two examples of a hooded garment with pendant tubular sleeves; his arms can leave the garment at the inner edges of the armholes. This garment frequently appears on travellers. Although its name is unknown, modern writers have sought to identify it with garments called a *garde-corps* and an *hérigaut*. The Jews pointing to the Tables of the Law and rejecting Christ's words (second from the top, right) are distinguished by their pointed hats and beards (as opposed to most of the Christian-looking Jewish protagonists in the Old Testament story). In these scenes dress is used to help tell a story, as well as to point to moral qualities, or to the lack of them.

After about a generation of looser clothing, it seemed that attempts were being made once again to produce clothes that fitted the body better. Sometimes buttons were used at the neckline. In fig. 35 the lower sleeves are uniformly tight and many are wrinkled, as though they are too long. One of the men wielding a club against Christ has raised his arms, revealing that some kind of pleating has taken place under the armhole seam. In the 1230s and 1240s, in German sculpture in particular, a crinkling of the fabric occurs just below the armpit – however the result was to be achieved, the aim seems to have been to make the sleeve and the bodice meet without affecting mobility. (Cutting a comfortable armhole is a lot more difficult than it appears to be.)

The quest for information on clothing construction takes us to a manuscript of c.1260, where two men wrestle, unconcerned by the display of their surprisingly baggy underpants, which can be tucked into the tops of stockings (fig. 36). One of the wrestlers is not even wearing complete stockings – they resemble modern ski pants in having a strap under the foot, rather than stockings proper that would require full feet to be included. Such footless stockings were presumably more economical than fully finished stockings, as they would not wear through at the toes, and might even have smelt less awful than stockings with feet – after all, these were garments that were made of wool, and wool was almost never washed, as far as can be ascertained. Rather worrying questions of hygiene are raised by the advice given around 1240 by Bishop Robert Grosseteste of Lincoln to the Countess of Lincoln, which implies that in some households dirty old clothing on servants was normal. The countess's knights and all the gentlemen who wore her *robes* (which may mean no more than the clothing she supplied) were to wear them daily in her presence and when they were serving her at table. These *robes* were to be clean and new. Some of that clothing could have been issued by the countess in *mi-parti*, which seems to have fallen down the social scale to servants' or squires' clothing (fig. 33).

In many ranks of society in England the wearing of more and more elaborate fabrics was gaining ground by the 1230s: the chronicler and illuminator Matthew Paris, who implies that he was present, says that when Eleanor of Provence, the wife of Henry III, was crowned in London in 1236, the whole city turned out dressed in

36
A wrestling match in which men brazenly show their underpants. That such a display of underwear is undignified is implied by a drawing by Villard de Honnecourt (c.1215–40) in which a figure of Pride falls from his horse, revealing his underpants and the stockings into which they are tucked.
(*Rutland Psalter*, England, c.1260: British Library, Add. MS 62925, f. 42r)

37
The *pellote* of Infante Don
Fernando (d. 1275) is about
51 inches (130 cm) long. It is
decorated with shields
containing lions and castles, and
retains scraps of its rabbit-fur
lining. The name *pellote* is linked
to the Latin word for fur (*pellis*),
indicating that a fur lining was
integral to the garment. Clothing
featuring lions and castles was to
be worn again at the coronation
of Alfonso XI of Castile in 1310.
(*Pellote* of Infante Don Fernando,
Spain, by 1275: Monastery of Las
Huelgas, Burgos, © Patrimonio
Nacional)

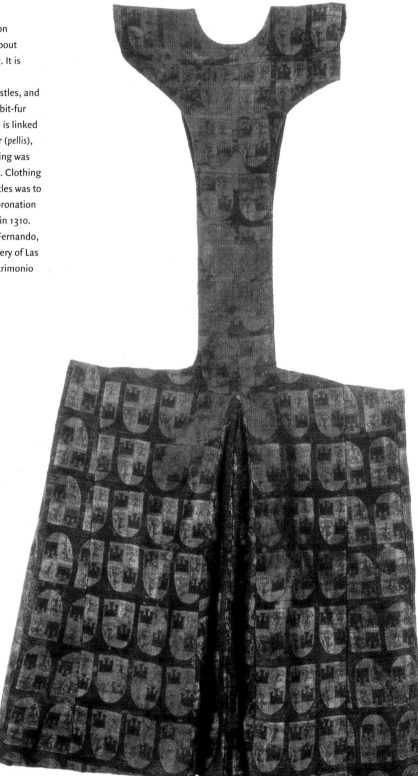

38 RIGHT TOP

In Alfonso X of Castile's *Law Code* clerics are instructed not to have long hair; and, indeed, the clergy on the right have considerably shorter hair than the king and his courtiers. The clerics are all bishops, holding crosiers and wearing mitres and chasubles, the latter garments worn by priests celebrating mass and deriving from a Roman circular cloak worn for warmth – originally eminently appropriate when one remembers that a bishop had a duty to travel around his diocese.
(*Law Code of Alfonso X the Wise of Castile*, Castile, c.1285–1300?: British Library, Add. MS 20787, f. 89r, detail)

39 RIGHT BOTTOM

In some of the images in Alfonso X's *Cantigas* and *Law Code* women wear almost turban-like wrappings made from striped material (stripes were very common in Spanish Islamic fabrics), and almost French-looking chin bands and pie-crust circlets. They also wear tall bonnets or layers of fabric strapped on under the chin, possibly a local variant of the French-style headdress.
(*Law Code of Alfonso X the Wise of Castile*, Castile, c.1285–1300?: British Library, Add. MS 20787, f. 105v, detail)

all-silk garments to greet her. In 1238 Henry gave his sister Eleanor baudekin worked with gold (a patterned silk, possibly originating in Baghdad, but apparently being copied in Europe by 1200). For Whitsun 1244 the royal couple wore mostly samites, in red, green, purple and blue; the reality of winter weather possibly forced them to wear woollens, including scarlets, for Christmas that year. (Around this time the English royal household saw the development of a specific department, known as the Great Wardrobe, whose responsibility it was to buy fabrics for the king's use.) By the 1250s Henry was acquiring silks and fabrics with gold in them from foreign merchants at the English fairs and from the mayor of London. But very little of this luxury is reflected in illuminated manuscripts, where fabrics could just as easily be plain wool as plain silk, unless a series of dots is to be understood as hinting at the presence of patterned silk (compare the cloak and cushions on the left in fig. 43).

Because the scale of manuscript illuminations rarely allows for the inclusion of many details of jewellery, it is easy to forget that jewels played a very important role in creating a splendid appearance. In Gerbert de Montreuil's *Continuation* (1226–30) of Chrétien de Troyes' *Perceval (Conte du Graal)*, the blood-red wedding clothing of Blancheflor is covered with stars and decorated with glittering jewels that seem to be aflame. The reality of contemporary jewellery is that it certainly was noticeable, if still rather crude by modern standards. Matthew Paris was also one of the few illuminators of this period whose names are known; in the middle of the century he made drawings of jewels given to the Abbey of St Albans (fig. 34). Many of the jewels were sapphires, fairly commonly in use, but perhaps less interesting than an ancient Roman cameo, said to have been a gift from King Ethelred, father of Edward the Confessor. It shows an armour-clad Roman emperor holding a figure of Victory on one hand. This figure was interpreted by Matthew Paris as being in rags and holding a boy. The misreading of the image seems to have led to its being regarded as an amulet, as he tells us that it was lent out to special friends of the abbey to aid in childbirth, but if a woman kept it too long, its powers were reduced.

Surviving jewels are rare; even rarer are surviving garments. Particularly interesting are the garments that have come from the thirteenth-century tombs of the Castilian royal family at Burgos in northern Spain. Some of them conform to the new fashion for having sets of garments (like the idea of modern suits) made from the same fabric to form what was called in Latin a *roba*. In many respects Castilian clothing is related to dress to be found elsewhere in western Europe at this time, but it also shows regional differences, especially in the very open-sided sleeveless over-tunic, called a *pellote* in Castilian (see fig. 37 and the man in fig. 38 whose hand is being held by the king), the *saya encordada* (a tunic with very obvious side-lacing), and in pillbox-type caps that were worn by men. One of the outfits from Burgos, that of the Infante Fernando, who died in 1275, consisted of a semi-circular cloak (*manto*), a *pellote* (fig. 37), and a *saya encordada*. They were all made from what was once a yellow and red samite brocaded with silver-gilt threads, featuring the heraldic lions of León and the castles of Castile. He also had a pillbox-shaped cap, embroidered to match, with lions and castles.

Fernando's father, Alfonso X the Wise of Castile (r. 1252–84), is perhaps most famous for his illuminated manuscripts of songs about the miracles of the Virgin (*Cantigas de Santa María*), but his law codes were also the subject of illuminated manuscripts. The British Library has the earliest known copy of the first part of his law code, the *Siete Partidas*, first compiled in the 1260s. It is related stylistically to the *Cantigas* manuscripts, though it may date from a few years after his death in 1284. Alfonso's manuscripts are invaluable because they contain a wide cross-section of Castilian society, some in the international dress of the Church (fig. 38) and others in more local styles (fig. 39).

In fig. 39 it is worth noting that the clothing of the man standing at the head of the queue looks uncomfortably tight at the junction of the arm and the torso – clearly tailoring had not yet managed to produce a successful armhole. Spanish clothing, however, was much tighter than dress elsewhere in Europe at this time, and Spanish tailors seem to have continued to wrestle with the problem of making clothes fit when tailors elsewhere had lost interest. This scene shows that Castilian women's clothing deviated more sharply than did men's from the north-western European 'norm', particularly in their headdresses.

Alfonso passed one of the earliest pieces of sumptuary legislation in 1258. Among its provisions was a general prohibition on making more than four pairs [sic] of clothes ('suits' of two matching garments?) in a year. These clothes were not to be lined with ermine or otter; nor were they to include silk, gilded or silvered leather (or gold or silver leaf?), gold or silver cloths, long cords, embroidery, ribbons or any decorations. They were to consist only of fur (presumably as lining) and woollen cloth. One garment was not to be worn on top of another; and only the king was allowed to wear a rain-cape of scarlet. (An ell, about a yard or a metre, of scarlet

40 LEFT

There is surprisingly little information on how women dressed while pregnant, but here the clothing of the late 1200s accommodates the pregnant woman (which the fashions of a hundred years before could not have) by allowing her simply to slide her belt down under her abdomen. A stomach-forward stance was also actually fashionable – compare fig. 41.
(Aldobrandino da Siena, *Li liures dou santé*, Lille?, c.1285: British Library, Sloane MS 2435, f. 27v, initial)

41 BELOW

A fashionably dressed lady, possibly the Queen of England, out hunting with her hounds. She offers proof that fashion has nothing to do with being practical – she presumably has to deal with her hounds, despite her elaborate headdress and trailing skirts.
(*Alphonso Psalter*, England, c.1281–4: British Library, Add. MS 24686, f. 13v, bas-de-page)

42 RIGHT

At the top left the figure for spring wears a *cote* and a sleeveless *surcote* with his hands tucked into the armholes and a hood at the back of his head, while below him the autumn figure, who should be dressed similarly, prefers the safety of a cloak. In summer, at the top right, a *cote* is worn on its own; below, in winter, the figure disappears into a hood and long pendant sleeves. (Aldobrandino da Siena, *Li livres dou santé*, Lille?, c.1285: British Library, Sloane MS 2435, f. 23r, initial)

would have cost an unskilled worker about forty days' wages.) No one was to make fur/leather rain-capes more than twice a year, and these had to last two years. No nobleman was to come to court in a *tabardo*. Perhaps it was too skimpy to be dignified: the Latin–French 'dictionary' compiled by John of Garland after 1218 as a means of learning Latin seems to define the French word *tabar* as meaning a mantle that reached only as far down the body as the level of the kidneys.

In 1254 Alfonso's half-sister Leonor married the future Edward I of England (she is known in English history as Eleanor of Castile). It was probably for their son Alphonso (the English spelling of his uncle's name) and his intended bride that the *Alphonso Psalter* was begun, shortly before his death in 1284 (fig. 41). Eleanor, who preferred hunting with hounds to falconry, is perhaps referred to in the image of a lady out hunting on foot with hounds. Her headdress is typical of Franco-English fashions of this period, with its wide-set hairnets under a short veil with a circlet on top. This fashion may be related to that criticized in 1273 when the Dominican Gilles d'Orléans preached against women who wore on their heads signs of Hell – horns and dead hair, which could have come from someone who was perhaps in Hell or Purgatory. The lady wears a blue sleeveless *surcote* and a white tunic, and gloves to protect her hands as the hounds strain on their leashes. The accounts for the clothing of Edward's and Eleanor's children survive for the year 1273–4, which included the coronation of their parents. Among the coronation items for the children were gloves with the king's arms on the thumb, at 3d. a pair. (The normal price for adult gloves, as given to one of Eleanor's ladies in 1289, seems to have been 2d. a pair.) The tombs of Eleanor's family at Burgos included pieces of patterned knitting, which was a Spanish-Moorish speciality; perhaps the children's gloves had been specially knitted in Spain. They could also have been decorated with heraldic enamel plaques: when Edward remarried in 1299, five dozen buttons enamelled with the arms of England and France were bought for the new queen, Margaret of France. Such minutiae are recorded only because the accounting systems were becoming more complex, as spending was perhaps becoming more diffuse, aided by the increasing complexity of clothing.

As well as elaborate accounting, legislation was very much in the air, which suggests that the authorities felt clothing manufacture needed to be controlled, presumably because it was too open to profiteering. The *Livre des métiers* (*Book of Trades*) compiled by Etienne Boileau around 1260 lists almost twenty trades in Paris related to clothing and textiles. In 1270 the cappers of London were forbidden to dye old caps black and then sell them as new because the colour ran in the rain. A similar decree was enacted in 1281, in Venice, when cap-makers there were forbidden to use burnt cork to dye grey caps, as that was little better than make-up, which would simply stain the wearer's forehead. In 1279 the French were told how many *robes* (suits) they might have in a year, by a law that was to have effect for five years. Great nobles were to have no more than five pairs of *robes* furred with miniver in a year; lesser aristocrats might have four or two, according to their rank; and finally no bourgeois was allowed more than one *robe*. In 1274 the scholars at the Sorbonne in Paris were the subject of one of the more unusual decrees – they were ordered to put ownership marks on their clothes. The marks, with their names, were to be put on a schedule that would go to a servant who would control the receipt and the return of their clothes, presumably for washing.

University educations had been available, to men only, from the twelfth century. The medical profession, trained in these universities, began to look less and less kindly on women who interfered with their own versions of medicine, even though the Paris census for 1292 listed eight women involved in aspects of medical practice. This may help to explain why in fig. 40 a pregnant woman is consulting a male doctor rather than a midwife. This and the next illustration come from the first medical treatise known to have been written in French rather than Latin, *Li livres dou santé* (The Book of Health). It was a compilation of received medical opinion, first produced in 1256 as a guide to good health by an Italian physician, Aldobrandino da Siena, for Beatrix of Savoy, Countess of Provence, who was planning a long trip to visit her daughters in France, England and Germany. The work includes advice on the clothing to be worn at different times of the year (fig. 42). Here it comes straight from Avicenna (980–1037), who practised medicine in Persia; and the origin of the advice shows. In spring (top left) one should wear *robes* that are neither too hot nor too cold, made of *tiretaines* and cotton cloths, lined with lambskin. *Tiretaine* was apparently a fine woollen cloth; although cotton was woven in Italy by the end of the twelfth century, cotton cloths were far more common in hot Middle Eastern lands than in north-western Europe. In summer (top right) one should wear cold [sic] clothes, such as linen, which makes the coldest of garments, and silks such as cendal, samite and stammes. (There may be a problem with Aldobrandino's translation, as stammes seems to have been a fine woollen cloth.) In September

43 ABOVE
On the left the Roman consul
Brutus wears a red cloak with
blue dots, a decorative effect that
may be visual shorthand for
patterned silk. Miniver shoulder-
capes feature in western and
Crusader manuscripts on figures
of high status, including other
consuls.
(*Histoire Universelle*, Acre,
Crusader states, c.1286: British
Library, Add. MS 15268, f. 161v,
detail)

44 OPPOSITE
Despite the limited colour
scheme, it is possible that the
artist was making some
comment about the characters,
especially those who wear grey.
The people in grey (often undyed
wool) are avaricious, humble or
poor: their clothing is cheap.
(*La Somme le roy*, France, end
1200s: British Library, Add. MS
28162, f. 9v)

MISERICORDE · AVARICE ·

ABRAHAM Q' RECO II A BONNE DAME

T I LAF ANGRES QUI DEPART SON HVITLE

(bottom left) one should dress as in the spring, though the cloth should be a little warmer; and in winter (bottom right) one should wear really thick fluffy wool with good fox fur because that is the warmest fur there is – thicker fur keeps in the heat better. In these scenes the illustrator has done little more than supply images of people clad in suitable contemporary French dress, and has not perceptibly differentiated the fabrics.

The link between France and the Crusader states remained strong, even though Jerusalem had fallen and most of the Frankish Christian population had fled to the cosmopolitan port city of Acre (now Akko, or Akka, in Israel). The *Histoire Universelle* (*Universal History*, fig. 43) is thought to have been produced there by a local illuminator, who is known to have had an associate who had worked in Paris. Yet the manuscript, which covers the history of the world from Creation to the time of Julius Caesar, offers a view of the dress of the past that would have been almost unthinkable in a contemporary, European-produced work because it calls on a knowledge of Byzantine dress. The Byzantine emperor (restored to Constantinople in 1261) remained an important figure in the lives of Christians living under Muslim rule as he claimed responsibility for them. On f. 203r of the *Histoire Universelle* the Greek Alexander the Great is shown, logically, as a Byzantine (i.e. contemporary Greek) figure in the *loros*. In fig. 43 Brutus, on the left, is shown as the first consul of Rome (in 509 BC) in a combination of contemporary western and Byzantine dress: a miniver shoulder-cape and a crown-like object with side pendants. This crown is remarkably like a royal Byzantine headdress, and rather strange, given that the Romans had just expelled their own royal family! The senators with Brutus, however, look like an assembly of western European citizens, some with linen coifs and round caps on their heads. One of them has a miniver shoulder-cape, another a shoulder-cape of strandling. In England Henry III (r. 1216–72) had worn miniver only on important occasions; under the next king, Edward I (r. 1272–1307), miniver seems to have become standard royal wear, with an average of over 119,000 skins being acquired annually for the royal household in the mid-1280s. Brutus and his fellow Romans are fundamentally important western Europeans, perhaps echoing in their dress the clothing of the kingdom of Jerusalem's Haute Cour, the assembly of the king, and the leading lords and churchmen.

The final image for this chapter (fig. 44) contains many of the garments that evolved in the course of the thirteenth century, and that would develop more specific significance in the following century. The short hanging sleeves of the miser (at the top right) are common in the second half of the thirteenth century. At the bottom left Lot welcomes into his home three angels disguised as travellers. The angels cannot have travelled far, however, as the one in blue is wearing rather fashionable and impractical shoes with long toes. This angel is also fashionable in having his hood and over-garment match, as a *robe*, like that worn by the boy at the door. Again, the over-garment would seem to imply that he is not a true traveller, unlike his companions, who wear more protective over-garments with cape sleeves (perhaps the garments called *houces* in the next century). All three do, however, carry the staffs and pouches used by pilgrims.

Between them the two female figures wear the basic components of the female *robe* – the charitable queen at the top left, giving clothing to a nearly naked man, wears a miniver-lined cloak over a tunic or *cote*, while the woman pouring out the oil wears her tunic under a sleeveless *surcote*, which is also miniver-lined. The historian Frédérique Lachaud's study of the wardrobe of Edward I of England has revealed that the English royal family lined their clothes with fur even in the summer, as a status symbol; the lower ranks were probably relieved to have silk linings. The queen in fig. 44 wears a simple veil – after all, she is the personification of a virtue, who cannot afford to compromise her standing by being too fashionable. Her 'human' counterpart, in the bottom left-hand corner, wears a fashionable arrangement of hair caught tightly into a veil at the sides and back of the head, with a chin band and a circlet, all apparently of white fabric.

Although the dress of the twelfth century is more interesting visually than that of the thirteenth century, the variety of clothing available in the thirteenth century, particularly from the 1230s onwards, demonstrates how far clothing had come towards the modern idea of fashion. Like Master Pierre the Chanter in France in the twelfth century, Berthold von Regensburg in Germany in the following century was appalled at the effort put into worrying about how clothes were made and looked. Several writers stressed the importance of novelty in dress. Laws existed to control the making and wearing of dress. And there was serious money to be made from providing clothing – according to Ottokar of Styria, writing a few years after the event, those who were skilled in cutting and decorating women's clothes became rich by making the clothes for the wedding of King Albrecht I of Austria in 1298. Fashion, and its particular association with women, had begun.

princeps nomme albuguafe. in libro suo
que sciencarum electione. z ubor no
mmaur pulcitudinem: dixit op hic p
tholomeus fuit ur in disciplinar scie
cia importens: prinensalijs in duabz ar
tibz subtili. id est. geometria. z astrolo

III

Fashion and Formality
c.1300–c.1400

THE FOURTEENTH CENTURY IS OFTEN SAID TO BE THE STARTING point of fashion. If by 'fashion' is meant an ever-changing appearance, based on novelty and not necessity, which is considered desirable and sought by as many people as possible, then, arguably, fashion developed at the start of the twelfth century. Modern writers have made much of the short clothes for men that appeared around 1335, as though men had never worn short clothing before. Far more significantly, the fourteenth century is marked by changes in clothing construction, such as experiments with the setting-in of armholes, the greater use of gores and centre-front closings; clearer regional differences in appearance, especially in women's dress; and by the increasing separation of clothing into fashionable dress and formal dress, which means that more garments were in use. The sum total of the changes perhaps justified the remark made towards the end of century by the Florentine Franco Sacchetti, who complained about the number of fashions he had seen in his lifetime, and the way people were rushing to adopt all the latest trends.

The economies of Flanders and England remained closely tied to the woollen textile industries. In 1337 Edward III banned the exporting of English wool and the importing of foreign cloth; in the hope of establishing a woollen industry in England, he encouraged foreign wool workers to settle there. Flanders began to concentrate on making only luxury woollens; and English and locally made cloths began to take over the markets abandoned by Flanders. By the early 1370s English cloth was being smuggled into Flanders, and England had become the chief manufacturer of woollen cloth. Edward III's claim to the French throne, which he pursued by waging war on France, destroyed most of the great fairs that had operated there in the previous century. However, the economic background was already becoming more complex, with the development of commercial centres such as Bruges in Flanders and Genoa in Italy, and the mostly Italian banks that operated across western Europe.

All the Italian silk-weaving centres produced the lightweight silk fabric called cendal, which was often used as lining in clothing, though by the end of the century cendal had largely been replaced by other light silks, called sarcenets, taffetas and tarteryns. The Lucchese silk industry was adversely affected by prolonged political disturbances in the city in the first half of the fourteenth century, and by the end of the century Lucca had lost most of its weavers, and its reputation as the major silk-weaving centre. Venice became famous for its velvets and satins, and forbade its own weavers to emigrate for fear of rivals benefiting from trade secrets, as it had done when it took in displaced Lucchese weavers. Genoa and Florence were among the other cities that also benefited from the influx of Lucchese workers.

A semi-automatic reaction to an assumed social or economic problem was the enacting of sumptuary legislation. What this legislation reveals, in hindsight, is a general increase in prosperity, and a concomitant desire to spend some of that prosperity on fine clothing. In 1337 in England there was a ban on anyone with an income under £100 wearing furs; in 1363 concern was expressed that the lower orders were buying finer clothing and food. Around 1350 Gilles Li Muisis, Abbot of St Martin of Tournai, said that women had previously had three outfits – a best one for great feast days; a second one for ordinary feast days and Sundays; and a third for daily life. But by that time new inventions were multiplying, and women were spending all morning arranging themselves. In Hainaut, in present-day Belgium, in 1354 servants (of both sexes) were forbidden to wear silks, miniver, ermine and lettice (a white fur, mimicking ermine) in their 'sourcos' and 'cottes hardies' (the latter apparently close-fitting outer garments). The comments and the assumed need for legislation suggest real growth in wealth, despite the drop in population levels caused by the Black Death (1348–9 in France and England). Peasant risings in Flanders between 1323 and 1328, in France in 1358, and in England in 1381 suggest increased expectations further down the social ladder.

The British Library has a few of the extant fourteenth-century English Great Wardrobe accounts dealing with the expenditure of the royal household. The bulk of the English material, however, is in the National Archives. Some of it has been published, but there is no systematic listing of its contents for those interested in dress. Equivalent material for France is held in the Archives Nationales and the Bibliothèque Nationale. French antiquarians have been busy transcribing and publishing material since the nineteenth century. Most Italian towns have their own archives, though the archives at Naples were destroyed towards the end of the Second World War; the material there had been published only sketchily. At a less elevated social level, one can find a wider range of chronicles and literature in the vernacular, coming from secular sources, which can aid understanding of the contexts in which clothing was worn and the attitudes to it.

In the first half of the fourteenth century splendid, but mostly undated, illuminated manuscripts were produced in northern France and Flanders. Comic border scenes continued into the fourteenth century, sometimes referring to the text they accompany (e.g. fig. 53). Although until around the middle of the century the preferred private prayer book in England remained the psalter, highly fashionable owners can be seen in the up-and-coming devotional book in England, the book of hours (fig. 56); and ownership of manuscripts becomes far easier to establish than in previous centuries. Unfortunately, the unstable conditions created on the Continent by Edward III in the early years of what was to become the Hundred Years' War, and by the Black Death, mean that for the second half of the century there are fewer illuminated manuscripts to use as sources for a study of northern European dress. In Italy the best sources for dress history are often to be found in the great fresco cycles in churches and secular buildings, but there are also a number of useful secular manuscripts.

It is perfectly clear that illuminated manuscripts were hugely expensive investments. The cost is most easily compared with the wages of masons, for whom there are the most complete wage figures. At a time when a master mason would be lucky to earn £10 a year, the scribe who wrote out the *Litlyngton Missal* (now in Westminster Abbey, London, MS 37) for the Abbot of Westminster received food and lodgings for the two-year duration of the work, as well as £5 in money and clothing. The parchment cost over £4. And then the illuminator had to be paid over £20. But there were many people rich enough to pay that kind of price – the sumptuary law passed in England in 1363 assumed that there were merchants worth £500 in goods, and even £1000. These men were equated, in terms of clothing privileges, with

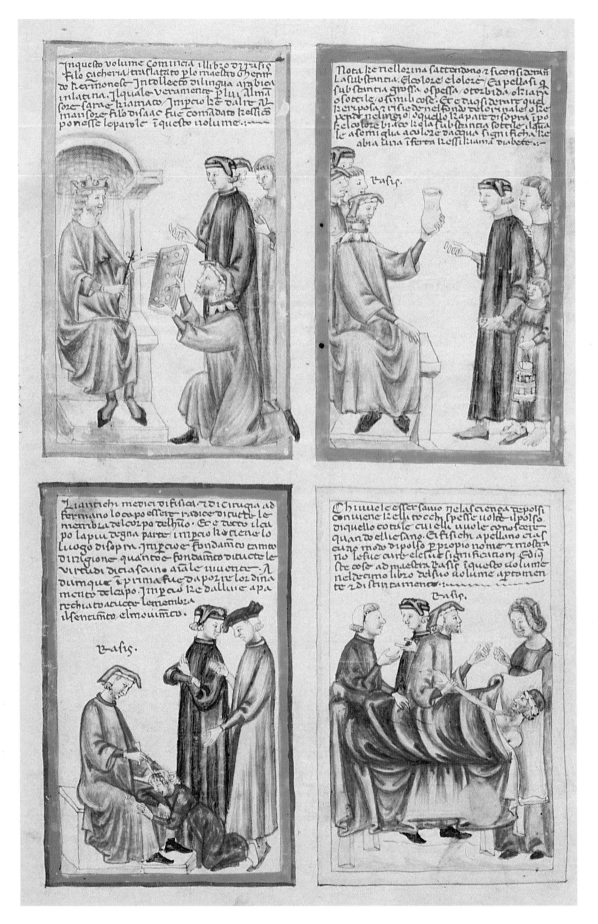

Inquesto volume comicia illibzo dyrasis
filo gacheria traslatato plo maestro ghenr
do hermonese. Intellecto dilingua ajabiou
inlatina. Ilquale veramente plui alma
sore sarae kiamato. Impero ke dal re al
mansore filo disaac fue comidata kessi e
ponesse leparole iquesto volume.:.

Nota ke nellozina sattendeno e si considrati
la substantia. Elcolore e lodore. Et pella si q
sub stantia grossa o spessa o torbida otriar
o sotrile o simili cose. Et e das si dermit quel
perposer virisede nelfondo delorinale o se
pede nelingo o quello kapa re disopra ipo
se color et bidet ke la substantia sottile ilqua
le asemiglia acolore dacqua signiffica re
abia una isterta kessi kiama diabete.:.

L antichi medici dufisica e di cirugia ad
fermano lo capo essere radice detuti le
membla delcorpo dethuo. Et e dicto ilca
po lapiu degna parte impero ke tiene lo
luogo disopra. Impero fondameto tamto
dirigione quanto e fondameto diuirtute le
virtudi dicascuno a tale muente. A
dumque iprima fue dapozte lordina
mento delcapo. Impero ke dallume apa
rechia vacuere lemembla
il sentimento elmouimeto.

Basis.

Chi uuole essere sauio nela scienga depolsi
conuiene ke elli tocchi spesse uolte ilpolso
diquello cotale cui elli uuole conoscieri
quando de ellie sano. Et fisicti apellano cias
cuno modo dipolso pproprio nome e mostra
no lesue carie elesse significatoni. Et di
ste cose ad maestra basis siquesto dolume
neldramo libro desuo dolume aptamen
te e distintamente.:.

Basis.

82

46 OPPOSITE
Transplanted to early fourteenth-century Florence and its dress are Rasis, a ninth-century Muslim doctor, his patron King Almansor, and his patients. (Rasis, *Liber medicinalis Almansoris*, translated into Italian by Zucchero Bencivenni, Florence, 1300: Florence, Biblioteca Medicea Laurenziana, MS Plut. 73.43, f. 6v)

47 ABOVE
This image of men in their underwear before surgeons suggests that, despite all the attention tailors had been lavishing on outer garments, little attention seems to have been paid to underwear. The drawers are little more than two lengths of cloth joined at the crotch and held up by a belt, which also doubles as a support for the stockings. Stockings were already available ready-made, not knitted, but cut from cloth, ideally on the bias so that they would have some 'give' at the knees. (Roger Frugardi, *Book of Surgery*, France, near Amiens?, early 1300s: British Library, Sloane MS 1997, f. 7r, detail)

esquires and gentlemen of annual incomes from land worth £100 and £200
respectively. (The master mason, not surprisingly, fell into the class with no clothing
privileges at all.) Figures drawn from tax records in England in 1436 give some idea
of the group of people whose wealth could have made them patrons of illuminators:
fifty-one peers, 183 greater knights, 750 lesser knights, 1200 esquires, and 5500 men
of 'esquire income'.

In keeping with the documentary evidence of growing expenditure on
clothing, patterned fabrics, whether embroidered or woven, become more common
in the illuminations; not surprisingly, given that patterned silks were woven in Italy,
Italian manuscripts often show the greatest interest in them (see figs 51 and 55).
However, at the start of the century documents show that even royalty was keeping
silks for special occasions. In England cloths involving gold were issued at court for
ceremonies creating new knights. Colours in dress remained little changed from
those used in the previous century – for instance, the trousseau of Isabella of France,
who married Edward II of England in 1308, was dominated by red and murrey
(a reddish-purple). Only one outfit was in crimson velvet; and only her wedding
robe was of cloth of gold. The accounts of Mahaut, Countess of Artois, for the period
*c.*1313–17 show that her clothing was dominated by vermilions and green.

The fourteenth century used colours to create a true uniform – indeed, the
liveries that royalty and the nobility issued to their households no longer simply
denoted the structure of the household, but allegiance to particular households,
thereby creating the modern understanding of the term 'livery'. It would appear that
at the start of the century in France, the royal administration was already creating
uniforms for those involved in government: in 1303 Philip IV took steps to ensure
that those attending the opening of the Parlement de Toulouse would have outfits
to wear. By the end of the century once-fashionable garments had established
themselves as clothing to be worn on formal occasions, or as professional dress.

From the early thirteenth century the University of Paris had been issuing
rules about the clothing of its students and teachers, with the result that by the
beginning of the fourteenth century, academics and some other professions were
easily recognizable by their dress. An anthology of academic texts produced in Paris
*c.*1300 (British Library, Burney MS 275) shows a number of teachers dressed in black
or grey. Black was worn by regent masters of theology and by masters of arts. The
garments depicted are sometimes clearly *houces* (see caption to fig. 66), and at other

times over-garments with long pendant sleeves complemented by matching hoods. The students are sometimes more colourfully dressed, and they too have matching hoods, as the university regulations demanded. Caps that look a little like modern berets tend to be worn by teachers or proven scholars. The rules forbade any clothing that could provoke scandal, but in fig. 45, from the Burney manuscript, one man wears shoes whose toes are so long (and therefore potentially scandalous) that one toe escapes from the scene on to the letter Q in which he and his fellow scholars stand. (The leading man must be the ancient Greek scholar Ptolemy.) They are dressed in a variety of pale colours, which removes them from contemporary academic practice, but their clothing is basically the same as that worn by contemporary scholars.

Apart from the sober colours expected of university teachers, doctors of medicine and law were, in many countries and cities, allowed to wear the expensive woollen cloth, scarlet; in Italy miniver was added to this fabric, often on the hood. Boccaccio's *Decameron* is set outside Florence at the time of the Black Death, and was probably started shortly thereafter, around 1350. One of Boccaccio's characters talks of Florentines who returned home after studying at Bologna, as judges, doctors or lawyers, resplendent in scarlet and miniver (day 8, story 9). It would seem that in Italy scarlet and miniver became so inextricably linked with universities, even after miniver and hoods had passed from fashionable use around 1430, that when students in Ferrara wanted to mock an unpopular teacher in 1478, they dressed a donkey up in scarlet with a red hood edged with miniver.

Miniver features in the dress of the doctor Rasis (fig. 46), as he presents his treatise on medicine to King Almansor and treats patients, in a translation into Italian made in Florence in 1300 by a Florentine notary, Zucchero Bencivenni. Rasis is dressed not as the ninth-century Islamic doctor that he was, but as a citizen of Florence, in a hood worn as though it were a hat, with the face-opening encircling the top of the head, the neck section hanging at the back and the tail flopping over the front. (For the basic shape of the hood see fig. 50.) Beneath the hood the men wear linen coifs. As their main garments, they wear tunics with tight under-sleeves and super-tunics with looser, three-quarter-length sleeves. These outfits, *robe* (the Italian equivalent of the French *robes*), come to constitute almost a uniform of citizenship, as in the statutes of the dyers and tailors of Perugia (British Library, Add. MSS 22497 and 21965). The version of the outer garment with the cape sleeves,

48 LEFT
Miriam and her companions, dancing after crossing the Red Sea, wear their hair down, suggesting that they are unmarried girls. They have two closely fitting layers of clothing, the outer one in two examples split at the side of the hips, and laced half-closed. Their slightly sway-backed posture is fashionable.
(*Golden Haggadah*, Spain: Barcelona?, c.1320: British Library, Add. MS 27210, f. 15r, detail)

49 OPPOSITE
King Priam of Troy, in imperial crown and fashionable lattice-patterned shoes, sends his son Paris to Greece. Like her English counterparts, Helen (the woman Paris is trying to seduce) has plaited her hair and bunched the plaits under her crown. Paris the dutiful son is a far less flamboyant figure than Paris the seducer.
(*Grandes Chroniques de France*, Paris, c.1320–30?: British Library, Royal MS 16 G VI, vol. 1, f. 4v, detail)

already seen in fig. 44, also occurs in Italy, apparently for men of some standing. Names for garments are often no clearer in Italy than they are in northern Europe at this period; and in Italy, to add to the problem, there are regional variations in the names for similar garments.

Only the beard marks Rasis out as not really belonging to Florence around 1300. The woman in the sickroom is typically Italian for this period, with her very high-waisted garment and her uncovered hair plaited round her head. She is also typically Italian in being blonde – women are far more likely to have blonde hair than men are in Italian art, a fact that must be attributed to artifice rather than genetics. Some of the hair was probably false, as it seems that false hair had been banned in Florence by 1326, and at some point between 1327 and 1336 the city of Modena forbade servants and lower-class women to wear false plaits made of silk. Modena also forbade these women to wear trains; in 1318 Florence had issued a prohibition on servants and wet-nurses wearing floor-length garments. The frescoes by Giotto in the Arena Chapel in Padua show that Italian women's garments could be very long indeed in the early fourteenth century, and they suggest that something like a series of vertical tapes was sewn inside the skirts, above the hems, to lift the skirts invisibly so that women could walk. Frederick III of Sicily decreed late in 1309 or early in 1310 that Sicilian women's trains were to measure no more than four palms' widths. Contravention of this decree would mean fines for the women who wore them, and for the tailors who made them. This double penalty is quite conventional in Italian sumptuary legislation, though much rarer elsewhere. Bizarrely, Frederick's spiritual mentor, the Catalan Arnau de Vilanova, suggested (1309–11?) that the queen, with two of her ladies dressed as Faith and Hope, should visit all the churches and hospitals wherever they went, to offer comfort to the suffering. Even more bizarrely, this suggestion seems to have been carried out. No personification of Faith or Hope, the wife of Rasis's patient is simply fashionable, with her high waistline, overlong skirt and blonde plaits. Without visitors in the house, she might have worn a peculiarly Italian garment, the *guarnella*, which was a type of dress for housework, made of cotton or hemp, and almost always white.

A conjunction (not fully worked out) of the sufferings of the sick and injured and the sufferings of Christ occurs in the *Book of Surgery* by Roger Frugardi of Parma, first written c.1180. The British Library's manuscript (fig. 47) is considered to be the finest medieval example of an illustrated book on surgery; it is thought to have been

made near Amiens in northern France around 1300–10. In most of the scenes the surgeons wear not the pendant sleeves of the academic, but a much more practical outfit of tunic and sleeveless *surcote*, with the coif, which can be a mark of status. There is some evidence, from images such as these, that the university-trained doctors did not want surgeons, who were less likely to have been to university, to wear their type of clothing. Several of the patients in fig. 47 have stripped down to their underwear. Underwear was not changed daily: around 1300 the Dominican Jean de Baume compared those who confessed infrequently to naughty children who, in cold weather, slept in their dirty shirts, while good children changed their linen fortnightly. *Le Livre des mestiers de Bruges* (*The Book of the Trades of Bruges*), a phrase book in French and Flemish written in the late 1340s, says that at night shirts should be put at the bed head, and underpants under the bed. The outer garments—*mantles, surcotes, cotes, houches, clokes* and *pourpoints* (doublets)—were to be kept on a pole. Illustrations suggest that clothes poles were suspended horizontally, like swings. (Compare the tailor's shop in fig. 70.)

The *houche* or *houce* can be found in use in France until the end of the fourteenth century, by then mostly as an academic garment. It was also the outer garment prescribed in 1363 for French Jews, who had to wear a special sign on it, and on whatever garment they wore under the *houce*, so that they could always be recognized as Jews. Sometimes Jewish clothing was prescribed by the Christians around them, and sometimes the Jews chose it for themselves, so as not to be ostentatious. Jewish illuminated manuscripts, such as the British Library's *Golden Haggadah* of c.1320 (fig. 48), were sometimes commissioned from illuminators who worked for Christian patrons as well. The clothing can be remarkably similar to that of Christians, especially in the case of women's clothing, although it is not clear why. This manuscript, produced in Barcelona where the Jews were still relatively privileged, has clear stylistic links to contemporary French illuminations, and much

50
Rabbits using a hood as a warren; the tail has been cut off to create a rabbit hole. In Bruges in 1309 it was decreed that a hood using miniver had to contain at least thirty skins. In England the accounts of Lady Elizabeth de Burgh for 1350–1 mention hoods using fifty miniver bellies each. Squirrel skins were usually 5½–7 inches (14–18 cm) long.
(*Gorleston Psalter*, England: East Anglia?, c.1310–20: British Library, Add. MS 49622, f. 202v, detail)

51 OPPOSITE

Although the elaborate textiles here help to denote the sin of Pride, throughout the manuscript one has a strong sense of the importance of patterns for the artist – he often almost loses his figures against their patterned backgrounds. Genoa had been weaving her own silks from at least the mid-thirteenth century. A Genoese silk (possibly a *samitum rotatum*) recorded at St Paul's Cathedral in London in 1292 had circles, yellow birds and leopards on it.
(*Treatise on the Vices*, Genoa or the Black Sea, *c*.1330: British Library, Add. MS 27695, f. 2v)

52 ABOVE

The woman here, with her fashionable high waistline, *mi-parti* garment and long hair, is to be understood as the embodiment of the sin of Luxuria. She has trapped a number of birds in cages; celibate churchmen often denounced fashionably dressed women as setting traps for men's souls, yet the Church could never speak with one voice on the relationship between women's appearance and the sin of Luxuria. St Thomas Aquinas, writing 1267–73, said that a woman who dressed up to please her husband was not guilty of sin. Other churchmen took the line that any self-adornment was sinful because it was done through pride, one of the major sins.
(*Treatise on the Vices*, Genoa or the Black Sea, *c*.1330: British Library, Add. MS 27695, f. 15v, detail)

53
In the early fourteenth century all women in England wore their hair in plaits drawn towards the front of the head, as shown above; married women increasingly made only a pretence of covering their hair, as their veils were growing thinner. The sleeves of super-tunics for the fashionable now stopped about the elbow, where they developed a tail at the back. (*Taymouth Hours*, England, c.1325–35: British Library, Yates Thompson MS 13, f. 88r, detail)

of the dress looks French-inspired too, with the most notable exception being the side-lacing on the dress of some of the women. Spanish dress continued to be obviously laced at the side until at least the middle of the fourteenth century (fig. 60). The twelfth-century Spanish rabbi Maimonides had decreed that a husband should provide his wife with new clothes every year in the rainy season, and with make-up to keep her attractive to him, in accordance with his wealth – this runs completely counter to the standard Christian view that women, and the men who were responsible for them, should be discouraged from such expenditure.

Artists were becoming increasingly adept at using dress to add silent meanings to the texts they were illustrating. The *Taymouth Hours* were illuminated in England c.1325–35 for an unidentified lady of very high rank. The woman at prayer in fig. 53 is dressed very much as the owner of the book is in other scenes, though one should perhaps hesitate to say that in this case she is the book's owner. The woman's veil and chin-cloth identify her as married. She is looking at a man who is more fashionable than she is because the tails (called 'tippets' in English) hanging from the sleeves of his super-tunic are longer than hers; he is also, therefore, probably younger. Behind her an almost bare-headed, and therefore unmarried, young woman, with fashionable horizontally set plaits, seems to be pulling at her veil, presumably to stop her from looking at a man who is forbidden to her because of her age and marital status. The image is related to the text above, which describes God – ignored by the lady, who is supposedly at prayer – as the source of holy desires, correct counsel and just works. The artist demonstrates by a number of means, including dress, that these are not in the lady's heart.

In a miniature in a copy of the *Grandes Chroniques de France* (*Great Chronicles of France*, fig. 49) the artist has worked without particular guidance from the text to produce an image that the original reader of the 1320s could have understood through its dress. The Trojan king Priam sends his son Paris to Greece, a visit that results in the seduction of Helen, the wife of Menelaus, King of Sparta, and the Trojan War. Priam's crown with its arched top makes him a venerable monarch in the mould of Charlemagne (who appears in fig. 81). While he is receiving his father's orders, Paris is dressed demurely in a violet super-tunic with modest tails (*cornettes* in French) on his sleeves. But when he reaches Greece he becomes a rather flashier dresser as the seducer of a married woman. The idea that a *robe* required garments of one colour is completely ignored – he wears a blue super-tunic with a red hood lined in green. He also wears very fashionable shoes, cut in a lattice-work pattern. Had Helen been as able to read the signs as a contemporary reader was supposed to be, she would have seen him for the wastrel that he was. Young men (and minstrels) were, it seems, always susceptible to the lure of flashy clothing: the Chevalier de la Tour Landry (fl. 1346–89) said that his father, when young, had once attended dinner dressed in a *cote hardie* in the manner of Germany (not explained), and had been told that he looked like a minstrel. (The early fourteenth-century *Manesse Codex*, now in Heidelberg University Library, shows Heinrich von Frauenlob, the German *Minnesinger* [singer of songs of courtly love], surrounded by minstrels dressed in *mi-parti* with horizontal bands, diagonal bands, and even zigzags.) Paris in fig. 49 has at least stopped short of adopting the returning fashion for *mi-parti*.

Three other examples of dress that help underscore a literary point come from an Italian work about the vices, and provide 'evidence' of the link between clothing and sin. This manuscript is often dated to the late fourteenth century, but the clothing suggests that it belongs to the later 1320s or early 1330s. The text seems to be datable between 1314 and 1324. It was illuminated in the republican city of Genoa, or a Genoese environment, possibly in a Genoese trading colony on the Black Sea. It now survives only in fragments. One of the most striking features of many of the outfits it depicts is the gold ribbon that often follows seam-lines, emphasizing their presence and perhaps serving the function of strengthening them, as though the tailor does not quite trust to his skill to hold the garments together. The most famous scenes show several men in Italian citizen *robe*, often in sober blues, browns and greys, as would suit good republicans. (Grey seems to have had a long history as a 'citizen colour' in Genoa.)

Fig. 51, set in a border of knights in tournament scenes, shows three male figures (possibly three generations of an aristocratic family) in clothing far richer

54

A Tartar potentate gives a banquet at which Europeans and one African are present as (very gluttonous) guests and as musicians. According to the Venetian traveller Marco Polo (who is said to have dictated the account of his travels while he was a prisoner of war in Genoa in 1298), whenever the Great Khan, leader of the Tartars, was about to drink at important banquets, the throng of musicians in the banqueting hall would start playing; and after the banquets jugglers and acrobats would entertain the diners. At his birthday feasts the Great Khan would wear a silk garment resplendent with gold, and his courtiers would dress similarly. The European banqueters here have not gone completely native, however, as they have retained their white coifs and remain clean-shaven.

(*Treatise on the Vices*, Genoa or the Black Sea, c.1330: British Library, Add. MS 27695, f. 13r)

55

The Judgement of Paris, in the dress of the 1330s. Paris (kneeling) wears a long *roba* of brocade; the goddesses, awaiting his judgement, wear super-tunics and tunics of different fabrics. Juno, as queen of the gods, wears a crown on her plaited hair, and her super-tunic is probably made from a Tartar silk. Seated on the viewer's left is Pallas Athena, the goddess of wisdom. The words on her chest are not part of her clothing, but her speech or thoughts: 'Paris spurns me because he does not see the light well, and he praises Venus who always cheats him badly.'
(*Address of the City of Prato to Robert of Anjou, Tuscany*, c.1335–40: British Library, Royal MS 6 E IX, f. 22r)

than that which republican Genoa should have tolerated for its citizens. In 1157 Genoa had already passed the first known sumptuary law since Carolingian times, restricting the use of rich furs to those of its citizens who were going to places where impressive clothing would have been necessary, such as the papal and imperial courts. At the end of the 1200s a poet known as the 'Anonimo genovese' enthused about the rich goods for sale in the city's shops, and the fine clothing of the Genoese, whose servants looked like ladies and knights. Every man seemed like a marquis. Small wonder, then, that to ensure republicanism in the fourteenth century, any nobleman who gained public office in Genoa had to resign his titles of nobility. The three men shown in fig. 51 are all dressed in very rich clothing, featuring many gold edges and seams. The man on the left has an extraordinarily lavish outfit of outer garment and hat-like hood, with gold-spotted vertical panels, lined with miniver. The man on the right has fur tails hanging from the hem of his *houce*-like over-garment. Outsize buttons also appear on the clothing. Quite reasonably, this scene is thought to depict Pride.

Fig. 52 depicts Luxuria, the excess of pleasures that can lead to lust. A figure in 'citizen' dress helps a lady, dressed in blue and gold *mi-parti*, with her cages and snares. Her hairstyle and her high waistline are typically Italian. The connection between women and Luxuria was fairly standard, as was the idea that women used their appearance to ensnare men; but the rest of the sinners in this manuscript tend to be men (as in penitential literature), even though grammatically the words for the vices are likely to be feminine.

Genoa expanded her trading interests to the east, to the Black Sea, where Caffa (now Feodosiya) in the Crimea became her most important link with the Mongol, or Tartar, Empire (and possibly part of the route that brought the Black Death to Europe). The trading colony at Caffa is thought to have been established in 1266; by 1290 there was an Italian tailor, called Pagano, living there in the house of a Saracen. There was a considerable amount of intermarrying with local Muslims and Christians. At the banquet at the court of a Tartar potentate (fig. 54) Europeans are present as guests and musicians. Several of the musicians wear European coifs, tunics and super-tunics with elbow-length sleeves, and the gold ribbon seam trimming common in the manuscript. The artist of this scene (dealing with the vice of Gluttony) knew a great deal about Tartar dress and customs. The potentate, seated at the centre top, and his European guests are depicted in clothing that is very similar in cut and shoulder decoration to a corn-coloured garment excavated from the late fourteenth-century tomb of Prince Zhu Tan in Shangdong province. The potentate's robe may be made of Tartar silk. Tartar silks had dominated the papal inventory of 1295, and the Neapolitan court bought Tartar cloths in 1316 and 1331–2.

In western Europe young men's clothing began to grow shorter and tighter from around 1335. But this was not seen at the time as a new phase of tailoring – rather, it tended to be considered a scandal, introduced by foreigners. In 1335 the fifty-eight-year-old King of Naples, Robert I of Anjou, made public pronouncements criticizing young men for introducing exaggerated and ridiculous fashions. Because of vanity or absurdity, the garments involved had been tightened, and they were so short that they scarcely reached the buttocks. (It must be remembered that the ruling house of Naples came from Anjou in France and spoke French. Naples could well have been the point of entry into Italy for the new fashions, if they came from the north, as it was to be for Spanish styles in the later fifteenth century.)

However, no signs of these disturbing new clothing trends appear in fig. 55, from a laudatory address to the king from the city of Prato that is thought to date from c.1335–40, the last years of his lordship there. Perhaps the artist was influenced by the recipient's known aversion to the new styles. The Latin text is a reflection of the impression that the king made on many in his lifetime as a seeker after justice and peace, in that it deals with justice; but the image here, of the Judgement of Paris, is one of faulty judgement, in that his judgement in favour of Venus in the goddesses' beauty contest was to lead to the Trojan War.

Pairs of peacocks, the birds associated with Juno, queen of the gods (the figure in the centre) appear not on her super-tunic, but on Pallas's, on the left. Pairs of birds, facing and turning away from each other, were very popular as decorative motifs in textiles at this time, and presumably featured among the garments recorded in Florence in 1343, when a number of wealthy women paid for lead seals that they then attached to clothing otherwise forbidden by law, to show that they had paid for the right to wear it. Much of this clothing was of silk, and patterned in a variety of ways, with birds, dragons, crowns, stars and butterflies. Animal decoration found its way into embroidery too – in 1330 Philippa of Hainaut, wife of Edward III of England, had worn a *roba* of five garments of purple velvet embroidered with golden squirrels when she first attended church after the birth of Prince Edward.

56 LEFT

The fashionably dressed Nevilles of Hornby kneel before the crucified Christ. An English poem, 'Against the pride of the ladies' (by 1340), says that all women wanted to wear their hair in 'boses' (lumps), with 'clogges' hanging at their jowls, declining to put the 'boses' in linen, and having them hanging like 'the ears of a slit swine'. The French chronicler Jean de Venette said that in the mid-fourteenth century, apart from the royal family, everyone (by which he meant every nobleman) began to be bearded, and was therefore mocked by the common people. (*Neville of Hornby Hours* [*Egerton Hours*], London, by 1335: British Library, Egerton MS 2781, f. 35r, detail)

57 LEFT BOTTOM

While some of the figures in the Luttrell Psalter wear dress from the 1330s, the heraldically decorated clothing of the women here has less to do with fashion than with status. All three figures display the martlets (birds) of the Luttrells, but Lady Luttrell also wears the lion rampant of her natal family, the Suttons, while her daughter-in-law Beatrice also wears the arms of her own family, the Scropes, perhaps embroidered. The most famous piece of fourteenth-century English heraldic embroidery, with the leopards of England, is now in the Musée de Cluny in Paris, and may date from 1338. (*Luttrell Psalter*, England, East Anglia, c.1325–40: British Library, Add. MS 42130, f. 202v, detail)

58 OPPOSITE

Alexios Apokaukos came from an obscure provincial background to immense wealth, and then to great political importance as Governor of Constantinople and *megas doux* (grand duke) or commander-in-chief of the navy. He was also a patron of learning: here he reads works attributed to the ancient Greek physician Hippocrates. Despite the emphasis on Greek culture, his clothing is Assyrian in origin. (*Hippocrates, Works*, Constantinople?, c.1342: Paris, Bibliothèque Nationale, MS gr. 2144, f. 11r)

Perhaps less charmingly to the modern reader, the *roba* was lined with squirrels in the form of miniver.

In 1342 the Lord of Florence was, briefly, the Frenchman Walter de Brienne, titular Duke of Athens and the nephew by marriage of Robert I of Naples. The Florentine chronicler Giovanni Villani blamed the introduction of the new male fashion into Florence on Walter de Brienne. His arrival had caused the city's knights to rush to wear a *surcotto*, or rather, a *guarnacca* (apparently both super-tunics), tight at the belt, with the points of their *manicottoli* (the tails on their short sleeves) reaching the ground, and lined with miniver and ermine. Young men were wearing a *cotta* or a *gonella* (both under-tunics) so short and tight that they couldn't get dressed without help.

Other aspects of men's dress were criticized. In fig. 56, from an English manuscript now known as the *Neville of Hornby Hours*, produced around 1335, Robert de Neville (an Englishman, despite his French-sounding name) wears clothing that could have been found in France, and was subject to criticism in both France and England. The *Grandes Chroniques de France* attributed the French defeat at the battle of Crécy in 1346 to God's judgement on men who had worn clothing that was too tight, too short (not de Neville's particular problem here), and too long in the tails on the sleeves and hoods. The vertical slit at the side of the super-tunic attracted adverse comments too – though the main function of the slit was apparently to grant access to the purse worn hanging from the belt beneath the super-tunic, some men seem also to have hung daggers from their belts. When the dagger hilts protruded from the side slits, the effect would cause preachers to draw comparisons with the hole in the side of Christ, caused by the lance of the Roman centurion who had delivered the *coup de grâce* at the Crucifixion. This image shows that de Neville had no qualms about such possible criticism, as he kneels beside the crucified Christ.

In two scenes his wife, Isabel de Byron, wears the same fashionable *robe* in blue-violet, with a wide neckline and miniver-lined tails on the super-tunic's sleeves. The increasing elaboration of women's hairstyles induced some women to wear only the filmiest of veils; but here, with plaits bunched over her ears and the ends drawn up over the top of the head, where they are presumably pinned together, Isabel de Byron seems to have abandoned veils altogether.

As noted earlier, *mi-parti* seems to have become fashionable again across western Europe in the 1320s, having recovered from its position as servants' livery.

Sometimes artists used this fashionable feature of dress to add a comment to their images. In the later 1330s Ambrogio Lorenzetti, working on the frescoes of *Good and Bad Government* in Siena, painted a figure dressed in black and white *mi-parti* (the colours of the city) and cutting itself in two, as an image of civil strife. The *mi-parti* effect of the coat of arms of the married aristocratic woman is found on the *surcotes ouvertes* (sleeveless, open-sided *surcotes*) of the women in fig. 57, the wife and daughter-in-law of Sir Geoffrey Luttrell (d. 1345), in the best-known scene from the *Luttrell Psalter*, of c.1325–40. It is not clear if women did actually wear clothes with heraldic decoration, but the purpose of the clothing in this scene is to identify the family who owned the book.

Leaving to one side the question of the 'reality' of the open-sided *surcotes*' decoration, it is worth noting that although these garments were currently fashionable, they would, in the course of the next generation, be increasingly reserved as garments of status, to be worn by women of at least the rank of lady on formal occasions. Some women seem to have preferred to be depicted on their tombs not in fashionable dress, but in the *surcote ouverte* because then there could be no question of confusing them with middle-class women of fashion and wealth. If some women did wear heraldic *surcotes ouvertes*, this could help to explain why the garment was retained as a symbol of rank.

The Byzantine Empire had had centuries in which to perfect its types of formal dress, and the Byzantines seem increasingly to have ignored clothing from the empire's Greek and Roman pasts in favour of that worn by their Middle Eastern neighbours. Fig. 58 shows the Byzantine dignitary Grand Duke Alexios Apokaukos around 1342. The work known as the *Treatise on the Dignities and Offices*, written between 1347 and 1368(?) by a writer referred to as Pseudo-Kodinos, ranks the position of grand duke eighth in the extensive hierarchy of the Byzantine court. The same writer indicates that some of the clothing of this rank was Assyrian in origin.

Apokaukos wears a garment unknown in western Europe, tightly fitting in the upper body, as a lot of western male dress was at this period, but closed all the way down the centre front. Modern writers often describe this type of garment as a kaftan, but the contemporary term seems to have been *kabbadion*: Pseudo-Kodinos says it was Assyrian in origin. The grand duke was among the group of highest officials who could exercise some choice in their uniforms: he could have his *kabbadion* made from any of the customary silks. Despite his position as commander

59

An assembly of those concerned with the authority of laws. In the centre, on the highest level, sits the pope, with, at a slightly lower level, an emperor with an arch-topped crown. Beside the emperor sit three kings or princes, with civilians in front of them. On the other side of the pope sit two cardinals (in red, wide-brimmed hats), and two bishops or archbishops. In front of them sit academic clerics, with clean-shaven faces and short hair. The small bars on the shoulders of the man at the extreme right, in *mi-parti*, resemble those worn by the presidents of the highest French law court, the Parlement de Paris, in the fifteenth century, and may therefore betoken membership of the legal profession. The pale, tongue-like shapes (*languetes*) on the chest of his neighbour allow his garment to be equated with the *houce* in a French royal wardrobe account of 1352, when they were perhaps a relatively new feature.
(Gratian, *Decretals*, Spain: Barcelona?, mid-1300s: British Library, Add. MS 15274, f. 3r)

60 LEFT
This figure, in very Spanish, very secular dress, appears at the start of a discussion on whether or not clerics can make wills. The immediate response is that clerics are ordered by many authorities to have no possessions. This figure, then, stands as a very clear example of worldliness, with his low-waisted garment laced tightly in red at the viewer's right, sharply set-in armholes, and his lattice-work shoes.
(Gratian, *Decretals*, Spain: Barcelona?, mid-1300s: British Library, Add. MS 15274, f. 185, initial)

61 BELOW
These scenes at the court of King Meliadus provide excellent examples of the diversity of dress to be found in Naples, an Italian city ruled by a French family, and open to influences from Spain. (Helie de Borron, *Roman du roi Meliadus de Leonnoys*, Naples, c.1352: British Library, Add. MS 12228, f. 220r)

of the fleet, Apokaukos appears, with his book, in civilian (and scholarly) guise, in a *kabbadion* made from a fabric decorated with roundels containing lions set back to back. This type of design probably originated in the Middle East and, through Byzantine versions of it, passed into early Italian silk designs; but whereas Byzantine silks seem to have retained the original Middle Eastern roundels, Italian silks were by this date using pairs of animals in asymmetrical patterns or in diagonal rows, under the influence of Tartar silks.

On his head Apokaukos wears a golden crown-like cap, with a red inner cap. Pseudo-Kodinos refers to a garment, also Assyrian in origin, called a *skaranikon*, made in gold and crimson for the highest officials, bearing images of the emperor standing (at the front) and seated (at the back). There is a trace of an image at the front of the cap. Modern authors cannot agree if the *skaranikon* was this cap or a type of tunic, but it seems reasonable to identify it with the cap worn here.

The British Library possesses a remarkable two-volume manuscript (figs 59 and 60) comprising the discussions of points of canon (or church) law known as the *Decretum* of Gratian. Gratian produced his text near Bologna c.1140, and it soon became a standard work in its field. This particular manuscript was produced in Barcelona in the mid-fourteenth century under the influence of contemporary Italian art; some of the 'official' clothing is shared with Italy and with France. The purely fashionable clothing it depicts tends to look Spanish. Fig. 59 includes the people to whom the work would have been of use: ecclesiastical and secular rulers, and, on the viewer's right, laymen who are almost certainly lawyers in occupational dress. This group includes elements of fashionable dress, such as a variety of sleeves, mi-parti, and a very tight waistline with buttons closing the garment over the stomach. The ridged high necklines of some of these figures are quite distinctive. Elsewhere in the manuscript these necklines can be seen to rise above scooped outer necklines; they are presumably doublet collars. Cape-sleeves and tailed sleeves can be found in France, but, unlike here, they are not usually worn simultaneously. This may be a local fashion in formal dress.

In fig. 60, once again a Spanish illuminator has shown how clothing is made to fit by lacing, and also by another attempt to create a smoother junction of sleeve and bodice on the body (though the sleeve itself wrinkles under the arm). Versions of this armhole seam that runs on to the chest can be found in Spain as early as the 1270s in the *Cantigas de Santa Maria* (see page 69) of Alfonso X, which may mean that

62

Two youths in doublet and hose (one pair in *mi-parti*) in a manuscript illuminated in the style favoured at the Austrian court in the early fifteenth century. One of the more extreme methods of setting in a sleeve involved cutting the armhole so deeply into the body of the garment that at mid-chest height the centre-front and the centre-back sections barely existed. The armhole then swooped around on to the body in a great curve called, in the French accounts, a *grande assiette* (big plate). In the examples here the upper body and the upper sleeve appear to be cut from the same piece of fabric. (Note also the centre-front lacing of the doublet, and the laces that attach the hose to the lower edge of the doublet.) (*Spiegel der Weisheit*, Austria, *c*.1415: British Library, Egerton MS 1121, f. 51v)

Spain pioneered this type of armhole. It was still in use in Austria as late as the beginning of the fifteenth century (fig. 62), which suggests that tailors still had some way to go before they gained complete mastery over cloth.

Helie de Borron's *Roman du roi Meliadus de Leonnoys* (*Romance of Meliadus, King of Lyoness*) was one of the Arthurian romances read in French in Italy. The British Library's manuscript of it (fig. 61) seems to have been made for the Francophone court of Naples, probably between 1352 and 1362. As there is little documentary material available for Naples, it is difficult to gauge the extent to which this outpost of France remained truly French. Both of King Robert's wives had been Spanish, the second one, Sancia of Majorca, having died as recently as 1345. One man in the manuscript has deep armholes on his super-tunic, suggesting that tailors in Naples were also trying the method used in Barcelona to make sleeves fit into bodices. Some men in the manuscript also wear garments like the Spanish *pellote*. Some of the female figures in this manuscript look more Italian than French, with their fat (almost inevitably) blonde plaits bound up on their heads. In fig. 61 the queen wears a very northern European veil with a crinkled edge; and on other pages some women wear *surcotes ouvertes*, which are difficult to find elsewhere in Italy. Yet some of the queen's ladies have very high-set *cornette* bands on their sleeves, which seem to be more characteristic of Italian dress at this period. The king's messenger to the queen has very long *cornettes* on his sleeves, and the tail on his hood (also called a *cornette* in French, but liripipe in English) is so long that he has tucked it into his belt; this is a common way of treating the hood's tail, and seems to have no regional significance.

Many of the men have the flat elongated torsos of the 1350s, with some flaring at the hips (flared skirts had been accused of contributing to the French defeat at Crécy in 1346). This must mean that the old way of cutting a garment's front and back from straight lengths of cloth, and adding smaller pieces where

63

At the coronation of Charles V of France in 1364 the Duke of Bourbon, the Great Chamberlain of France, puts the special stockings or boots of the King of France on the new king. The whole process of dressing the king turns him into a walking symbol of France. As Louis XIV is reported to have said in 1655, 'I am the state'.

(*Coronation Book of Charles V of France*, Paris, Master of the Coronation Book of Charles V, 1365: British Library, Cotton Tiberius MS B VIII, f. 48r, detail)

64

At the coronation of Jeanne de Bourbon, women's fashion is represented, without a qualm about its level of dignity, by the two young women near the queen (possibly members of the royal family), with their stiffened plaits at the sides of their heads and their wide-necked, tightly fitting super-tunics. A sleeve *cornette* flies out behind the Countess of Artois (in brown), as its wearer moves forward to help the queen. One of the men at the left has a sleeve tail that reaches his ankle.

(*Coronation Book of Charles V of France*, Paris, Master of the Coronation Book of Charles V, 1365: British Library, Cotton Tiberius MS B VIII, f. 67v, detail)

65
This scene, of the Old Testament figure Hosea writing, is attributed to an illuminator called the Master of the Bible of Jean de Sy, one of a small group of illuminators who worked for the King of France, Jean le Bon, and then for his son, Charles V. He was therefore in a prime position to find out about and record the latest trends, including sway-back postures. (*Bible Historiale*, Paris, Master of the Bible of Jean de Sy, formerly called the Maître aux Boquetaux, 1357: British Library, Royal MS 17 E VII, vol. 2, f. 99r, detail)

necessary to increase the width, as with garments found in Greenland, had been abandoned, and that a horizontal seam had been introduced at the waist, with the flaring starting there. The clothing of the messenger and the king feature the slashed edges (dagging) that returned to popularity, and to criticism, towards the middle of the century. Elsewhere in the manuscript some men wear two new features of fundamental importance to western dress – a centre-front closing and a line of buttons down it. Since centre-front closings were adopted, they have never been abandoned in western clothing. Buttons were now so crucial in making clothing fit tightly that they became fashionable items in their own right, and were frequently used in unnecessarily large quantities. In Venice in 1351 the *signori di notte* – judges responsible for maintaining order, especially at night, and for collecting fines for abuse of the sumptuary laws – noted sixty silver-gilt buttons on a man's scarlet *tunica*.

Even if one ignores the novelties in dress in fig. 61, the variety alone suggests that the dress in this manuscript is neither French nor Italian, but Neapolitan – as befits that culturally diverse city.

In a *Bible Historiale* (*Historiated Bible*) of 1357 (fig. 65) a much more clearly French figure is to be found – in the young man with the typical whiplash stance of the period and upper-arm *cornette* bands and *cornettes*. This *Bible Historiale* seems to have been made for the future Charles V of France, who would have been twenty-one at the time; men of Charles's age would have dressed like the young man here.

In May 1364, when he was twenty-six, Charles V was crowned King of France in ceremonies at which dress was profoundly significant, for himself and for the nobility of a country being ravaged by the King of England in pursuit of his own claim to the French throne. Charles cast aside the secular dress of his previous worldly state and took on clothing that symbolized his entering into the quasi-ecclesiastical state occupied by the kings of France. The queen, Jeanne de Bourbon, participated in this change too, but to a lesser extent. The ceremonies are recorded in the Coronation Book of Charles V, produced under the king's supervision in 1365. Two scenes, one for the king and one for the queen, have been chosen here (figs 63 and 64). The book contains a description, in French, of a coronation ceremony drawn up c.1230, and a description, in Latin, of Charles's and Jeanne's coronations. To these have been added nearly forty miniatures through which the ceremonies can be followed. These miniatures raise questions, to be considered shortly, about the accuracy of the clothing depicted on other male participants.

On ff. 44v–47v the king is shown in the early stages of the coronation ritual, dressed in a miniver-lined hood and ankle-length super-tunic with elbow-length sleeves and short tails on them. This second garment would have been fashionable about twenty-five years before, and it was made in a most unimpressive colour, plain brown, presumably to emphasize the contrast with his later splendour. Beneath it he wore the special red silk tunic (*cote* in the French text) and shirt that would be unlaced on the chest and the back to allow him to be anointed – the rings for the lacing on the chest and arms of the tunic can be seen in fig. 63. This scene, the first after the removal of his brown super-tunic, shows him being dressed in the special stockings or boots of the King of France, with fleur-de-lys (the French royal emblem) in gold. (The Latin text says the stockings/boots are hyacinth-coloured; the French text says they are violet, though this has been corrected, perhaps by the king, to 'azure'.) Gold fleurs-de-lys on a blue ground permeate the rest of the coronation clothing, which includes a tunic like a priest's dalmatic, the final confirmation of the king's semi-clerical status.

Both texts agree that the royal boots or stockings are put on the king by the Great Chamberlain of France who, in this instance, is identified by the heraldry on his mantle as the queen's brother, the Duke of Bourbon. Apart from the presiding archbishop, the Archbishop of Reims (also wearing a version of the fleur-de-lys), and an attendant bishop, all the other figures visible at full length are in entirely secular and fashionable dress. The only figure in completely short clothing is the humble mace-bearer at the left, with his dagged hemline and his chokingly tight hood. The other men, who must be peers of the realm and are therefore present as participants in the ceremony, rather than as observers, make various concessions to the notion that longer clothing is more suitable for the occasion because it can hide some of the excesses of fashion and is more dignified. Their outfits also suggest that the comparative sobriety of the self-coloured *robe* is disappearing from fashion.

66 LEFT

A debate between a churchman and a knight takes place in an orchard in front of a king, a queen and a crowned nun. The *houce* of the churchman is red, the colour prescribed for doctors of canon law in Paris from the 1340s. In 1352 Charles V's father had a *houce* lined in squirrel belly fur, with the body of the garment taking 440 bellies, the 'wings' (sleeves?) ninety-six, the hood 110, and the crucial identifying elements, the 'tongues' (*languetes*) taking six.
(*Le Songe du vergier*, Paris, Master of the *Bible of Jean de Sy*, formerly called the Maître aux Boquetaux, *c.*1378: British Library, Royal MS 19 C IV, f. 1v)

67 OPPOSITE

St Ursula and some of her virgin companions in fashionable north Italian dress of the late fourteenth century. Garments like these made Giovanni de Mussis in Piacenza splutter with indignation in 1388. The garments the women of Piacenza called *cyprianae* would have been beautiful, he said, had they not had such large necklines that the breasts seemed to want to leave them. The costs of *pellande* (voluminous, high-necked garments) worried him too; but at least *pellande* covered the breasts, as does the red one on the right.
(*Hours of Bertrando dei Rossi or Giangaleazzo? Visconti*, Lombardy, *c.*1380–5: Paris, Bibliothèque Nationale, MS lat. 757, f. 380)

In fig. 63 the cloak of the man supporting the king opens to reveal a fashionably tight-waisted, doublet-like garment, with dagging at its lower edge. The man immediately next to him, perhaps the king's brother and heir-presumptive, the Duke of Anjou, wears a long garment with a sleeve left unbuttoned and wound around his arm. The garment is possibly also meant to be understood as being buttoned all the way down the centre front, in which case it is probably a version of the relatively new type of super-tunic called a *houppelande*, introduced around 1360, and disapproved of in 1362 because its length (after so many years of once-derided short clothing for men) made men look like women from behind. (In England, where the aristocracy were abandoning Anglo-Norman French for the English vernacular, the garment was known by both its French name and by its English name, goun. To contemporaries the word 'goun' apparently suggested foolishness because it was pronounced 'goon', which even today means 'fool' or 'madman'.)

The queen entered the cathedral dressed entirely in red – mantle, super-tunic and tunic, prescribed as silk – with her hair loose (compare fig. 64). Among married women, only queens wore their hair loose, and then only at their coronations. Normally, loose hair was the prerogative of unmarried girls, especially at their weddings, and nuns at their consecrations. There may be some symbolic link here in that the queen was enjoined to behave as much like a virgin as possible; and she was, like the king, entering into a quasi-religious state.

The queen, Jeanne de Bourbon, is described somewhat conventionally in Christine de Pisan's biography of Charles V, written in 1403, as being in the habit of wearing royal outfits and very rich jewels, with mantles of cloth of gold. Much more interestingly, she is also said to have changed her clothes at various times of day, according to royal and priestly customs. Obviously, one would expect a queen to change for special ceremonies, but the frequent changes within one day, with demands made by custom, would not have been possible without the larger wardrobe that the fourteenth century provided, and without a range of specifically formal garments.

Formalized dress is also to be found in the brown clothing of the woman behind the queen in fig. 64. She has been identified as Marguerite de France, Countess of Artois in her own right, and thus a peer of France. She had been a widow since 1346. A widow's clothing, like that of a nun, was meant to indicate that its wearer was in effect dead to the world, with the shrouding of the head and neck

68

The doublet associated with the Blessed Charles de Blois is made from a fabric identified as a Tartar silk and apparently so precious that every scrap of it was used, with the result that the garment is made from more pieces than are strictly necessary for its shape. In 1376 the city of Lucca ordered that velvet be woven to a width that corresponds to 23¼ inches (59 cm), presumably as part of the continuing demand for narrower fabrics to reduce wastage.

(Doublet, France, c.1364?: Lyons, Musée des Tissus et des Arts décoratifs, No. 30307)

in veils, and the dull (but not necessarily black) colouring of the rest of the clothing. Black was very difficult to dye, as is suggested by the most common black being known as *brunette* (dark brown cloth), and apparently being obtained by dyeing fabric in a dark woad blue, and then twice in a dark red.

The cut of the widow's outfit in fig. 64, with the simple three-quarter-length sleeves on the *surcote*, would have been fashionable about fifty years before. She was regarded as an exemplary widow; perhaps less so was the Countess of Tonnerre, widowed in 1334, and shown by an inventory of her possessions in 1360 to have only one *robe* of *grosse brunette noire* (coarse brown cloth). The rest of her clothing, though of wool rather than silk, was dominated by colours ranging from violets (violet was sometimes a widow's colour) to reds.

One point that may have struck the reader is how lacking in pattern the clothing of the peers at the coronation seems to be – can no one have worn figured silks, and would they really all have worn plain woollen clothing, sometimes with fur linings, especially in the middle of May? Sumptuary legislation passed in England in 1363 implies that silks were being worn even by the gentry and merchant classes. It is therefore inconceivable that the aristocracy of any country in western Europe would not wear silks to a coronation. The so-called doublet of the Blessed Charles de Blois (fig. 68), who died a few months after the coronation, is made from a Tartar silk of Near Eastern origin that uses a thread of almost ninety-nine per cent pure gold. Charles de Blois was at the coronation, and his son-in-law, the Duke of Anjou, was an active participant in the coronation ceremonies. In the manuscript interesting fabrics are reserved for the hangings in the cathedral. Perhaps the depiction of the textiles worn at the coronation was toned down to help focus attention on the king and on those individuals who had to be identifiable. Identification is possible chiefly through heraldically decorated clothing, which appears only when an individual is actively involved in some part of the ceremony – irrefutable proof, as has been argued recently, of the legitimacy of Charles's coronation and of the loyalty pledged by nobles who might face divided loyalties in the course of what was to become the Hundred Years' War. As with women's heraldic *surcotes ouvertes*, it is difficult to be sure of the extent to which such clothing was really used. In this respect the manuscript, though depicting actual events and people, is not a simple piece of

69 LEFT
A highly fashionable couple drink barley water for the good of their health. It is unusual for the hem of a woman's garment to be dagged like the one shown here, perhaps because dagging in that area might have risked exposing feet and ankles. As can be seen here, men did not worry about the length of their toes, or the difficulties they might experience in walking. De Mussis said that everyone, men and women, in Piacenza in 1388 was wearing pointed toes stuffed with ox hair. (*Tacuinum Sanitatis*, Lombardy, 1390s?: Paris, Bibliothèque Nationale, MS nouv. acq. lat. 1673, f. 52)

70 OPPOSITE
Although the purpose of this scene is to illustrate a short passage on the benefits and problems of wearing woollen clothing, it has been extended to encompass the activities in a tailor's workshop where the types of clothing made of wool can be seen – both main garments and accessories such as hoods and hose.
(*Tacuinum Sanitatis*, Lombardy) 1390s?: Paris, Bibliothèque Nationale, MS nouv. acq. lat. 1673, f. 96r)

de ſuo

Veſtes de ſiri i lane.

ſames eē ſ. deſcindendū erea de p̄ br ulr marinis et fiſi-
ſſanorum coualir calorem. nocumēntz tunentibz caloꝛē
riſono noi al ueſtibz lineis ſubtus eos.

reporting, like a souvenir, but a vital piece of statecraft in which dress acts as evidence when it is needed. Not until the sixteenth century were illuminated manuscripts almost mass-produced as souvenirs of important events (e.g. fig. 107).

Charles V, once crowned, developed a very particular image of himself as king, and dress was a crucial part of that image – he was Charles *le sage*, not just wise, but an intellectual, a sage. He encouraged scholars and commissioned illuminated manuscripts, often appearing in the dedicatory miniatures not as a crowned monarch, but as a learned man, in an outfit based on the cape-sleeved *houce* worn by university-educated (and hence often priestly) scholars. Thus he appeared in the now-damaged presentation scene of his own copy of a work called *Le Songe du vergier* (*The Dream of the Orchard*), translated into French from Latin at his command in 1378. Fig. 66, from this manuscript, shows the writer asleep, in a *houce*, dreaming of a King of France, accompanied by two ladies, witnessing a dispute on the relationship between the papacy and the King of France, and whose authority is greater in France. The ladies, a crowned nun and a queen, representing spiritual and worldly power, have chosen as their advocates a cleric and a knight.

In this scene the King of France, identified as such by his mantle with fleur-de-lys, is not Charles V so much as any King of France, since the problem was not Charles's alone; the queen is identifiable by her crown, and by the *surcote ouverte*, which had ceased to be fashionable and had become a garment of aristocratic status. Only her hairstyle is related to fashion. The outfit of the nun differs most obviously from widows' dress through the black veil on top of her white one; it resembles the clothing of the Franciscan Poor Clares.

The knight and the cleric highlight the gulf between clerical/academic and secular dress. The knight's curled hair, forked beard, egg-shaped torso, hip-level sword belt and long toes are all highly fashionable. His adversary has a shorter beard (clerics were supposed to be clean-shaven) and he wears a beret-like cap, one of the items worn at the university in Paris. Even in images as the philosopher-king, Charles V did not wear such a cap. Instead he is often shown wearing a fine linen coif, in recognition of the idea that the head of the King of France had to be kept covered after it had been anointed, and therefore sanctified, at the coronation.

In 1389 Charles V's son Louis, later the Duke of Orléans, married his cousin Valentina Visconti, daughter of the ruler of Milan. It is difficult to assess how far her trousseau was geared towards French, as opposed to Milanese, tastes, but it was certainly a most lavishly decorated one. Some of the garments sound similar to those worn by St Ursula and her virgins (fig. 67) in a Lombard book of hours, now in Paris, but formerly belonging to a Visconti vassal, Bertrando dei Rossi, or even to a member of the Visconti family, and dating from around 1380–5. Several of the girls wear super-tunics so tightly fitting that they resemble garments called, in French, *cotes hardies* (daring under-tunics). Valentina Visconti's trousseau contained five *cottardite* (*cotes hardies?*), four of which had matching hoods. Two of the girls in fig. 67 have hoods, a red one flat on top of the head, and a blue one slung over one shoulder. Valentina's *cottardite* were elaborately decorated, mostly with pearls; flowers were a favourite motif. The dark *cottardita* at the front of the illustration is perhaps to be understood as being decorated with birds worked in clusters of pearls. Such decoration would have fitted in with the contemporary passion for personal badges or devices: a dove was a device of Giangaleazzo Visconti, Valentina's father.

When women wore the high-necked garment called the *houppelande*, whether in France, England or Italy (where it was called a *pellanda*), it was always belted immediately under the bust, as here in the red example on the right. In artistic terms there was considerable unity of style in the period between *c.*1380 and *c.*1420, dominated by the so-called International Gothic style in art and architecture, but regional differences can still be detected in dress, particularly in the way that women adorned their heads. One girl has a version of the French plaits seen on the queen in fig. 66, but the rest look very Italian, with their hair bound around with ribbons and then wound around their heads, or else with a padded roll or garland of jewels encircling the head. Only St Ursula, holding the standard at the right, wears her hair loose in token of her virginity, and at the same time avoids displaying too close an adherence to fashion by draping much of her body in a large mantle.

Fig. 69, despite its northern Gothic architectural setting, betrays its Italian origin through the woman's relatively simple hairstyle. It comes from another Lombard manuscript, probably of the 1390s, a manual on health that once belonged to Verde Visconti, the cousin of Valentina Visconti's father. Both figures (drinking barley water) wear elaborately dagged garments, the woman a hood and a *cottardita*, the side-lacing of which explains how the garment fitted so tightly; and the man a version of the *pellanda*. Dagging is one of the most important hallmarks of the International Gothic period in dress, and, as here, could vary from simple slashes to elaborate patterns, almost like leaves. In Florence, according to Franco Sacchetti

71 ABOVE

Many figures in this scene of a couple adoring the Virgin Mary as the Woman of the Apocalypse, wear fashionable quantities of buttons. The wide use of buttons in western Europe worried the authorities. According to Franco Sacchetti, a government official in Florence, a woman denied that she was wearing buttons because there were no buttonholes to go with them. In Milan in 1396, in one of the city's very rare pieces of sumptuary legislation, men were permitted to wear as many buttons as they wished, but only knights, doctors of law, lawyers in general, and physicians were allowed to wear gold ones. (*Carmelite Missal*, England, c.1393: British Library, Add. MS 29704, f. 193v, initial)

72 OPPOSITE TOP

The coronations of the Queen of Sheba, the Virgin and Esther, from a Dutch manuscript of the *Biblia Pauperum* (Bible of the Poor). Apart from the unfashionably dressed figures of Christ and the Virgin in the centre, the other figures wear elements of dress of the 1390s, such as overlong cuffs covering the hands, or turned back at the wrists, and standing collars. Esther, in the scene on the right, wears a form of the *houppelande*, high-waisted as women's were. (*Biblia Pauperum*, Holland, The Hague?, c.1395–1400: British Library, Kings MS 5, f. 28)

73 OPPOSITE BOTTOM

Philippe de Mézières presents his treatise to Richard II of England in a scene of the English court as imagined in France. Nonetheless, the courtiers' clothing is compatible with English fashions. *Mi-parti* stockings, like those shown, could still be subject to criticism. Chaucer specifically denounced the wearing of one red and one white stocking with short clothing because it made the wearer look as though he had a hernia and was half-flayed. Red and white were, however, the colours of Richard II, who presumably did not share Chaucer's point of view. (Philippe de Mézières, *Epistre au roi Richart*, France, 1395–6: British Library, Royal MS 20 B VI, f. 2, detail)

who was involved in the city's government in 1384, a woman who was asked to give her name to the relevant official because she was wearing a dagged tail (*becchetto*) on her hood, was able to unpin it and claim it was in fact a garland.

The next image (fig. 70) also comes from Verde Visconti's manuscript. This tailor's shop shows how much clothing was made of wool – the *cottardita* of the customer, whose sleeve-length he is checking; the dagged garments behind her; and behind the tailor stockings and hoods, with long tails and slightly padded face-openings. These hoods would have been worn like those in fig. 46, as hats rather than hoods. Despite the inconvenience long sleeves must have caused to anyone who had to work with his hands, as a provider of fashionable clothing the tailor has chosen to wear a fashionable under-sleeve that comes down over his hand. The best kind of woollen clothing is said in the text to be that which comes from Flanders, and such clothing is useful because it protects the body against the cold and keeps the wearer warm. The still-recognizable problem with woollen clothing, that it can irritate the skin, is dealt with by the advice that thin linen clothing should also be worn (presumably between the skin and the wool).

There is some disagreement among scholars about the date of the English *Carmelite Missal* (fig. 71), but elements in the dress suggest that it dates from no later than the early 1390s. The woman kneeling on the right wears a slightly outmoded form of the *houppelande*/goun, with a low neckline and very narrow sleeves; by the end of the 1380s the goun, for both sexes, had developed a standing collar and funnel-shaped sleeves. The goun is closed down the centre front with lots of tiny buttons, and buttons close the *cote hardie* of the saint behind her. Those on the *cote hardie* of the Virgin (standing in the centre) are more difficult to see. The kneeling woman is recognizably English because of her headdress, square and thick at the front, as though it were composed of a series of veils with fluted front edges, such as can be seen on contemporary English tomb brasses and effigies. Similar fluted veils, though not set so rigidly around the head, can be found in Germany and in the Low Countries at this time, as on the left in fig. 72.

The final images in this chapter show dress at a contemporary court, that of Richard II of England, as visualized by a French artist *c*.1395–6 (fig. 73), and a surviving example of the shoes worn then (fig. 74). The figure on the throne is not identifiably a portrait of Richard so much as a king (because of his crown and the ermine lining and trimming of his mantle), and a King of England (because of the heraldry behind him). The courtiers wear long and short *houppelandes* with widening sleeves and standing collars. One wonders how the wearer of the floor-length *houppelande* coped with it and his long-toed footwear at the same time.

Men were criticized once again for the shortness of some of their garments, and the length of their footwear. In order not to disrupt the flow of leg into foot, the stockings here are probably fitted with leather soles, a practice more common, and more reasonable, in the warmer and dryer climate of Italy than in northern Europe. This scene is one of those delightful instances where the artist has responded to the nature of the clothing he is depicting by, in this case, having these seemingly impossible toes run on to the border of the miniature, emphasizing just how much space these fashionable men would require. The Museum of London has in its collections a late fourteenth-century shoe, minus the ankle strap that would have held it on (fig. 74). While not as exaggerated in the length of its toe as the stockings of the courtiers, it must still have been difficult to walk in. As always when there are so few extant examples of dress on which to base comparisons, it is necessary to remember that images convey what people wanted to believe they looked like, not necessarily how they actually looked. And moralistic commentators always seized on extreme examples to criticize, which can create the impression that 'problems' with fashion were more widespread and pernicious than they actually were.

Fashionable clothing in the fourteenth century reached the point where it changed perceptibly by the decade, and sometimes even within a decade. Some forms of clothing, though they ceased to be fashionable, were not discarded, but acquired new life as ceremonial or professional dress. (Sometimes that new life has proved to be very long – even today a state opening of Parliament calls forth, if not quite the *surcote ouverte*, then mantles that hark back, in their scarlet and ermine, to the Middle Ages.) The marked upsurge in sumptuary legislation in the fourteenth century, which has been just hinted at here, suggests that more and more people were not only aware of the fashions evolving among the upper classes, but actually had the money to try to emulate them. And illuminated manuscripts at last depict some of the wonderful fabrics that caused such anguish to the authorities, and such joy to their wearers.

74
A shoe found at 'Baynard's Castle', London. A wardrobe account of 1393–4, once thought to belong to Richard II, but now identified as being for his heir, the Earl of March, refers to whalebone in the 'pikes' (pointed toes) of his shoes. During the siege of Nicopolis in 1396 French knights took to wearing shoes with beaked toes 2 feet (60 cm) long, and then had to cut them off in order to go into battle. (London, late 1300s: Museum of London Archaeology Service)

IV

Dressing Everybody
c.1400–c.1500

THE TITLE OF THIS CHAPTER REFLECTS THE EXTRAORDINARY
increase in the amount of information available for studying the dress of all ranks
of society, almost all of whom, except the very poor, seem to have been able to afford
some aspect of fashionable dressing. This growth in information comes about
because of the increasingly secular emphasis of illuminated manuscripts themselves.
In the second half of the century some manuscripts show evidence that more
sophisticated ideas were developing about the clothing of other countries, and of
the past. Documentation related to dress increases too, with chronicles, inventories,
wardrobe accounts and private letters and diaries surviving in considerable profusion.

  At the start of the century Paris dominated the trade in luxury illuminated
books, whether secular or religious works. The temporary English victory in the
Hundred Years' War led to the English occupation of Paris in 1420, as a result of
which some illuminators seem to have drifted away to provincial centres. Others
followed the French court to west-central France, where one of the most impressive
illuminators, Jean Fouquet (fig. 91) worked for courtly patrons. At the same time the
Duke of Burgundy, Philip the Good (r. 1419–67), moved away from Paris to his
northern territories in Flanders, where, despite years of political and personal
antipathy to their sovereigns, Philip and his son Charles the Bold (r. 1467–77)
presided over courtiers whose culture and clothing styles were shared with France.
The presence in Flanders of the Burgundian court, the richest in Europe, fostered the
development there of extremely sophisticated illuminated manuscripts. Flanders was
to enjoy a period of remarkable prosperity from the early 1430s to the early 1470s,
with the city of Bruges attracting merchants, and potential book buyers, from all

over Europe. Even the collapse of Burgundian power with the death of Charles the Bold in 1477 and the marriage of his heiress to the heir to the Habsburg Empire (as the Holy Roman Empire tends to be referred to in this period) did not destroy the Flemish book trade; instead of producing as many secular texts as it had done previously, it built up an unrivalled market for devotional works. The chief strength of the British Library lies in Flemish manuscripts, partly because of the manuscripts commissioned by Edward IV of England (whose sister was married to Charles the Bold), and it would have been easy to concentrate on them here to the detriment of manuscripts from other parts of Europe.

Italy at this time was still mostly a series of city states, which by the middle of the fifteenth century had allied themselves, willingly or not, with one of the five most powerful states – Venice, Milan, Rome, Florence and Naples. Each of these five states had its own distinctive clothing styles, especially for women; and smaller cities had their own as well. The kingdom of Naples remained an anomaly in the Italian peninsula, and in the early 1440s it changed rulers and cultures, replacing Frenchmen with Spaniards. Although the period may be defined by historians as the Renaissance, the clothing should not be described in that way, as it, unlike the architecture of the period, makes no obvious reference to the ancient world. Contemporary scholars of classical antiquity were also far less concerned with studying classical dress than with studying classical literature, and even in the new humanist manuscripts, illustrations were often secondary to the calligraphy involved, if they were included at all. The continuing obsession with controlling society through sumptuary laws shows that as far as attitudes to clothing and personal appearance were concerned, Italy remained medieval, hence the appearance of some Italian images in this chapter.

Something is known of the costs of Italian manuscripts in relation to other items, including dress and paintings. Between spring 1455 and December 1461 work was proceeding on a remarkable two-volume bible for Borso d'Este, Marquis of Ferrara. (It is now in Modena, in the Biblioteca Estense Universitaria.) The manuscript, without its covers, weighs 34 lb (15.5 kg), and for it Borso d'Este paid what seems like the considerable sum of 2200 ducats, yet in 1480 the dowager Duchess of Milan had a sleeve embroidered with so many jewels that it was worth 18,000 ducats. It has been noted that at the end of the century the Milanese illuminator Giovan Pietro Birago placed a value of 500 ducats on a part of manuscript that had been stolen from him; and that Leonardo da Vinci, by contrast, thought his painting of *The Virgin of the Rocks*, now in London, was worth only 100 ducats. In 1492 Ludovico Sforza of Milan presented his style-conscious sister-in-law, Isabella d'Este, with fabric worked with gold and silver loops, costing 600 ducats, to make herself a *camora* (gown). Art cost less than clothing.

The majority of the clothing of the upper classes in north-western Europe, at least in the first half of the fifteenth century, continued to be made of high-quality woollens. By about 1430 an elaborate type of patterned velvet had been created in Italy, involving a gold background with gold loops drawn up in the velvet; it was called *riccio sopra riccio* ('loop over loop', probably worn by the two men at the front of fig. 92.) Italian textile towns enacted a series of protectionist measures to prevent the importation of fabrics that could compete with locally made ones – fabrics were therefore either for home consumption, or export to areas without such prohibitions (or industries). The wearing of silks seems to have become more common in the second half of the century; and by the end of the century every self-respecting ruler is depicted in cloth of gold, which documents reveal was sometimes *riccio sopra riccio* (known as 'tissue' in English).

The drapers' guild in Bologna in northern Italy was the most prestigious guild in the city. The statutes of the guild contain an illumination of c.1411 (fig. 75) that shows mostly the making, trying on and selling of clothes at the city's Porta Ravegnana. In 1401 Bologna decreed that women would have to register and pay for the privilege of wearing velvets and fabrics involving gold and silver, and features of clothing that must refer to *pellande*. Women's sleeves were to be no more than two *bracci* around (about 4 feet or 1.2 metres), and no longer than the arm and hand of their wearer. However, the wives, daughters and daughters-in-law of knights and doctors of civil or church law or of medicine were allowed to wear sleeves two and a half *bracci* around. No garments were to be more than ten *bracci* around at the feet. In two days 210 garments were registered by 131 people, mostly by the women who wore them, but a few by their husbands or fathers. Many of the fabrics were striped or decorated with patterns, such as chevrons. The list shows that most of these women owned only one forbidden garment each, but some owned several. One woman, who lived in the area of the Porta Ravegnana, owned five *sacci* (which seem to be the local equivalent of *pellande*), three of them being of velvet and one with cape-like sleeves.

The scene here, of the marriage of Philip III of France to Marie of Brabant, gives some idea of one of the outfits provided for the twelve-year-old Philippa of Lancaster, who married King Eric of Denmark, Norway and Sweden in 1406. It was a *robe* of blue velvet, made as tunic, *surcote ouverte* and trained mantle, edged with thirteen ermine and lined with a total of 2114 pured miniver (miniver trimmed to leave only the small white area). Such clothing posed an increasing threat to wildlife species' survival.
(*Grandes Chroniques de France*, France, c.1400: British Library, Royal MS 20 C VII, vol. 2, f. 10r, detail)

Louis of Orléans, seen here receiving a book from Christine de Pisan, is recorded in a wardrobe account of 1393 as having had a black satin *houppelande* embroidered in gold with a wolf in front and behind, and as giving each of 116 members of his household a black woollen *houppelande* with a wolf embroidered on the sleeve. The 'simple' accessories seen here were not necessarily cheap – in 1387 the French king had two straw hats lined in silk and decorated with gold fringing; in 1427 Louis's son Charles trimmed his peacock-feather hat with gold butterflies.
(*Collected Works of Christine de Pisan*, Paris, *Cité des dames* Master and shop, c.1415: British Library, Harley MS 4431, f. 95r, detail)

78

In an attempt to prevent her son Achilles from being taken with the Greek army to besiege Troy, the goddess Thetis disguised him as a girl and sent him away to what she thought was safety. Here, to complete his disguise, Thetis hands him a small, fashionable padded headdress known as a *bourrelet* (from the French verb 'to stuff'). (Statius, *Achilleis*, France, early 1400s: British Library, Burney ms 257, f. 230r, detail)

Dress as an aid to narrative plays an important part in figs 76 and 78. In the former, a scene from the *Grandes Chroniques de France*, Philip III of France marries Marie, daughter of the Duke of Brabant in 1274. The artist has dressed most of the figures in the clothing of around 1400, with the addition of ceremonial clothing and one hint of awareness of the dress of the recent past. The groom wears a fashionable *houppelande* with the high collar that men would shortly find competing for space with their forked beards; miniver-lined sleeves with gold fringes at the top; and long under-cuffs. The bride and groom are united in being dressed in clothing that features the royal French arms, the fleur-de-lys, with the bride in the *surcote ouverte* of ceremonial dress. The text merely describes the bride as being beautiful and wise, and full of good habits, and as being sent to the French court adorned with jewels and dressed as befitted her. Two of her attendants wear *cotes hardies*, with one having long white tails on the sleeves, a suggestion that the artist is trying to hint at the past (actually of *c.*1370). With the king is a man who wears *mi-parti* hose in red and white, with a green *heuque. Heuques*, sleeveless, open-sided garments, were frequently issued to bodyguards. As red, white and green were colours worn by the royal household, this figure is almost certainly meant to be Philip's chamberlain, Pierre de la Broce. He was to try to break up the royal couple's mutual affection (perhaps hinted at by their heraldically matched outfits) because it weakened his considerable influence over the king, by accusing the new queen of poisoning her stepson.

In fig. 78 clothing is judiciously chosen to emphasize the significance of the moment in the story. Thetis disguises her son Achilles as a girl in a vain attempt to prevent his being taken with the Greek forces to Troy. Few people living around 1400 would have misjudged the gender of the wearer of a *houppelande*, as women's were usually belted higher than men's, and only men's had breaks in the 'skirt' which would reveal the legs. In order to drive home the point that the young Achilles is a boy disguised as a girl, he is shown displaying a leg.

The next two images to be discussed come from one of the most famous manuscripts in the British Library, the *Collected Works of Christine de Pisan*, made for the Queen of France, Isabella of Bavaria, around 1415 (figs 77 and 79). The manuscript was perhaps written out by Christine herself, and as she had very clear views about dress, the illuminations presumably reflect them. Christine (fig. 77) is immediately identifiable by the dress she wears in this and other manuscripts of her work. In 1389, at the age of twenty-five, she was left a widow, and she always appears with a

79 OPPOSITE

The goddess Venus, seated at the top, drops hearts to the mostly expensively dressed people who are under her influence. Female dress tends to be the *cote hardie*, with Venus's having long over-sleeves; her headdress is a large, horn-shaped *bourrelet*. Male dress is the *houppelande*, one with an inner sleeve, and a belted *heuque* (the northern equivalent of the *giornea*).

(*Collected Works of Christine de Pisan*, Paris, *Cité des dames* Master and shop, *c.*1415: British Library, Harley MS 4431, f. 100r, detail)

80 RIGHT

The annunciation of the birth of Christ to the shepherds. Their mainly dull-coloured clothing helps to explain why brightly coloured clothing (particularly red) was widely coveted by the peasantry. In 1430 in Scotland, the working classes living in the countryside were forbidden to wear dyed clothes with bag-shaped sleeves (*houppelandes*?). In 1458 the same people were told that on working days they were to wear only white or grey (presumably undyed) cloth, while on holy days they were to wear only light blue, green or – they must have been pleased – red.

(*Bedford Hours*, Paris, Bedford Master and shop, *c.*1423–30: British Library, Add. MS 18850, f. 70v)

cloth wrapped around her neck, in reference to the neck-cloth of widows (compare the Countess of Artois in fig. 64). Christine also wears a modest version of the fashionable horned arrangement of veils, and a surprisingly tight-fitting *cote hardie* with wide, square tails hanging from the ends of the sleeves. These tails are another of Christine's hallmarks, and would seem to derive from the fashions of her childhood (again, compare fig. 64). At the time of the manuscript's completion she would have been in her early fifties. She kneels before a figure identifiable through the badges, or devices, in the scene as Louis, the Duke of Orléans, son of Charles V. Louis' badge of the porcupine hangs from the collars of two of his attendants. The animals 'walking' across Louis' sleeve appear to represent another of his badges, the wolf.

In her concern that clothing should reflect social status, Christine was fairly conventional. She was unusual in offering aesthetic, rather than moral, judgements about fashions, and in comparing the costs of dressing well in France with the costs in Italy, where she had been born. Her views were expressed in her *Trésor de la cité des dames*, written in 1405. In this she remarked that a *cote hardie* with the wide sleeves described as *à la bombarde* (in the style of a cannon), reaching the wearer's feet and trailing on the ground, worn with a tall headdress constructed to balance the *cote hardie*, constituted extreme ugliness. She thought that anyone who looked properly at it would agree with her. Hence, perhaps, the modest horns she always wears, and the modest tails to her *cote hardie*'s sleeves. She complained of the increasing elaboration of clothes in France, for both men and women, and the way in which they changed annually. She thought that, although Italian clothing was initially more expensive, in the end it was better value, as it was worn for longer.

Fig. 79, also from Christine's manuscript, shows the goddess Venus at the top with a more exaggerated version of the sleeves worn by Christine, and one of the large headdresses she disliked – an interesting contradiction in a manuscript perhaps produced under her supervision. Another example of exaggerated fashion, this time on a man, is to be seen on the figure left of centre, in an additional cuff turning back over his *houppelande* sleeve. When the wearer of such a subsidiary cuff lowered his or her arm, the hand was effectively rendered useless – a clear sign that the wearer had nothing more strenuous to do than be fashionable.

The *Bedford Hours*, made in Paris in the 1420s, demonstrates the great gulf between the fashionable aristocracy and the peasantry. Fig. 80 shows that for shepherds there was still no such thing as fashion – there was simply clothing. It was clothing that was not very well cut, as can be seen from the way in which the leggings are tied or drawn in around the ankles; and it was clothing made in a fairly limited range of colours, in which naturally black and white wools could be mixed to produce serviceable greys. Blue dye was still widely used, and is often shown in manuscript illuminations as the colour of lower-class clothing; red could be obtained from a variety of dyes, but none with the intensity and durability of kermes, which remained extremely expensive. In the *Bedford Hours* it is the shepherdesses who seem most determined to inject a little fashion and colour into their lives, with their close-fitting outfits, like overalls (possibly called *rochets*), from under which red or pink breaks out. These colours are repeated in their long-tailed hoods, standard items in the wardrobes of working- and middle-class French and Netherlandish women (as can be seen in fig. 94). Around their hips the shepherds and shepherdesses wear an item that looks remarkably like the pouches worn by modern tourists; in the Middle Ages, only peasants seem to have used these pouches, presumably as large pockets. Fig. 81, focusing on the Virgin of Mercy protecting humanity, omits the working classes altogether, to concentrate on the upper and middle classes, and those in religious orders.

There are two stupendously expensive-looking outfits in the *Bedford Hours*, worn by the book's original owners, John, Duke of Bedford (regent in France for his nephew, Henry VI of England), and his wife Anne (fig. 82), sister of Philip the Good, Duke of Burgundy, the richest man in western Europe. These outfits complement each other, being *houppelandes* made of the same elaborately patterned fabric, which must be an Italian silk. Dressing alike was more than a visual conceit – it implied equality. In 1421 Anne and her sister Agnes both had green woollen *houppelandes* decorated with 300 small silver buckles and lined with a total of 4000 miniver skins. Here on her head Anne wears a vast horned and jewelled *bourrelet*. Women's huge horned headdresses attracted the attention of Franciscan preachers in Flanders and Paris at the end of the 1420s, and small children were encouraged to mock their wearers in the streets. Anne of Burgundy, however, seems not to have attracted any personal criticism because of her clothing, as she possessed the rank that Christine de Pisan had said entitled some women to dress richly. (She was also so full of good works among the poor and the sick that she contracted a fatal illness on one of her charitable outings.) The other form of vast horned headdress worn in the late 1420s

81 LEFT

The Virgin, as Queen of Heaven (on right, with crown and ermine-lined mantle) shelters a king of France (front right, fleurs-de-lys); Charlemagne (beard, arch-topped imperial crown, fleurs-de-lys and imperial eagle); a queen (crown and *surcote ouverte*); and various important and fashionable people. On the left she shelters a pope (triple-crowned tiara); cardinals (in red); and bishops (with mitres). Lesser persons are grouped in marginal scenes. The men are, left to right, an Augustinian (black habit); a Franciscan (grey habit); and a Carthusian (white habit). The female religious on the right is a Cistercian (all-white, with the standard black veil of a nun). The second woman may be a Benedictine novice (black). The only major order missing is the Dominican (black cloak over white). The three final figures are probably to be understood as middle-class lay people. The woman has swathed herself in a dark cloak, as non-aristocratic women are often shown doing when they are in church. (*Bedford Hours*, Paris, Bedford Master and shop, c.1423–30: British Library, Add. MS 18850, f. 150v)

82 RIGHT
Anne of Burgundy, Duchess of
Bedford, kneels before St Anne,
the Virgin and Christ. For her
wedding in 1423 her brother
Philip the Good gave Anne
vermilion velvet, worked with
gold loops, to make a long
houppelande (that is, one with a
train) with open sleeves. The
loops were the latest weaving
technique. The fabric here is not
that worn on her wedding day,
but the illumination does give
some idea of the elaboration that
her wedding *houppelande* must
have involved.
(*Bedford Hours*, Paris, Bedford
Master and shop, c.1423–30:
British Library, Add. MS 18850,
f. 257v, detail)

consisted of veils held together by pins, and presumably heavily starched (fig. 83). Somewhat improbably, it is shown here, along with the *cote hardie*, as being worn at the court of Philip II of Macedon in the fourth century BC.

As has been seen, the large, flowing garments known in French as *houppelandes* did not disappear from fashion simply because the fourteenth century ended; indeed, they continued to be worn into the 1420s, although they are rarely seen after about 1430. The French term went out of use, along with the garment, to be replaced by the word *robe*, which lost its previous meaning of a suit of clothes, and took on a new meaning, an outer garment with narrower sleeves and body, and no dagging. The English word 'goun' continued in use to describe this new form; it is not clear why the French and English languages reacted so differently to the change in style.

The artist to whom fig. 85 is attributed, the Master of the Munich Golden Legend, like his colleague, the Bedford Master, worked for French and English patrons. The clothing of the book's female owner, however, would seem to be completely French (English headdresses are more likely to include a veil) and aristocratic (her belt and *bourrelet* are decorated with gold). She kneels to receive communion, not wrapped in a middle- or lower-class cloak, but fully displaying her fashionable high-waisted *robe* with the new narrower sleeves and long, trailing belt. The fur appears to be *gris*, the back fur of the squirrel; squirrel furs would shortly be replaced by darker furs, such as marten and sable. Not only have the *bourrelet*'s horns shrunk in size since the late 1420s, the artist has failed to turn them forward to match the angle of her head to the viewer. The red garments are presumably meant to be understood as being made of scarlet, which was the subject of sumptuary control that cost ought to have rendered unnecessary – purchasing a length of about 30 yards (27.5 metres) of the cheapest scarlet in the wardrobe of Henry VI of England would have consumed the wages of a London mason for 405 days. Nonetheless, in 1439 in Brescia, Italy, the lower orders, such as builders and weavers, were criticized for dressing their wives in very fine scarlet and even in crimson velvet; the clothes of these women in particular were regarded as the cause of the city's misfortunes.

Women and their clothes were seen as a problem in Italy, in a way that did not appear in northern Europe – yes, in the north women liked expensive clothes, which their husbands said they couldn't afford, but in Italy the cost of providing wives with clothing was often stated to be detrimental to the birth rate in various cities, as young men were reluctant to marry and take on such a financial burden. This was a reason given for sumptuary legislation in Florence in 1433, and the problem was noted in a letter written by the Florentine Alessandra Strozzi in 1466. In extreme cases, women's clothing was blamed for a perceived increase in incidents of sodomy (what was meant by this is not always clear) among men. The long-term economies that Christine de Pisan had seen in Italian clothing do not seem to have been noticed by the Italians themselves. It is the case, however, that some cities tried to ensure, through legislation, that clothing was worn for several years. Italians also seem to have had wardrobes that distinguished more clearly between winter and summer clothing than northern European wardrobes did, which presumably meant more clothes, which perhaps therefore had to last longer. In Florence during the summer, for instance, women seem to have abandoned the combination of *cotta* (underdress) and *cioppa* (gown), worn in winter, for a more expensive, and more visible, type of underdress called a *gamurra* (or *camora*), and a long version of the *giornea* (the equivalent of the northern *heuque*). Comparisons between French and Italian images in the 1430s and later do suggest that Christine had been right in remarking that clothing styles changed more slowly in Italy than in France.

By the 1430s (fig. 85) Frenchmen had abandoned the wide sleeves of the *houppelande*. But an Italian (possibly Venetian) scene of a king and his courtiers, learning from a philosopher how to play chess (fig. 84) shows (on the right) that huge sleeves were still in use on gowns in Italy at this time. A purely Italian exaggeration of the hood required it to be rolled round and round on itself, as at the back right. Italian men also retained the *giornea* for much of the fifteenth century. San Bernardino of Siena loathed the *giornea*: he said in a sermon in Siena in 1427 that it was made like a horse cloth, which showed that the humans who wore it were animals at heart. He was outraged that young men would remove the *giornea* when they entered their homes and thus expose to their female relatives all sorts of disgustingness because of the gap between the stockings and the short doublet worn beneath the *giornea*. The saint also disapproved of the way in which the male leg was exposed in tight stockings.

A number of 'messages' through dress are contained in a scene (fig. 86) from the *Book of the Seven Philosophers* who had educated the son of an unnamed Roman emperor. The youth is shown as having acquired, as a result of his education,

bellare decreuit.

83 TOP

According to this version of the life of Alexander the Great, Alexander was the son of the Eygptian king and sorcerer Nectanabus, who had fled to Macedon, where, in disguise, he slept with the queen, seated here among her ladies. Nectanabus, on the right, is described as wearing 'white samite, like the prophets of Egypt'. Many other figures in the manuscript wear turbans, standard 'exotic' garments. Nectanabus's strange hat is even more exotic. (*Histoire d'Alexandre le Grand*, Paris, late 1420s: British Library, Royal MS 20 B XX, f. 7r, detail)

84 OPPOSITE BOTTOM
A bearded philosopher, on the
extreme left, uses chess pieces
to explain to a ruler and his
courtiers how society works.
He wears an unfashionable,
unbelted long gown, as befits a
man of serious disposition. The
courtiers wear Italian fashions,
such as huge hoods piled up on
themselves (back right), gowns
with bag-shaped sleeves, and
the *giornea* (extreme right).
(Jacobus de Cessolis, *De ludo
scachorum...*, Venice?, *c.*1440?:
British Library, Add. MS 15685,
f. 2v, detail)

85 RIGHT
The owner of this book of hours
at Communion, with male
members of her family kneeling
in the border. Narrower sleeves
came into fashion for both sexes
in the 1430s, as the *houppelande*
passed from fashion and was
replaced by the *robe*. The male
members of the family still wear
standing collars on their *robes*, a
relic of the garment's origins in
the *houppelande*, forcing them to
wear short hair. The lumpy areas
of black and pink behind the
shoulders of two of these figures
are the *bourrelets* of their hoods,
introduced around the face opening in the 1420s; over the front
hangs the hood's very long tail.
(*Book of Hours*, Paris, Master of
the Munich Golden Legend,
*c.*1435: British Library, Add. MS
18192, f. 196)

a clothing style that would not have disgraced a sober Italian citizen several years his senior. The youth's stepmother, a very beautiful woman, fell madly in love with her stepson. Her beauty is emphasized by her having, yet again against statistical probability in Italy, blonde hair, bound up on top of her head. Because the youth said nothing in his father's presence, the stepmother undertook to encourage him to talk in the privacy of her chamber. The scene shows us, in continuous narrative, the next stages of the story. The youth is sent along; she declares her passion; he still says nothing. She says that if he refuses to sleep with her, she will tear her clothes and tell the emperor that it was the youth who wanted to sleep with her. Had the youth been a little wiser, he would have recognized the danger inherent in her being only in her *cotta* rather than in her *pellanda*. As he leaves the room, she begins to carry out her threats, and undoes her hair.

Women's hair, real or false, was a marked feature in Italy in the fifteenth century, and it provoked serious reactions at the highest levels of the Church. In 1437 a Venetian canon asked Pope Eugenius IV about the authenticity of a decretal that was attributed to Pope John XXII (1316–34), denying absolution to women who wore false hair. By 1440 a formal response was being composed on behalf of the Church by a commission that argued that the making and the wearing of jewels, false hair and elaborate clothes would be sinful only if the intention behind them were sinful. However, if a woman were to use them to please her husband, or even to attract a potential husband, then she would not be sinning. The decretal about false hair was itself declared to be false. It is clear that the empress in fig. 86 is false through and through. The story finally ends happily for the youth, but less so for the stepmother, who is burnt at the stake – in a *cotta*.

Although, as noted above, dress in Italy could be highly regionalized, especially for women, there was usually a relative homogeneity about men's dress, despite the interesting, but unexplained, reference to men's shirts in the style of Florence in a letter of 1450 written by Alessandra Strozzi. However, in one part of Italy, the kingdom of Naples, the continuing influences from outside Italy make dress connected with Naples difficult to assess in the mid-fifteenth century. On her death in 1435 Giovanna II of Naples left her kingdom to be fought over by the heirs to whom she had bequeathed it at different times – her French relative, René of Anjou (fig. 92) and Alfonso V of Aragon (figs 87 and 88). Alfonso's territories encompassed Aragon, Valencia, Majorca, Catalonia, Sicily and Sardinia. After his conquest of Naples in 1442 the language of the court ceased to be French; instead, Catalan and Castilian were spoken, and most of the leading officials at court were Spaniards, whom the Italians tended to describe indiscriminately as 'Catalans'. Alfonso's wardrobe in Naples was under the charge of two Spaniards, and sometimes he ordered clothes to be made for him in Spain. Alfonso's long-term ambition seems to have been to unite Naples with the great northern Italian power, Milan, and make himself ruler of the whole of Italy. Ironically, it was only at the end of the fifteenth century, many years after Alfonso's death in 1458, that Spanish-Neapolitan influence reigned supreme in Milan and much of northern Italy – but only in clothing styles apparently introduced by a series of marriages between the Neapolitan royal family and the ruling families there.

The visual images of Alfonso's clothing in his prayer book (figs 87 and 88) make for an interesting contrast with the verbal images created by fifteenth-century biographers, and perpetuated by modern biographers. The book bears the date 1442, the year of the conquest of Naples. This means that the book could have been produced in Aragon, before Alfonso's acquisition of Naples, or in Naples afterwards. Art historians are not agreed on the provenance of the manuscript, but the clothing and the heraldry suggest that we are looking at Alfonso as Alfonso V of Aragon, rather than as Alfonso I of Naples. In Naples Alfonso's retainers sometimes wore hose made in the Italian manner, with the left stocking green and the other stocking half white and half red, which identified them as his servants. It is not easy to discern such liveries in the present manuscript, which may argue for its having been made outside Italy.

The images of Alfonso in this manuscript are not those propagated by two fifteenth-century biographers, the Florentine Vespasiano da Bisticci, and the Sicilian humanist Antonio Beccadelli, known as Panormita. The former presented Alfonso as dressing usually in black, with just a brooch in his hat, or a gold chain around his neck, and as not making much use of brocades or silks. Panormita described Alfonso as dressed moderately and no differently from his courtiers, and saying that he wanted to be seen as king because of his virtues and his authority, rather than because of royal trappings.

It is difficult to check the accuracy of these statements because the Neapolitan archives were destroyed in the Second World War, before there had been a thorough investigation of their information on dress. Alfonso's literary image as

86 ABOVE

A Roman empress tries, and fails, to seduce her serious-minded stepson. The informality of the situation is indicated by the empress's having removed the *pellanda* in which she appears elsewhere in the manuscript, to reveal her red high-waisted under-dress (*cotta*) with its blue sleeves. Sleeves were usually made separately and readily changed. In 1465 Alessandra Strozzi of Florence recorded her efforts to see a prospective daughter-in-law in an under-dress to check on her figure for her son's benefit. (Jacobus de Cessolis, *De ludo scachorum...*, Venice?, c.1440?: British Library, Add. MS 15685, f. 84v, detail)

87 OPPOSITE BOTTOM

Seen here is the hybrid nature of dress at the court of Alfonso V of Aragon. The great sleeves, slit to hang like capes, on the queen's gown (bottom right) are also found in Italy; but the front V-necklines of the ladies are more common in Spain than in Italy at this date. Most of Alfonso's closest courtiers came from his Spanish territories, but some of the clothing seems Italian – large, saggy hoods and a type of pleating seen occasionally in Spain from the mid-1430s, but much more common in Italy. The pleats begin in a sharply defined horizontal line on the upper body, and are most clearly seen on the man second to left from the queen. In 1449 Florence outlawed the permanent pleating, pinning or stiffening of silk garments, presumably because of the extra effort involved in making such clothing. (*Prayer Book of Alfonso V of Aragon*, Aragon?, c.1442: British Library, Add. MS 28962, f. 281v, detail)

88 RIGHT

Alfonso V of Aragon, seen here at prayer, wears a garment that would be a *giornea* in Italy (or, in Spain, a *jornea* or a *huca*), were it not joined at the sides above the hem. According to the Spanish dress historian Carmen Bernis Madrazo, a short closed cloak with side-slits for the arms was typically Castilian. It can, however, also be found in Siena, Italy, in Domenico di Bartolo's fresco *Distribution of Alms* (1441–4). (*Prayer Book of Alphonso V of Aragon*, Aragon?, c.1442: British Library, Add. MS 28962, f. 302r, detail)

clad in black was perhaps created in response to a treatise on the meanings of
colours, written for him in the Low Countries by a northerner whom he appointed a
herald with the title of Sicily. The treatise stated that black was to be equated with the
virtue of prudence; but dark colours did not accord with contemporary Italian taste,
which tended to reserve them for citizen dress, or for mourning.

Alfonso did not actually shy away from magnificent clothing for himself and
others: he had one garment so covered in pearls that it took fifteen embroiderers two
weeks to sew them all on. In 1447 he paid 745 ducats for a piece of gold brocade.
The wages of a labourer in Apulia in the period 1452–4 have been calculated as
18 ducats a year, plus food. So much for Alfonso's moderateness – the fabric would
have cost that labourer thirty-one years' wages. A report sent to Barcelona from
Naples in 1451 mentioned how Alfonso paid 2000 ducats (about the cost of Borso
d'Este's bible, mentioned on page 124) to dress his mistress, Lucrezia d'Alagno,
in gold brocade lined with sable for her sister's wedding, and how he dressed her
relatives in gold brocade too. The thrice-annual distribution of silks to all his men-
at-arms was said to have made the merchants of Florence and Milan very rich.
The king who appears throughout the prayer book is not entirely the sober figure
encountered in the fifteenth-century biographies. In addition to many blue gowns
and mantles, he also wears violet-pink and gold gowns, and black and gold or
purple and gold doublets (*jupones*). As the herald Sicily equated blue with justice,
gold with faith and purple with temperance, there may be present in the manuscript
other layers of Alfonso's image as a king identifiable because of his virtues.

If anyone dressed soberly, it was the queen. She died a few days after
Alfonso, in 1458, in the great silk-producing city of Valencia. The inventory of her
possessions drawn up there after her death contains little clothing of any splendour;
apart from rich jewelled collars, much of her clothing is described as old, or used,
or black. Of the few garments that had anything approaching colour in them, most
were described as *morado*, the dark morello-cherry colour that could do duty as
mourning in Italy. Two of her gowns in *morado* had even been dyed black, to be used
as mourning clothing. The most clearly local elements in the inventory were ribbons
described as Moorish, and *aljubas*, identified today as a type of loose, thigh-length
jacket, also of Moorish origin. According to a chronicle written by the Neapolitan
court official Loise de la Rosa, she adopted the habit (of a nun) because she had been
deprived of her husband (they never met again after she had been left in Catalonia as

regent in 1433), and because of her grief at his obsession with an Italian woman (the gold brocade-wearing Lucrezia d'Alagno).

In the middle of the fifteenth century there seems to have been considerable awareness of how people dressed in various parts of Europe, and a willingness by the fashionable to adopt elements from dress abroad, and by artists to try to depict foreign dress. Republican Florence in particular seems to have objected to borrowed styles, perhaps because it was in many respects the most insular of the Italian states, not welcoming aristocratic influences from elsewhere in Italy, and not allowing citizenship to men who could not demonstrate that their fathers had been citizens and that their mothers had been the daughters of citizens. Nonetheless, French styles (fig. 89), as they were called, seem to have exercised a fascination over much of Italy, including Florence, at this time. The front V-neckline was regarded in Italy as French, and was banned in Florence in 1449, with women being instructed to dress in 'an honest [i.e. modest] manner' (fig. 90). In 1449 and again in 1456 Florence banned horned headdresses in the styles worn on the other side of the Alps.

The V-necklines did not pass without comment in France either. In 1445 the bishop of Laon advised his brother Guillaume Jouvenel des Ursins, recently appointed chancellor of the kingdom, to encourage the king, Charles VII, to prohibit the wearing of openings at the front that allowed women's breasts and nipples to show (which must refer to low V-necklines and nothing more outrageous). The cause of this outburst was probably the middle-aged king's young mistress, Agnès Sorel, whose group of young male friends had begun supplanting the king's older advisers, who included men of the bishop's generation.

There are also scenes where the artists are trying to depict not transplanted versions of foreign styles, but foreigners themselves. Fig. 91 offers a Frenchman's view in the late 1450s of Italian dress, supposedly in the third quarter of the fourteenth century, and fig. 92 gives an Italian view of a fellow Italian among Frenchmen, also in the late 1450s. The artist of fig. 91, Jean Fouquet, is believed to have been in Italy in the 1440s; it is well known that some of the architecture in the scene is Italianate. A very typically Italian round cap, apparently called a *berreta alla capitanesca* (cap in the style of a captain's) is held by the kneeling Boccaccio, and worn by his patron, Mainardo dei Cavalcanti, and by a third man. The patron's stockings are doubly Italian in being soled (rather than worn with separate shoes or boots) and *mi-parti*. Fouquet has also recorded the Italian fashion for wearing a

90 OPPOSITE

Famous lovers from antiquity gather around Love's triumphal car. Although the scene was painted in Florence, 'French' fashions (horned headdresses and V-necklines) have clearly infiltrated the dress of the women of that most resolutely Italian city. However, some Italian elements do survive. Cleopatra, on the viewer's right in blue and red, embracing Julius Caesar in 'Roman' armour, wears Italian hanging sleeves and a 'French' headdress. The courtesan Phyllis (riding on the back of the philosopher Aristotle) has an Italian-looking cap. Miniver, a mark of the scholar in Italy, trims the clothing of Aristotle; several men are bearded, showing that they belong in the past.
(Petrarch, *Trionfi*, Florence, attributed to Francesco d'Antonio del Chierico, 1457: Paris, Bibliothèque Nationale, MS ital. 545, f. 11v)

89 ABOVE

The wedding of Raymond of Poitiers and Melusine, who, according to legend, turned partially into a serpent every Saturday, and fled when Raymond discovered her secret. Many of the characteristics of north-western European styles of the mid-fifteenth century can be seen here. Men's gowns, pleated from ever-wider shoulders to hem, were open at the chest to reveal their shirts and the ties that held their doublets in position across the chest. Often they wore ankle-length boots with pointed toes. Women wore gowns with increasingly narrow sleeves and V-necklines at the front, and, echoing the V shapes, tall horned headdresses. False hems were attached to under-dresses.
(Jean d'Arras, *Roman de Melusine*, Flanders, c.1445–50: British Library, Harley MS 4418, f. 36r, detail)

giornea belted at the front and left free at the back, and decorative points (laces) hanging from the doublet sleeves. The *giornea*'s short sleeves, however, are less convincing, and its folds go too far up on to the shoulders. In doing so, the folds look more northern European than Italian. In the main, however, this is a reasonable attempt at depicting male dress in Italy at the time of the manuscript's creation.

The colours of Cavalcanti's clothing accord well with Italian images showing that dress for young people was remarkably colourful. Basing his comments on the effect of flowers among grass, Filarete in his *Treatise on Architecture* of c.1464 said that any colour went with green – yellow, red, even blue; blue went with red; red went even better with green than it did with blue. White and red and white and black went well together. But red did not go with yellow (so much for the collars, in the heraldic colours of Aragon seen in fig. 88, worn by the cats patrolling for rodents in the royal wardrobe in Naples).

René of Anjou never gave up hope of reconquering Naples, and in pursuit of Italian aid he maintained contacts with potential and actual supporters in the peninsula, such as the Venetian aristocrat, humanist and soldier Jacopo Antonio Marcello (fig. 92). In 1453 René even visited the court of the Duke of Milan. René had therefore fairly recently been in northern Italy when he was portrayed in fig. 92 with Marcello, who is presenting him with a translation into Latin of the works of the ancient Greek historian and geographer Strabo. This Italian view of northern dress seems to concentrate, quite reasonably, on its bulk at the shoulders; the stand-away collars of doublet and gown; the open front of the gown, revealing the shirt; and the (somewhat exaggerated) points on its footwear. The Burgundian ducal accounts for 1454 show that Duke Philip the Good's gowns had sleeves pleated with extra fabric inside the sleeve-head. Beneath such gowns Philip the Good (and René of Anjou) would have worn doublets with sleeves whose puffed upper sections were shorter and stiffer than those worn in Italy, hence the greater bulk of the northern men's shoulders seen here. It is doubtful, however, that a northerner would have understood the skull-caps.

The image of Marcello presenting the book to René can be dated to 1458–9, a period during which Marcello was involved almost non-stop in government affairs in Venice itself, where he would have had to wear what amounted to a uniform for his class. In this scene, however, he is represented not as a Venetian nobleman, but simply as a nobleman, in cloth of gold, and one who dressed perhaps rather too young for his age (he was born in 1398), in *giornea* (or *zornea* in Venetian dialect), *zupone* (doublet) and soled stockings. Marcello was happy to have some humanists liken his rather uneventful military career to those of the great soldiers of antiquity, in a remarkably self-aggrandizing and totally un-Venetian way. Here he is basically a private citizen, but one still deeply conscious of his rank – like René of Anjou, a former king, he can afford cloth of gold. (In reality, René's preferred colours in dress were black, grey and violet, in accordance with northern taste.)

The 1460s saw the first real signs of interest in the dress of the classical past (as opposed to the much older interest in classical literature and other achievements), chiefly in the humanist circles of northern Italy. In 1464 the term 'Middle Ages' was first used to describe all that lay between the current period of classical revivals and the lost world of ancient Rome. In 1468 the pope took great exception to a group of scholars who called each other by classical names and had dinner parties while wearing what they thought was ancient Roman dress. He accused them of sodomy and heresy, and banned their gatherings.

Petrarch's *Triumphs* (*Trionfi* in Italian), probably begun in the 1350s, had clear links to the triumphal processions of ancient Roman generals; and it is surprising to find that the young Cardinal Francesco Gonzaga (1444–83), from the northern Italian city of Mantua, did not seek more actively to have the latest ideas about classical dress (apart from a few draped mantles) incorporated into his Petrarch manuscript, probably of the late 1460s (fig. 93). Instead we have thoroughly contemporary-looking young people, with the men in *giornee* and *mi-parti* soled stockings; one youth on the right even has a Gonzaga device, a sun, on his *giornea*. The girls resemble many of the young women in the famous frescoes in the Palazzo Schifanoia in Ferrara, painted in the late 1460s, with their high-waisted gowns and their hair dressed in horns.

The dress of the women of Mantua and Milan was long considered to be similar, and was twice the subject of correspondence about costume dolls. In 1460 Cardinal Francesco's father, Ludovico, the Marquis of Mantua, wrote to his wife, telling her that an ambassador in Milan, who had already had dolls made to show the dress of women in Siena and Florence, wanted a Mantuan one, even though Mantuan and Milanese women dressed similarly. She was to get one made as quickly as possible, showing both the clothing and the hairstyles of Mantuan women. Over fifty years later, Francis I of France, anxious to give ladies in France clothing like that

91 LEFT
The Florentine Boccaccio, writing in his study before the people who are the subject of his book, wears ordinary scholarly dress. Presenting his book, he wears clothing suitable for a journey on horseback (compare the boots and short gown in fig. 97). Doffing the cap was a widespread symbol of respect, but it is doubtful whether a good mid-fifteenth-century Florentine republican would have removed his hat before most people. (Boccaccio, *Cas des nobles hommes et femmes*, France, Jean Fouquet, c.1458: Munich, Bayerische Staatsbibliothek, Cod. Gall. 6, f. 10r, detail)

92 OPPOSITE
Jacopo Antonio Marcello of Venice presents a book to René of Anjou. The wearing of cloth of gold was perhaps becoming widespread in Italy around this time, as in 1464 Florence concerned itself for the first time with the dress of men, prohibiting a number of clothing luxuries, including cloth of gold and cloth of silver, to men under the age of forty-five. San Bernardino had equated the wearing of the *giornea* with young men; Jacopo Antonio Marcello was sixty when this manuscript was begun. (Strabo, *Geography*, translated by Guarino da Verona, Venice?, 1458–9: Albi, Bibliothèque Municipale, MS 77, f. 4r)

CLEMENTIAE
AVGVSTAE

worn by the stylish Isabella d'Este, Marchioness of Mantua, asked that she supply him with a doll, dressed as she dressed, including her hairstyle. Side-stepping the request somewhat, she replied that he would not see anything new because 'What we wear, the ladies in Milan wear'. (Francis I had recently occupied Milan.) For full-size clothing, Mantua's chief claim to fame in the fifteenth century lay in its production of knitted woollen caps.

It is time to turn to see how dress was developing in north-western Europe in the course of the 1460s and the early 1470s. The scene by the Master of the *Harley Froissart* (fig. 94), in a manuscript owned by Philippe de Commynes, a counsellor of Charles the Bold, Duke of Burgundy, depicts the crowd gathered in Paris to watch the execution of the robber baron Amerigot Marcel. As is often the case with group scenes, there are insights into the clothing styles of different social classes; here there is the bonus of information on how clothing affected mobility. The condemned man wears the short shirt (and much smaller underpants, because they are no longer visible) necessitated by the shorter clothing of fashion. The executioner has stripped down to his doublet and hose, with his underpants visible at the hips, because he has had to undo some of the lacing so that he can move freely. The well-to-do young man mounted on the bulging white horse in the foreground is almost a caricature of the fashionable ideal – with his tall hat (which echoes the spiky headdress of a woman at a window on the right), the exaggeratedly wide shoulders and narrow waist of his short green gown, and the slit in his gown sleeve, revealing the red lining, and the slinging of that sleeve up on to his shoulder. Most of these features are spoken of by a chronicler in Arras, Jacques du Clerq, in 1467, as the latest things. Many other men wear rather longer gowns of a far less exaggerated shape, with old-fashioned hoods. They are to be seen as a sober, middle-class contrast to the extremes of aristocratic fashion. The farmer's wife in the foreground, with her baskets of eggs, wears the hood typical of her class, and she has hitched up the skirt of her loosish gown to allow her to walk.

In 1468 Charles the Bold, an inveterately lavish dresser, married Margaret of York, sister of Edward IV of England (fig. 95). Charles, in his wide-shouldered gown, fits in with the new fashions noted by du Clerq in 1467. But Margaret, though she eventually settled into her new homeland (and became a noted collector of manuscripts), seems initially to have had problems adapting to the new clothing she was expected to wear. She seems here to be clinging to what she knew in England.

Her gown looks mostly Franco-Flemish, with its very narrow sleeves, deep belt and flaring skirt; but her sway-back posture and headdress are more commonly seen in English images. The courtier Jehan de Haynin noted in his memoirs that during the festivities after the wedding Margaret changed back and forth between the clothing styles of her old and new homes. Later manuscripts that include images of Margaret of York show her with an upright posture and a tall, steeple-shaped headdress with a black frontlet and a veil in the Franco-Flemish fashion of the 1470s (seen with two more fantastic ones in fig. 97, made for Margaret of York's brother). Fig. 97 shows that the back neckline of women's gowns was curved, but visually matched the V-shape at the front by means of a strip of fur that hung over the belt. The hybrid being playing a harp in the right-hand margin wears a simplified version of the fashionable headdress. Theatrical designers at the time were prepared to go to great lengths to make 'real' versions of such fantastic creatures, even producing a mechanism whereby an actor dressed as an ancient Greek centaur could make 'his' rear legs seem to walk with his front legs (fig. 96).

Fig. 98 gives a view of the type of dress worn at the court of Edward IV of England, around 1480, with velvets (rarely seen so clearly before now), cloths of gold and the royal fur par excellence, ermine. The woman in the gown edged with ermine must therefore be a queen, and the child in cloth of gold beside her is presumably her son. The other figure wearing ermine is the god of love. The most obviously English features of the scene are the women's pillbox caps, typical of around 1480, and the veils suspended on top, a version of the headdress seen earlier in fig. 95.

Edward IV spent lavishly on clothing, and perhaps had to spend even more in 1480, when his sister Margaret, by then dowager Duchess of Burgundy, returned to England to visit him. The two young princes (later to be known as the Princes in the Tower, the supposed victims of murder committed to benefit their uncle, Richard III) were given gowns of white cloth of gold, the elder prince's being distinguished by being of a more expensive type of the fabric, known in English as 'tissue' (that is, *riccio sopra riccio*). After Edward's death in 1483 over 118 yards (108 metres) of cloth of gold and over 128 yards (117 metres) of cloth of silver, still unused, were inventoried in his wardrobe. For his coronation in 1483 Richard III bought more cloth of gold, including red cloth of gold 'wrought with nettes' at fifty-three shillings and four pence a yard. It perhaps resembled the pattern of the cloth of gold of the boy's gown and of the god of love's doublet sleeves and collar in fig. 98.

93 ABOVE

Fashionably dressed young people are present as Love passes in triumph under a Renaissance archway. The dress of the young women seen here is very plain when considered beside that worn by Susanna, the sister of Cardinal Francesco Gonzaga, for whom the manuscript was made: in 1451 she had a green velvet *vestito* (gown) decorated with gold apples, oranges and leaves. (Petrarch, *Triumphs*, Mantua, attributed to Pietro Guindaleri, 1463–83 (late 1460s?): British Library, Harley MS 3567, f. 149r, detail)

94 OPPOSITE TOP

People of all classes and ages gather to witness a public execution. On the bottom left there is a sharp contrast between the short, tight-waisted clothing of the young aristocrat on horseback (left of centre), and the longer gowns and hoods of the bourgeoisie. Henry VI of England's chaplain, John Blacman, says that a long gown and such a hood were the preferred garments of the pious king (r. 1422–61 and 1470–1), who thereby looked like a townsman. (Jean Froissart, *Chroniques*, Bruges, Master of the *Harley Froissart*, c.1465–70: British Library, Harley MS 4379, f. 64r, detail)

95 RIGHT

Charles the Bold, Duke of Burgundy, who was very fond of *riccio sopra riccio* fabrics, here wears one of the many plain golden gowns in which he is depicted in manuscripts. Margaret of York wears an altogether much less expensive-looking greyish gown. Her rank is indicated by the ermine collar and cuffs, and her nationality by the kite-like English headdress. (Pierre de Vaux, *Vie de Sainte Colette*, Bruges, Master of the *Ghent Life of St Colette*, c.1468: Ghent, Convent of the Colettine Poor Clares, MS 8, f. 40v, detail)

The queen in fig. 98 wears a gown of crimson velvet, a fabric that featured prominently in the gowns worn by the ladies of various ranks who attended Richard III's queen, Anne Neville, at her coronation. Crimson was the most expensive of the velvets, costing up to twenty-six shillings and eight pence a yard. Three duchesses and one countess (the Countess of Richmond, mother of the future Henry VII) were given white cloth of gold to trim their crimson velvet gowns. The other countesses and ladies of lower rank had white damask to trim their gowns, with less and less of the fabric being given to them as their status diminished. These outfits were a visual reflection of the kinds of distinction that sumptuary laws sought to make: earlier in the year, parliament had decreed that cloth of gold of tissue should be worn only by those of the rank of duke and above.

In ermine each black tadpole-shape, known as a 'powdering', was supposed to be the tail of an ermine, but in reality the 'tails' were usually faked with tiny pieces of black lambskin, called in England 'bogy shanks'. Anne Neville's coronation mantle, lined with 860 ermine skins, had 8500 powderings of bogy shanks. Dress at the time of the coronation was probably not particularly subtle in its colourings, as in addition to their crimson velvet and white gowns, the queen's ladies had blue velvet gowns trimmed with crimson. The noble young male attendants of the royal couple were dressed in crimson velvet over doublets of green satin, with the front of the doublets covered by stomachers of green and crimson satin. The effect must have been somewhat similar to that of the gown of the god of love's female companion, with its dark pink velvet trimming on a green gown. The god of love himself wears a green velvet stomacher over his cloth of gold doublet.

Local dress manifested itself perhaps most forcefully in the traditional styles required for men of the Venetian aristocratic class, a fixed group of 150–200 families (about four or five per cent of the population, with all noblemen being forced into political life at the age of twenty-five, or even younger in the case of certain families). Also subject to clothing rules were men of the citizen class, who provided the civil service and amounted to about five to ten per cent of the population. The Venetian ideal of social cohesion and stability was promoted by a variety of means, including the imposing of a uniform on all men of these classes over the age of twenty-five. It consisted of a full-length, front-closing black cloth gown (*vesta*, also called by the Latin word *toga*, the dress of ancient Roman citizens), a black doublet, a black cap (*bareta*) and a strip of black cloth or velvet (*beccho* or *becchetto*) worn hanging over one

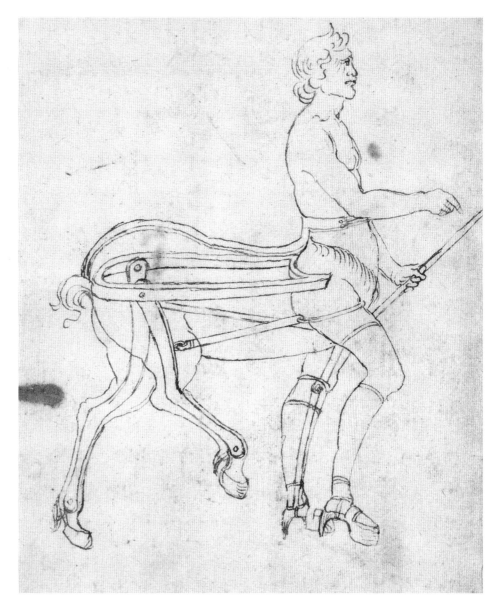

96

During his lifetime Francesco di Giorgio of Siena (1439–1501) was a painter, a sculptor, an architect and, as we see here, an engineer. Such a design was perhaps used in Rome in 1473, when Cardinal Pietro Riario entertained Eleanora of Aragon on her way north from Naples to marry Ercole d'Este, Duke of Ferrara. The cardinal arranged a type of early ballet on the theme of famous lovers of ancient times; it included troops of nymphs who were attacked by centaurs, which were chased off by the hero Hercules (Ercole in Italian). (After Francesco di Giorgio, *Treatises on Machines, Natural Philosophy*..., Italy, early sixteenth century?: British Library, Add. MS 34113, f. 176v)

shoulder. The sense of equality was reinforced by men not uncovering their head for anyone except the doge, the head of state (compare fig. 99). The group identity, as expressed through clothing, mattered a great deal in Italy; Venice is unusual only in the extent to which it mattered for two social classes. It was also unusual in not regarding participation in trade as a bar to noble status, as trade was essential to the well-being of the community.

157

Cy commence le tiers liure de ce piit
wlume intitule le chemyn de vaillance
et parle prudence a lact~

C onime amy y lors
du bosquage
fus yssu a mon ad
uantage

T ant que ces vii. mortels perils
N estore vraiant ne paix
Par les vertus des vii. pucelles
Le sens et la prudence dicelles

Qui bien men orent deliure
Sans estir a la mort liure
Aue non obstant celle victore
Auoie le des dangiers encore
A passer pour ma voie tendre
Com prudence me fist entendre
Quant en ce lieu fus arreste
Sy fut du parler appreste
Et me dist amis ne tes maix
Se longue est encores la voie
A paruenir a ton entente

97 OPPOSITE

Jean de Courcy is led from the
Forest of Temptation by the
Seven Virtues. By the late 1470s
northern European men had
longer hair, shorter caps, and
gowns that tended not to be
pleated or belted, with small
lapels being created by the
turning back of the front edges.
The gap across the front of the
doublet was covered by a
stomacher, here a piece of pink
velvet over the black-and-gold
doublet. Unless they were high-
ranking enough to have girls
carry their trains, women seem
to have had to loop them up over
their fashionably stick-like arms
when they walked, especially
outdoors.
(Jean de Courcy, *Chemin de
vaillance*, Bruges, Master of the
White Inscriptions, late 1470s:
British Library, Royal MS 14 E II,
f. 194r)

98 ABOVE

A queen presents her son at the
court of Love. Although velvet
had been worn for almost two
hundred years, it was not often
depicted so clearly in manuscripts
as we see it here, especially in
the red and the green on the
right. The colours become much
darker and smudged as they
wrinkle or fall into shadow.
(*Poems of Charles d'Orléans and
Other Works*, London? and
Flanders, c.1480 and
c.1495–1500: British Library,
Royal MS 16 F II, f. 1r, detail)

The tendency to keep upper-class women invisible at home, except when important visitors had to be impressed by a public display of the splendid clothing and jewels those women could command, and the discouraging of individual portraits, mean that it is very difficult to learn much about Venetian dress for most of the fifteenth century, hence the value of fig. 99, showing a doge, his young grandson, and a female personification of Venice in 1486.

Men of the noble class who rose to public office always wore crimson or violet-purple garments. Their clothes, by law, had to be made in Venice. On special occasions other men were expected to replace their black clothing with garments in shades of red, or face criticism for lacking the festive spirit. Only the doge, the holder of the only life-long office in the state, could wear white. He could also wear cloth of gold; and he never wore any colour below the status of crimson. Like Venetian noblewomen, he had to reflect the power of the city through clothing. The doge had especially wide sleeves, known, appropriately, as dogal sleeves; no one else, except doctors of medicine and the nine procurators of St Mark (from whose number a doge was usually elected), was allowed to wear them. His cap with the point at the back, the *corno*, was his everyday wear as a version of a crown. Since ambassadors too reflected the power of the state, they would be given silks worked with gold to wear abroad, and such fabric seems to have been considered an appropriate gift to give to departing Venetian ambassadors: when a delegation was about to leave Milan in 1475, the Duke of Milan, Galeazzo Maria Sforza, gave each of them a *veste* (gown) of gold brocade lined with marten fur, and made 'with wide sleeves, according to their Venetian custom'.

The personification of Venice shows the peculiar appearance of Venetian women, which involved a wide neckline and hair piled up on top of the head and in ringlets at the sides of the face. The Milanese cleric Pietro Casola, who visited Venice on his way to the Holy Land in 1494, marvelled at how Venetian women kept their bodices in place, as well as at their lack of fear of having their exposed flesh bitten by insects. Venice's high-waisted bodice and her sleeves are golden; her skirt is in those two important Venetian colours, crimson and gold. Among Venetian women cloth of gold was allowed only to female members of the doge's family living in his palace; therefore Venice herself can hardly be shown in less than a type of gold fabric. Her splendid collar of jewels is a reminder of the spectacle Venetian noblewomen were expected to provide – yet Venice, along with many other Italian states, frequently

legislated against excesses in dress and jewellery. Such splendour was forbidden –
except when the state needed it, therefore women clearly had to own, or have access to,
what was otherwise prohibited, and did not get many opportunities to display legally.

Italy, used to a certain amount of interference from the north in the shape
of imperial policy, was shortly to be convulsed by a major invasion from France, as
Charles VIII sought to make good the claim to the throne of Naples that had been
taken over by the French crown on the death of René of Anjou in 1480. New fashions
entered Italy with the invaders, and added to the local styles, as well as to the
versions of Spanish and Neapolitan styles that had filtered into northern Italy
through marriages and alliances with Aragonese Naples. In France itself Catalan
dress seems to have had a degree of attraction for Charles VIII. This chapter finishes
with a look at some of these styles at home and abroad.

One of the most famous manuscripts in the British Library is a copy of one
of the most popular texts of the Middle Ages, the *Roman de la rose*, begun around 1220
by Guillaume de Lorris and completed around 1280 by the much more cynical Jean
de Meun. This particular manuscript (fig. 100) is important not just because of its
rarity as secular illumination produced around 1490 for a patron at what was left
of the once-magnificent Burgundian court, but because it shows that a more
sophisticated sense of the clothing of the past was developing. Crucial to this were
pointed toes and areas of dagging, derived from the International Gothic period, and
replacing a standard set of elements such as turbans and short sleeves, hitherto used
fairly indiscriminately for both the past and the exotic. In some other respects the
illuminator is reacting to the text: the man at the back in the yellow stockings
leading the dance (Sir Mirth, as Chaucer called him) wears dagging because that is
how the artist has understood de Lorris's description of his *robe*, as 'cut up in many
places', and his shoes have also been slashed to correlate with the text. Yet his long
hair and flat cap come from around 1490. His clothing, to match the text, should be
decorated with birds worked in gold. Behind him the god of love wears a huge,
contemporary hat, like that seen on the man in green and red; these are the artist's
additions. The floral pattern and the lion on the god's gown are part of an attempt
to deal with the text's description of his clothing, which was made of little flowers,
combined with what sounds like an extreme mixture of textile designs from the
thirteenth century – lozenges, little shields, birds, lion cubs, leopards and multi-
coloured summer flowers of all kinds.

99 ABOVE
Doge Marco Barbarigo (1413–86),
seen seated here, receives a
panegyric composed by his
young grandson, Vittore Capello,
who kneels before him. They are
watched by the personification of
Venice. Barbarigo seems to have
had some personal peculiarities
in his dress, noted by the
Venetian diarist Marin Sanudo,
one of which was to wear his
golden *becchetto* round his neck
in an attempt to disguise his
neck's excessive length. Vittore
Capello wears clothing that
mimics adult Venetian citizen
and noble dress, but does not fit
in with it completely. Adults
would have had a black *becchetto*,
and they seem not to have

draped it across the chest; this
may be a child's way of dressing,
as a portrait of a boy of *c.*1480 in
the National Gallery, London, by
Jacometto Veneziano, also shows
the *becchetto* draped across the
chest.
(Vittore Capello, *Panegyric for
Marco Barbarigo, Doge of Venice*,
Venice, 1486: British Library, Add.
MS 21463, f. 1r, detail)

100 ABOVE
A dance in the garden of Sir
Mirth, watched by the narrator
of the *Roman de la rose*, dressed
in blue, at the viewer's left. The
dagging and belts with golden
'tails' fashionable at the start of
the fifteenth century, and the
long-toed shoes of the narrator,
are called upon to evoke the
1220s, when the poem was
written. Most of the rest of the
men's dress (and that of the
women) belongs to around
1490, when this manuscript
was produced.
(Guillaume de Lorris and Jean de
Meun, *Roman de la rose*, Flanders,
Master of the Prayerbooks of
*c.*1500, *c.*1490: British Library,
Harley MS 4425, f. 14v, detail)

101 OPPOSITE
A Catalan noblewoman kneels
before St Mary Magdalene. The
saint's dress is largely obscured
by the crimson mantle she wears;
but the lady before her is dressed
in clothing that marks her
awareness of dress at the
Spanish court. Typical of that
style is the hair wrapped in a veil
at the back of the head, and
long, exposed shirt sleeves.
(*Book of Hours*, Catalonia, Spain,
after 1461 [1480s?]: British
Library, Add. MS 18193, f. 143v)

Love's companion, Beauty, wears her long blonde hair hanging to her heels. Her looped-up train, like those of three other women, is an interpolation of the late fifteenth century. Other 'modern' features are women's tight bodices with narrow belts; and the black-fronted French hoods, made of silk, and worn in France and the Netherlands by upper-class women. The wardrobe accounts of the French queen, Anne of Brittany, show that she was wearing wide sleeves in 1492. Here the sleeves are just beginning to widen out over the hand, but the slashed and puffed lower sleeve of the golden gown at the front is an element of fantasy. The girl in pink (Candour) is perhaps the most fantastically dressed of all, with her large, beret-like cap and her baggy blue lower sleeves. Her main garment seems to be the product of the artist's having lit upon a word in the text that he understood, *cote*, when in fact the text says that she wore a white garment he would not have understood, a *sorquenie* (still not fully identified), which is said to be more becoming to a woman than a *cote*.

Candour's companion and the other man at the front are both very fashionably dressed, the one in a gown with wide lapels and the other showing the layers worn beneath such a gown: a V-necked doublet, with matching stomacher, and very elaborately patterned hose. Elaborate hose had long been a part of Italian male dress, particularly in the context of court liveries and the groups of young men known as the Companies of the Stocking, whose function was to organize entertainments, and whose identifying mark was, not surprisingly, an elaborately decorated stocking. Perhaps the idea entered northern Europe with the growing interest of Charles VIII in Italy. On their feet most of the men wear very bulbous-toed shoes, the kind worn by the French invaders of Italy and matching the description in the *Ferrarese Diary* as 'wide at the front, at the point of the foot, which an ox's foot could enter'.

As Spanish aristocratic dress for women successfully invaded northern Italy towards the end of the century, it is useful to look at it at home before examining how it looked in its transplanted version. Probably belonging to the 1480s is fig. 101, from a book of hours whose internal evidence suggests it belonged to a Catalan lady called María or Maddalena, on the basis of the identity of the saint before whom she kneels, Mary Magdalene. The heraldry suggests that the lady was connected to the old Catalan family of Vallgornera. Although local styles of dress can still be identified in Spain in the next century at levels below the aristocracy, and the large noble class dressed alike in what is often referred to today as Spanish dress,

'Spanish' aristocratic dress should be regarded as the aristocratic dress of the dominant region in Spain, Castile. The Catalan lady here would indicate that this cultural accretion was already taking place.

The upper-class 'national' style consisted of a hairstyle in which the hair was drawn towards the back of the head and wrapped in a long scarf attached to a small coif at the back of the head, in the style known as the *cofia de tranzado* (literally 'coif of plaits'), or, more simply, the *tranzado*. The queen, Isabella the Catholic, and her daughters wore *tranzados* made of fine Holland linen, embroidered in red (as here) or in black; the coloured embroidery was repeated, again as here, on their great trailing shirt sleeves, another 'Spanish' feature. (In 1477 Brother Hernando de Talavera criticized the wearing of 'very bagged' shirt sleeves.) The Spanish dress historian Carmen Bernis Madrazo says that when the embroidery was done in coloured silks (as opposed to gold thread), it was known by a name that betrayed the decoration's Moorish origins, *punto de almofarán*. (A Milanese inventory of 1501 describes a woman's shirt worked in black silk as being *a punto moresco* – in Moorish stitch; this type of embroidery, when it reached England in the sixteenth century, was known, rather less accurately, as Spanish work.)

The gown on top, known as a *brial*, is of cloth of gold; in the 1480s every fashionable noblewoman owned *briales*, usually made of sumptuous fabrics. The commonest decoration for the *brial* was a series of strips of contrasting fabric placed horizontally on the skirt, often containing rolls of fabric acting as hoops that held the skirt away from the body. The hoops were said to have been invented in 1468 by the wife of Henry IV the Impotent of Castile to hide an inappropriate pregnancy. Equally 'Spanish' is the cloak with its long side-openings. It may be the upper-class *mantilla de aletas* (winged mantle), in which the back of the wearer was covered by one piece of cloth and the front by two narrower pieces attached to the back at the shoulders. (A version of it is to be seen in the *Neapolitan Chronicle*, now in the Pierpont Morgan Library in New York, on women involved in an event that took place in 1486.)

In northern Italy women at this time wore a much smaller mantle, called the *sbernia*, which was worn under one arm and over the other shoulder. The ultimate origins of the *sbernia* are disputed among dress historians, though it almost certainly came from Spain to Italy. It is most readily seen in Milan, the dominant city in northern Italy and the one with the strongest links to Naples (fig. 102, the investiture

102 LEFT

The investiture of Ludovico 'il Moro' Sforza as Duke of Milan in May 1495. (The duke stands under the pillars on the left, the central figure in dark clothing, facing the man holding the banner.) The documents relating to the investiture of the duke state that part of the significance of putting on the ducal clothing was to show that its recipient had become a new man. In 1494 in the *Ferrarese Diary* (written in the duchess's home town) women's *sbernie* are described as short mantles fastened on the shoulder in the manner of the apostles (compare St Peter in fig. 7). (*Arcimboldi Missal*, Milan, attributed to the Master 'B.F.', 1495–7: Milan Cathedral Library, MS D.1.13, f. 1r)

103 OPPOSITE

Charles VIII of France receives a book from Pierre Louis de Valtan. The king wears cloth of gold and a black cap fashionably decorated with a gold medallion. In France an edict of 1485 limited the right to wear cloth of gold, and cloth of silver, to nobles who lived nobly and had an annual income of 2000 *livres tournois*; this suggests, as does a contemporary English law, that more and more (unsuitable) people had access to luxury goods. When Charles entered Naples in triumph in 1495 he wore a black cap like the one here, decorated with a gold medallion showing the Virgin and Child, embellished with diamonds and rubies. (Pierre Louis de Valtan, *Credo fidei militanti*, France, before 1498: British Library, Add. MS 35320, f. 2v)

of Lodovico 'il Moro' Sforza as Duke of Milan). At the centre front kneel Sforza's wife, Beatrice d'Este, and her ladies in *sbernie*. The Neapolitan, and hence Spanish, element in Beatrice's background was pronounced. Her father was Ercole d'Este, Duke of Ferrara, who had spent many of his formative years at the court of Alfonso V of Aragon in Naples; her mother was Alfonso's granddaughter, Eleanora of Aragon. When Eleanora returned to Naples in 1477 for the marriage of her widower father to the Spanish princess Juana of Aragon, she had taken the two-year-old Beatrice with her. Beatrice was left in Naples, at her grandfather's request, from 1477 to 1485. In Naples in 1481 Beatrice was given a *briale* of crimson silk and a number of ribbons embroidered in the Moorish style. Ten years later, aged sixteen, she married Lodovico 'il Moro', at that date only the *de facto* ruler of Milan.

The position of the women in fig. 102 provides a view of the long tails of hair hanging down their backs and wrapped in veils. This style clearly derives from the Spanish *tranzado*, though it was known in Lombardy as a *coazzone*. Beatrice and one other woman wear scarlet or crimson *sbernie*; all the rest would appear to be in some livery-type combinations of colours. The *sbernia* allowed women to seem to be modestly wearing cloaks while at the same time displaying the fine fabrics of their outer sleeves, tied to the gowns at the shoulders, and slashed to display the undershirt sleeves as a series of puffs. It is possible that the women were also wearing skirts with hoops. In 1492 the trousseau of Ippolita Sforza of Milan, who was marrying a fellow Italian, featured a number of Spanish-style garments, including three *faldilie*. They must have been related to the *faldie*, or hooped underskirts, prohibited in 1498 in one of Milan's very rare sumptuary laws.

The scene is not a true record of any one moment in the investiture, but a composite in a manuscript made for the archbishop (centre back) who conducted the cermony. 'Il Moro' is in profile on the left in dark clothing. By the stage at which the banner would have been entrusted to the man holding it, Galeazzo da Sanseverino, the captain of the Sforza troops, 'il Moro' would have been dressed in his red ducal mantle with a deep collar lined with ermine, and the ducal *berretta* (cap) of red satin and miniver, decorated with gold. He would thus have been less readily distinguishable from the many fellow princes, also in red, who face him, and from the members of the legal profession at the front left.

The Spanish monarchs Ferdinand and Isabella were irritated by French influence in Catalonia; yet Charles VIII of France had many Catalans at his court, including the queen's physician and the Archdeacon of Angers, Pierre Louis de Valtan, seen before the king in fig. 103. Dark colours, worn by many of the courtiers here, had become so much a part of northern dress that at the wedding festivities of the Duke of Milan in 1490 the men and women of the dancing troupe who were dressed up in French-style clothing wore black. In 1490 Charles had a full-length, wide-sleeved *sayon* (a type of gown, apparently characterized by a large number of gores in its 'skirt') in the Spanish style, with twenty-four wide gores, twelve in black velvet and the other twelve in violet cloth of gold. (It seems that when such contrasting gores appeared in women's dress in Spain, they were regarded as Moorish.) The pleating of the 'skirt' of the guard in the background would have lent itself readily to this treatment (and compare figs 104 and 106). In 1492 Charles had four shirts gathered in the Catalan manner, and he was presumably pursuing his taste for such garments when he sent back to France from conquered Naples a married couple who made shirts in the Catalan fashion. Along with them went a tailor who could make women's clothes 'in the Italian style, of all sorts'. This means that either the French had a very poor grasp of the complex regional variety of clothing styles to be seen in Italy, or that the tailor was remarkably well informed. Unfortunately, the French invasion of Naples in 1495 sent more than interesting tailors back to France: some of those in the returning army who fell for the limited charms of the few women to be seen in public contributed to the spread of syphilis to northern Europe. In 1509 the English priest Alexander Barclay was able to say in his version of the satirical poem *The Ship of Fools* (which originated in Germany in the previous century) that 'disgysyng' (new, strange and ostentatious clothing), like the pox, came from France. Other things, however, were to come from there too – including illuminated manuscripts that served as souvenirs of contemporary events.

While this chapter has, of necessity, given the nature of the material, still concentrated on the dress of the upper classes, a far greater variety of clothing has been available for study in far more situations than before. Much of that clothing was worn by contemporary figures, rather than figures in historical accounts. Manuscripts have offered images of the highest and the poorest in the land; a pagan goddess and a man dressed up as a centaur; Venetians and Spaniards; a royal wedding, and mass being sung for the King of Aragon. They have shown how the French saw Italian dress, and vice versa. Indeed, they have shown the clothing of (almost) everyone.

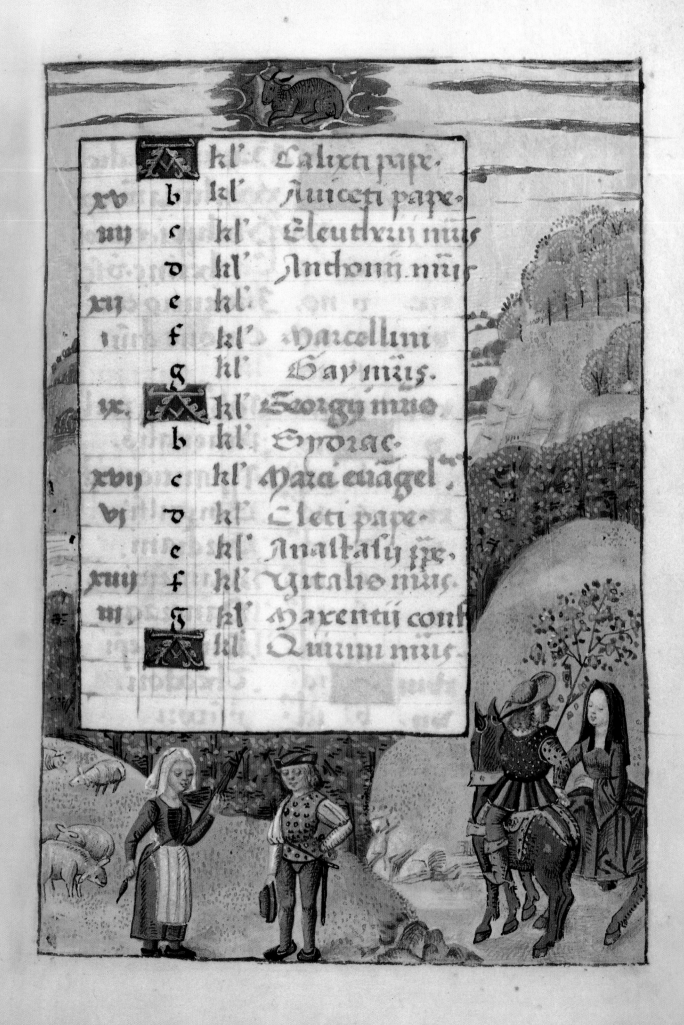

	A	kl'	Calixti pape.
xv	b	kl'	Aniceti pape.
iiij	c	kl'	Eleutherij mris
	d	kl'	Anthonij mris
xij	e	kl'	
viij	f	kl'	Marcellini
	g	kl'	Gay mris.
ye.	**A**	kl'	Georgij mro
	b	kl'	Syriac.
xvij	c	kl'	Marci euagel'
vj	d	kl'	Cleti pape.
	e	kl'	Anastasij pe.
xiiij	f	kl'	Vitalio mris.
iij	**g**	kl'	Maxentij conf.
	A	kl'	Quirini mris.

V

Dressing the Present and the Past
c.1500–c.1570

104 OPPOSITE
Two young couples out in the
countryside on a calendar page
for April, from a Flemish book of
hours. The upper-class woman,
on horseback on the viewer's
right, wears a French hood and
the square-necked, wide-sleeved
garment known as a 'French
gown'. Around 1500 women's
sleeves became wide enough to
develop large turn-backs that
showed the lining, thereby
affording an opportunity for the
display of expensive silks or furs,
depending on the season.
(*Hours of Joanna of Castile* [Joanna
the Mad], Bruges or Ghent,
Master of the David Sequences in
the *Grimani Breviary*, 1496–1506:
British Library, Add. MS 18852,
f. 5)

THE ILLUMINATED MANUSCRIPT AS A SOURCE FOR DRESS HISTORY
remains unsurpassed until the mid-sixteenth century; but as a book form, its days
were numbered because of the invention of movable type in the mid-fifteenth
century. Those all over western Europe who wanted luxurious books of hours
continued to turn to Flemish illuminators, who continued to provide in these books
calendars with scenes of the months, and people of various ranks engaged in
appropriate activities. French illuminators who worked for the court circle were
called on to produce manuscripts that related to events involving the court, thereby
creating a considerable volume of visual and allied documentary information about
real people in real events. As for purely documentary sources, the by-now usual
range – from wardrobe accounts to private letters – can be called upon.

Clothing as it was worn in various parts of the ever-expanding world was
part of the growing interest in what would today be called ethnography, and was
therefore one of the obsessions of the age. The extensive correspondence of Isabella
d'Este, Marchioness of Mantua, about her own clothing and that of other people,
while partly prompted by her considerable vanity, is symptomatic of the interests
of the age, and she was taken seriously by crowned heads as the arbiter of style.
Knowing about the dress of other nations (as opposed to imitating it) was not
frivolous; it was part of being educated. As will be seen at the end of this chapter,
the general interest in clothing would also eventually be extended to attempts at
recording accurately the clothing of the past.

Dress took on a political aspect of far greater importance than it had ever
done before – outside Italy a sense of nationhood was emerging, fostered by a

number of factors, including resistance to the authority of the Church in Rome. The Habsburg Empire encompassed peoples with vastly different clothing styles. The emperor Charles V's abdication speech in 1555 makes clear the areas that concerned the European part of that empire – among other journeys he had made, he had travelled to Flanders ten times, to Germany nine times, to Italy seven times, to Spain six times, and to North Africa twice. Modern writers have assumed that Spanish styles therefore dominated Europe, but that represents a gross simplification of the complexity of styles available. Black, seen with increasing frequency, is often said to have been a peculiarly Spanish colour in dress; but if black had a 'natural' home, it was probably at the Habsburg court in Flanders. There for almost fifty years (1509–55) the regents (Margaret of Austria and her niece Mary of Hungary) were widows whose sober black clothing could well have given black an aura of power, to add to its already recognized ability to confer dignity on the wearer. In Flanders black woollen cloth was worn by the middle classes, with small areas of black velvet or satin as trimming; and black silks of all kinds were worn by the upper classes.

It was French styles, especially for women, that came to dominate the wardrobes of aristocratic women in Flanders and England, despite the political antagonisms of Habsburg-ruled Flanders and Tudor England towards France. In the case of Flanders the attraction of French styles was probably historical, given that in the fifteenth century the Burgundian court had imported French culture to Flanders. In the case of England, there was a strong tendency, criticized at the time, to imitate foreign styles of dress, and possibly a suspicion that the French were simply more stylish because they took novelty in dress far more seriously than any other nation. Certainly Italian observers of the Anglo-French meeting at the Field of Cloth of Gold in 1520 thought that the French were more elegant than the English; and an Italian in London in 1493 had already noted that the French-style clothing worn by the English looked less good on them because they were physically bigger than the French.

In Italy there was felt to be strong French sartorial influence, which came about because of continuing French political intervention in the peninsula. Louis XII (r. 1498–1515) and Francis I (r. 1515–47), inheriting a claim to Milan from Valentina Visconti, Duchess of Orléans, established themselves for a while in Milan. Looking back on the events of the first half of the century, the Ferrarese courtier Agostino Mosti concluded that although Spaniards, Germans and others had introduced some new clothing habits, none had been so varied or imitated as those brought by the French. Baldassare Castigilione, in *The Book of the Courtier* (first drafted between 1508 and 1516, and more or less finished 1516–18), includes a debate on clothing. The lack of distinctive Italian dress (presumably only for men) was offered as proof of the subjugation of Italians to all the foreigners who had invaded the peninsula. German dress was skimpy; French dress was overdone. But the application of Italian taste to both could correct their deficiencies. Illuminated manuscripts and documentary sources, however, are far more likely to show the French fascination with Italian dress.

The clothing worn in Habsburg-ruled Flanders can be found in the *Hours of Joanna of Castile* (also known as Joanna the Mad: 1479–1555). This book was created probably around 1500, during her marriage to Philip the Fair (1478–1506), son and heir of the Habsburg emperor Maximilian I. Fig. 104, from the calendar for April, shows two couples of different ranks, the one on horseback upper class, and the other couple presumably working class, as the second woman wears an apron, a skirt clear of her feet, and a linen headdress rather than the black silk French hoods worn by the upper classes.

The manuscript includes images of Joanna wearing the French-style clothing of the upper-class woman here, as was appropriate for her as a loyal Habsburg wife living in Flanders; but when the death of her older siblings left her, unexpectedly, the heiress to her parents' kingdoms, her wardrobe had to change when she returned to Spain, with her husband, to be sworn in as heiress to Castile. Travelling from Flanders by way of the French court in December 1501, she and some of her ladies wore Spanish dress. When the couple reached Saragossa in October 1502, where they were to take an oath as the heirs, Philip wore Castilian dress, but on the next day, at the oath-taking ceremony, although Joanna (correctly) wore Castilian dress, Philip wore the clothing he had been used to at home. This was probably a major display of insensitivity.

The young man in fig. 104 wearing only doublet and hose as his main garments may be lower class, seeking to be unencumbered by his clothing. But his shoes are fashionably chunky, and he can afford the two caps worn by fashionable men at this time. He may therefore be a servant in a great household, or an upper-class potential seducer, as the upper classes tended to discard their gowns only in intimate situations, or when they indulged in physical exertion, a respectable example of which was tennis (even with shoes like these – compare fig. 114).

105 OPPOSITE
Anne de Foix, wearing cloth of
gold in the middle of the
procession, is closely surrounded
by attendants in French dress,
and farther out by Bohemians in
a variety of headgear. At the front
of the scene are peak-fronted
hats of the type worn many
centuries later by Errol Flynn
playing Robin Hood (actually a
type of travelling hat to keep the
sun out of the eyes), and even
(to the right, behind the queen)
a modest fifteenth-century-style
blue hood. Other men wear
turban-like head coverings.
(*Journey of Anne de Foix and Her
Marriage to Ladislas of Bohemia and
Hungary*, France, c.1513?, after
original of 1502: British Library,
Stowe MS 584, f. 71v)

106 ABOVE
Henry VIII of England, at front
on horseback, passes before
Katherine of Aragon and
courtiers, including men
with large gold chains, shortly
before Thomas More mocked
Englishmen's love of such chains
in *Utopia* (first edition printed in
1516). In Utopia chains of solid
gold were used to restrain slaves,
and criminals were liable to be
forced to wear gold necklaces,
crowns, rings and earrings. A
Venetian observer of the English
contingent accompanying Mary
Tudor into Abbeville in France in
1514 described them as having
great gold chains, some worn
'in the manner of prisoners'.
(*Westminster Tournament Roll*,
England, 1511: London, College
of Arms)

In France the queen, Anne of Brittany, had a major interest in illuminated manuscripts, commissioning not just devotional works but also works that portrayed the lives of the royal couple and their immediate circle. When Ladislas, King of Bohemia and Hungary, selected her cousin, Anne de Foix, as the bride who would seal his new alliance with France, the queen sent her herald, Pierre Choque, with the bridal party to provide her with a detailed account of the journey in 1502. Fig. 105 shows the party, in their French clothes, being accompanied by heralds from France and Brittany (Anne of Brittany's coat of arms involved stylized ermine), and a Bohemian escort who have joined the travellers. The French interest in illustrating foreign clothing could take strange turns – the Bodleian Library in Oxford has a book of hours made for a member of the de Scépaux family (Douce MS 264), who had presumably been to Italy, as it includes, inserted quite gratuitously, images of women from various Italian cities and regions, in their local dress.

The transformation of Englishwomen into pseudo-Frenchwomen was all but complete by the end of the 1530s. A glimpse of the early stages of the process is afforded by fig. 106, a record of a tournament held at Westminster in London in February 1513 to celebrate the birth of a first (short-lived) son to Henry VIII of England and his wife, Katherine of Aragon (a sister of Joanna of Castile). Under a canopy decorated with Tudor emblems, such as the portcullis, sit ladies and gentlemen of the court. The queen sits under her own canopy beside another woman, possibly Henry VIII's sister, Mary. All the women wear headdresses of the type to be found in England at this time, and called by modern dress historians the 'gable' headdress. The queen (who had arrived in England in 1501 wearing a Spanish hooped skirt) and two of the women with her have wide sleeves on their gowns, in the French fashion; the rest have much narrower sleeves, which seem to have been an English fashion. (When the princess Mary married the widower Louis XII of France in 1514, the wardrobe she took with her included not just French gowns, made with French advice, but English-style gowns, some with narrow sleeves.) The male courtiers are more international in their appearance, with their flattish, fan-shaped bonnets worn on shoulder-length hair, and fairly loose gowns with wide sleeves. However, the large gold chains around the necks of some of the men were a feature of English (and German) dress.

Some men wear their hair in gold nets, which seem to be another German fashion. The knights have adapted the current fashion for coats with gored skirts (*sayons*, or base coats in English) in contrasting fabrics to provide 'skirts' to wear over their armour. The writer of *The Great Chronicle of London* interpreted the gold letters H and K on the king's outfit as standing for Henry and King (rather than, as one might expect, Henry and Katherine). Henry VIII wore a considerably more elaborate arrangement of his attendants' colours at the proxy wedding of his sister Mary in 1514, when he had a gown of cloth of gold and ash-grey satin in a chequer pattern. The queen wore plain ash-grey satin; and the bride and her proxy bridegroom wore cloth of gold and purple satin in chequers. The fashion for chequered clothing clearly provoked disapproval in Italy, as *The Book of the Courtier* says that a gentleman in a *roba* (gown) quartered in different colours was not necessarily mad; he had perhaps just lived in Lombardy for some time, where everyone dressed in that way.

Mary married Louis XII of France a few months after the death of Anne of Brittany. Appropriately enough, Anne's funeral arrangements (fig. 107) were the subject of thirty-four known copies of a description by her herald Pierre Choque, mostly made for French aristocrats. Comparison of the description of dress in the text with what appears in the illuminations shows that this version is not one of those most concerned with accuracy of detail – for instance, sometimes the ermine trimming on the clothing of the effigy of the queen on her coffin, mentioned in the text, is missing, as here. Anne had twice been Queen of France, her first husband, Charles VIII, having accorded her the most unusual honour of being anointed at her coronation in 1492 in the same manner as he had been at his. When she died after fifteen years of marriage to her second husband, Louis XII, he organized the most splendid funeral seen for a queen of France, based on those for French kings.

The text tells us that the men in scarlet beside the coffin are the four presidents of the Parlement de Paris (the highest law court in the land); what it doesn't explain is why they are exempt from wearing mourning. This was where the effect of Anne's anointing came into play. Those men, whose role as judges required them to wear scarlet, wore scarlet at the funerals of kings to signify that although an individual king might be dead, royal justice, which they administered, lived on. After their accessions, French kings would wear violet or red, not black, in mourning for their predecessors because the kingdom was deemed never to be without a king.

Within a few months of this elaborate funeral, Louis XII was proposing to make peace with England and marry Henry VIII's sister Mary, as noted above. The

The coffin of Anne of Brittany
was, in the usual manner, topped
by a temporary memorial, known
as a funeral effigy, made by the
royal painter and illuminator Jean
Perréal, and dressed in a version
of the robes of state (*habit royal*)
in which the body itself had
already been dressed. The four
men in scarlet beside the coffin
are the four presidents of the
Parlement de Paris.
(*Account of the Funeral of Anne of
Brittany, Queen of France*, Paris,
c.1513: British Library, Stowe MS
584, f. 35v)

108

A pageant scene of the peace between England and France, as devised by Pierre Gringoire, who described it as showing God the Father with a large heart in his hand, and below him a king and a queen 'in their triumph and magnificence dressed and garbed royally'. Below are seated personifications of France and England, with standing figures of Friendship, Alliance and Peace. The sleeves of Alliance (*Confederacio*, in the centre) derive perhaps from a version of Milanese dress.
(*Pageants for the Marriage of Louis XII and Mary Tudor, Paris, 1514:* British Library, Cotton Vespasian MS B II, f. 8v)

109

Pageant figures personifying the virtues expected of a queen of France. Most of the Old Testament heroines gathered around a queen (in a *surcote ouverte*) look as though they belong in the France of *c.*1515 because of square necklines, wide sleeves, or caps like French hoods. Rachel (top left), Leah (below her), Rebecca (top right) and Esther (below her) had all been mentioned in a prayer at the coronation of Jeanne de Bourbon in 1364 as examples for the queen to follow. With the heroines are four figures of Prudence, Generosity, Justice and Temperance, in clothing suggestive of that of Benedictine nuns.
(*Pageants for the Coronation of Claude, Queen of Francis I of France, Paris, 1517?:* British Library, Stowe MS 582, f. 32v)

pageants (actually *tableaux vivants*) that greeted Mary's entry into Paris as queen on 6 November 1514 are the first known set created by a single writer, in this case the comic poet Pierre Gringoire (fig. 108). The British Library manuscript contains Gringoire's account of the event, perhaps brought back to England by Mary. The personification of France, at the left, wears, naturally, a French hood and ermine-lined wide French sleeves; but England, at the right, is a little more mysterious, as French-style sleeves and a hat like a man's, worn over a sort of French hood, are not the most obvious attributes of Englishwomen at this period. (Mary on her journey to Paris had worn a crimson hat set at an angle over her left eye; perhaps the hat here was a last-minute, complimentary, addition to the scene.) Friendship, second from the left, wears a kind of short overskirt, found in other theatrical or exotic figures. The sleeves of Alliance, in the centre, with the shirt puffing out at the shoulders and elbows, could have been inspired by late fifteenth-century Italian, possibly Milanese, dress. Included in Mary's trousseau were Milanese-style gowns, clear proof that the Venetians were correct in their suspicion that the pope wanted the French king to have Milan. (A copy of Mary's clothing list is in the British Library in Egerton MS 3800.)

Gringoire was also responsible for the pageants for the 1517 entry into Paris of the next queen consort of France, Claude, Louis XII's daughter by Anne of Brittany. This included (fig. 109 at the top right) a figure in 'Italian' dress, so similar to one in the pageants for Mary Tudor that perhaps the design was reused. Claude's husband Francis I soon set out to recover Milan. He seems to have been very interested not just in Italian women, but also in their clothing styles. Isabella d'Este was told by her son's secretary that a festivity at the French court in the summer of 1516 involved fourteen young ladies wearing rich Italian clothes Francis I had brought back from Italy.

Collecting information on clothing styles seems to have been fairly common in Germany; a very personal version of this phenomenon was created by Matthäus Schwarz of Augsburg, in an autobiography illustrated with all the clothes he bought and wore. In fact, nothing he wore even before he started the book in 1520 seems to

have been omitted. He went to Milan in the autumn of 1514, aged seventeen, and sometimes wore the extremely wide-brimmed hat typical of southern German dress. He was still in Milan when Francis I entered the city in 1515; Schwarz on that occasion wore a kind of base coat striped in blue and yellow, the French royal colours. In Milan in June 1516 he bought the black clothing in fig. 110 and wore it in Venice. While there he bought himself the long black gown of a Venetian gentleman (which, of course, he was not entitled to wear because of his nationality and age).

Back in Augsburg that October he recorded his first outfit, again in the German style, which he wanted to be like that of a young nobleman out hunting (fig. 111). This suggests that not only did Schwarz like clothes, but also that he saw them as a means of adopting other identities. One of the motives behind sumptuary legislation had been to stop dress being used to blur class identities; as the sixteenth century progressed, it was thought that national boundaries were beginning to blur too. As if aware of this, Schwarz has an outfit of wide hat, low-necked doublet, broad-toed shoes and elaborately slashed hose, marking, after the sobriety of his previous Venetian outfit, a most aggressive return to the flamboyance (and the skimpiness noted by Castiglione) of German dress.

Another German obsessed with recording himself and his life was the artist Albrecht Dürer. Although his obsession was less exclusive in its focus than Matthäus Schwarz's, it seems to have extended on at least one occasion, in 1525 or 1526, to designing his own shoes (fig. 114). Most shoes of this style must have been bad for the feet, as they usually had little or no sides to them, and, with their flat soles, offered no support to the arches of the feet.

112 OPPOSITE

A personification of Concord (bottom) holds Tudor roses and French lilies, symbolizing the friendship between the kings of France and England. Her black and gold neckline goes back in a slight slope towards the centre back, where it probably meets in a V-shape, as is suggested in a drawing of an English lady by Hans Holbein. In a book commissioned by Katherine of Aragon about the education of a Christian woman (1523), the Spaniard Juan Luis de Vives became almost apoplectic when he wrote of how wrong it was to allow girls to go out of doors baring their necks, breasts 'and between the shoulders on the back, and almost the shoulders'.
(*Garter Statutes for Francis I of France*, England, 1527: British Library, Add. MS 5712, f. 1v)

113 RIGHT

A dance in a great household, from a calendar for February. The male maskers are in white fancy dress. Of the fashionable garments worn by the rest of the men, one of the more interesting appears in the lower right-hand corner. It looks like a base-coat with a flap-front on the bodice. The women in the scene wear French hoods and French gowns, the one at the front allowing us to see that the gown's square front neckline is not repeated at the back. To keep such wide necklines in place Netherlandish women seem to have had quite high, scooped back necklines.
(*Golf Book of Hours*, Flanders, workshop of Simon Bening, *c.*1525?: British Library, Add. MS 24098, f. 19v)

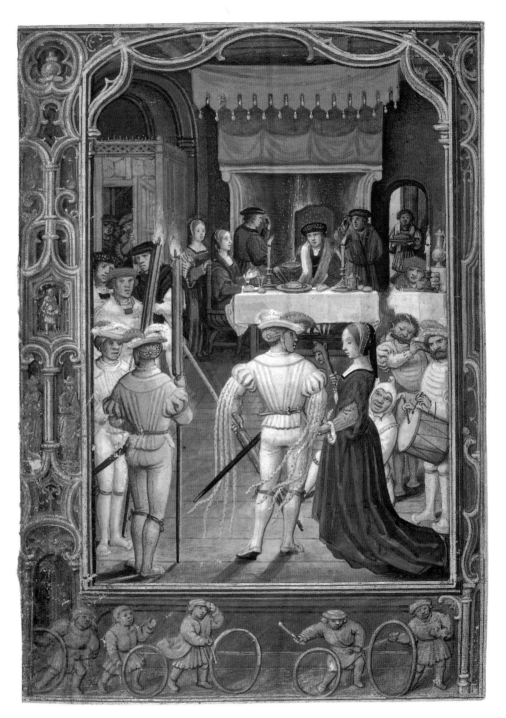

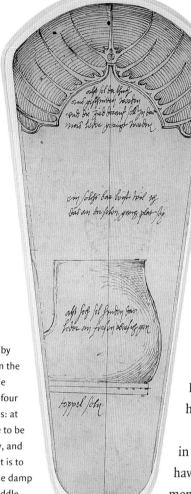

114

Design for a shoe by
Albrecht Dürer. On the
pattern for the sole
Dürer has written four
sets of instructions: at
the top, 'The shoe to be
cut out in this way, and
the ornament on it is to
be pressed into the damp
leather'; in the middle
'I want a pair of lasts like
these to be made so that the
whole sole lies flat'; in the sketch
of the heel, 'So high is the leather
at the back at the heel to come
up'; and below the heel, 'Double
soles'. He also wanted straps
and rings (presumably to pull
the straps through). Shoes were
made from this pattern in
Germany in 1974, and showed
that Dürer would have taken a
modern size 41 (UK 7, US 8½).
(*Design for a shoe*, Germany,
Albrecht Dürer, 1525 or 1526:
London, British Museum, Sloane
5218–200)

While male dress in the south German-speaking lands was marked at this period by a certain degree of exaggeration in its elements, such as large hats and extensive slashing of hose, there was a particular group of men in that part of the world who carried these tendencies to extremes. They were mercenary soldiers, known as *landsknechts*, and highly valued by whoever could afford to pay for their services (fig. 115). The Swiss had won in battle their independence from the Habsburg Empire in 1499, and a Swiss army had driven the French from Milan in 1512. These successes perhaps helped to spread their style of dressing to soldiers elsewhere (though no distinction was generally made between Swiss and German mercenaries). In 1515 Henry VIII of England had his guards dressed in the German fashion 'with certain slashed hoods' (possibly the 'night-cap' seen in the Dürer self-portrait of 1498 now in Madrid). In 1517 the Castilians, nervously awaiting the arrival of their new king with the outlandish name Carlos (the future Emperor Charles V), found he had a bodyguard of two hundred halberdiers dressed in German-style doublets and hose.

The French defeat of the Swiss mercenaries at Marignano in 1515 and the subsequent return of the French to Milan seem to have had little or no effect on the popularity of aspects of 'German' men's dress, even at the French court. Federico Gonzaga wrote from there to his mother, Isabella d'Este, saying that as Francis I and some of the nobles were wearing German-style shirts with high collars, he would like her to have some made for him. She did not approve, as she thought his neck was too short and thick for this style, but ordered a couple for him and said that he need not wear them more than two or three times, after which he could return to his usual French shirts.

The influence of French styles for women was steadily growing in England. In 1527, when a French marriage was arranged for Henry VIII's daughter Mary, Francis I of France was made a knight of the Order of the Garter, and provided with a copy of the order's statutes (fig. 112). The royal lady, identified as Concord, tying together the Tudor roses and the lilies of France, could be read as joining the two nations through her clothing. She is dressed in a French gown with turned-back ermine-lined sleeves, but she wears it in a peculiarly English way, with, on top of it, a tiny, scarf-like strip of linen over her shoulders. Hans Holbein's drawings of the women in Sir Thomas More's family at this date show similar hybrid outfits.

Concord's headdress remains resolutely English, being of the gable variety with its golden front flaps (lappets) turned up on to the sides of her head. However, this type of headdress was on its way out of fashion: the Great Wardrobe accounts show the purchase of French hoods for Mary in 1531, and although her stepmother Jane Seymour, as queen of England, would try to enforce the wearing of the English headdress among her ladies-in-waiting in 1537, by then only older women seem to have chosen to wear it.

Fig. 113, from the workshop of the greatest Flemish illuminator of the time, Simon Bening, shows a mixture of old and new in dress and behaviour. In an aristocratic Flemish household, in the month of February, a group of men in fancy dress has been performing a *morisque*, a rather old-fashioned type of group dance in which the participants dressed identically and often fantastically. Crucial elements in their appearance were (as here) ribbons hanging from the sleeves (vestiges of the dagging of a century or more before) and masks. Also old-fashioned is the cut of their doublets, with the V-shaped setting of the folds recalling the fashions of the third quarter of the fifteenth century. More fashionable elements are their shoes with hammer-shaped toes, and the gold nets in which their hair is caught up. Their bonnets resemble those seen in portraits of the time, with rather more flamboyant (and hence theatrical) trimming.

The lady at the front, in fashionable dress, seems to be joining in the dance without a mask. In the fifteenth century all participants in *morisques* had been masked, and had been known to each other. Edward Hall's chronicle of the reign of Henry VIII indicates that a shocking new development occurred at the English court on Twelfth Night 1512, with the arrival of the Italian fashion of masked dancers inviting

115

Versions of contemporary *landsknecht* (mercenary) dress, with plumed hats and elaborately slashed doublets and hose, in a manuscript in which Francis I and Julius Caesar discuss their defeats of the Swiss. The women's clothing includes garments commonly worn across southern Germany and Switzerland, most famously recorded by Albrecht Dürer in his drawings of the dress of the women of Nuremberg in 1500: a beehive-like headdress (*Schleier*) and a small shoulder-cape (*Goller*).

(François du Moulin, *Les Commentaires de la guerre gallique*, France, Godefroy le Batave, 1519: British Library, Harley MS 6205, f. 9v)

116 OPPOSITE

Descendants of John of Gaunt (1340–99) and Constance of Castile (m. 1371, d. 1394) are shown in dress that ranges from clothing rather like that of *c.*1530, to elements that meant 'the past'. The attire of King Juan of Aragon (top, third from left) is the most like the dress of the 1530s. Among the women there are strong suggestions of Iberian hairstyles of *c.*1530, with hints of the *tranzado* hairstyle in veils draped at the back of several heads, and puffs of hair at the sides of the faces.
(*Genealogy of the Infante Dom Fernando of Portugal*, Lisbon and Bruges, António de Holanda and Simon Bening, 1530–4: British Library, Add. MS 12531, f. 10r)

117 RIGHT

This scene at the French court shows, on the small prince seen from behind, the square back edges to the gown collar, and the virtually useless lower halves of the gown sleeves, hanging from the elbows as tubes. Black was a popular colour in the 1530s – Francis I's ally and future son-in-law, James V of Scotland, wore it for the Christmas festivities in Scotland in 1532 and 1533. Black and a shade of pink known as carnation in English were a popular combination in the early 1530s.
(Diodorus Siculus, *Histoires*, France, attributed to Jean Clouet, 1534?: Chantilly, Musée Condé, MS 1672, frontispiece. © Photo RMN-Ojeda)

unmasked observers to join them. The lady here looks down demurely, perhaps in an attempt to avoid the flirtation that this new practice seems to have encouraged.

A far more elaborate mixing of past and present occurs in the contemporary *Genealogy* produced for Dom Fernando, brother of John III of Portugal, by António de Holanda, apparently a northerner, working at the Portuguese court and providing the drawings to be illuminated by Simon Bening. Fig. 116 shows the contribution to the royal house of Portugal by the fourteenth-century figures John of Gaunt, Duke of Lancaster, a son of Edward III of England, and his second wife, Constance of Castile, and notables to whom they were linked. Regardless of the date at which they lived, the women tend to have headdresses or hairstyles that reflect the current Iberian mode for pulling the hair forward over the ears in loose puffs. Constance of Castile, at the bottom left, has her headdress completed by a horned cap, which she would not have worn, but which António de Holanda would have known came from the (fifteenth-century) past in northern Europe. (She lived in England for most of her married life.) Constance's short over-sleeves were part of the old visual shorthand for clothing from the past or from exotic lands. Other women can be linked to what is recorded of the appearance of Eleanor of Austria, the widowed Queen of Portugal, when she arrived in France in 1530 as the second wife of Francis I, wearing sleeves made of bands of cloth of gold, held together with silk ribbons. This type of sleeve underlies the billowing blue sleeve, with puffs of shirt pulled through between the clasps, of Queen Joanna of Castile towards the top right.

John of Gaunt, at the centre bottom, and several of the men wear golden armour; his is exoticized by the tabs at the waist and the embossed decorations at the shoulder and the knees. Like many of the men, he wears a large plumed hat, similar to those to be found in contemporary Germany. Third down from the top right, with a moustache he would never have worn, is Charles the Bold, Duke of Burgundy (compare fig. 95). The red and gold of the cloak of the emperor above Charles the Bold recall the red and gold of the mantle of Roger II of Sicily (fig. 27), by then part of the imperial regalia.

Francis I of France (r. 1515–47, fig. 117) and Henry VIII of England (r. 1509–47, fig. 118) had inherited their countries' traditional enmity; but they also met, more than once, in the pursuit of peace. The clothing to be worn at the meetings at the Field of Cloth of Gold in 1520 was carefully planned and discussed to ensure that no one took umbrage at being outdressed; and for a meeting in 1532

Francis sent Henry 'rich apparel wrought with needle work purled [looped] with gold' so that the two kings 'were both in one suite' on the same day when they went to Mass together. Both kings are rendered bulky by the fashions of the 1530s and early 1540s – gowns had wide revers and deep collars turned back over sleeves that were puffed and slashed on the upper arm.

In fig. 117, probably recording an event of the first half of 1534, the three sons of Francis I (the dauphin, born 1518; the future Henry II, born 1519; and Charles, born 1523) are dressed alike in red-pink gowns, gold doublets, black bonnets and beige stockings. Black features quite strongly in the scene, being the colour of the shoes, hose, gown and cap worn by both Antoine Macault, reading to the king his translation of the work of the ancient Greek historian Diodorus Siculus, and by the king himself. But the reader's black belongs to his occupation (notary and secretary of the king), whereas the black of the king is fashionable. Francis's gown is easily the most lavish in the room, with its incrustation of pearls on its revers and the panes (slashes) of its sleeves. Francis and Henry VIII shared a love of jewelled clothing: at the meeting in 1532 Francis wore a doublet that those amongst the English contingent who knew about such things valued at £100,000 because of the gemstones and diamonds all over it.

The English writer Sir Thomas Elyot, who wrote the political treatise *The Boke Named the Governour* in 1531, must have despaired of ever seeing his sartorial advice to monarchs being taken seriously – he advocated that princes should dress between sobriety and luxury, following the examples of the best emperors of ancient Rome. He felt that taking up a new fashion too quickly was likely to make its wearer be considered 'dissolute of manners'. The French satirical writer Rabelais, in his *Gargantua* of 1534, has his hero wear a hat medallion with a Greek inscription and an image of a hermaphrodite deriving from Plato's *Symposium*. This may be a jibe at the fashionable quest for classical erudition that we see the court indulging in in fig. 117.

One item that we do not see here in this world of seemingly very well-built men is the codpiece. Gargantua's, like that of Henry VIII in fig. 118, was made of the same fabric as his upper stocks (stockings for the upper legs) and, like them, was slashed, with puffs of the lining coming through. Apparently, Gargantua's was not like the fraudulent, empty codpieces being worn by so many young men at the time. The codpiece seems to have been the subject of ribald comment at the time, as Rabelais said that his next book would be *On the Dignity of Codpieces*.

1400.

Een burghers wijf

Een burghers rijck wijf __ Een jongste dochter

Een boerinne. Zoo clie mi gaer.

Een rijcke burghersche

Een ghemeÿ borghers wijf

Dit was een groote Edel vrouwe

118 OPPOSITE

Henry VIII appears as King David, with his fool, Will Sommer. The inventory drawn up after Henry's death in 1547 lists many lavish gowns, but none in fabric that matches the one here. However, he had many *cotes*, hose and doublets, some in crimson with gold trimming. Several of the doublets, like the one here, were 'sett owte with camericke' (had the fine linen known as cambric in puffs on the surface).
(*Psalter of Henry VIII*, England, Jean Mallard or Maillart, 1542?: British Library, Royal MS 2 A XVI, f. 63v)

119 ABOVE LEFT

Contemporary Englishwomen: from left to right the wife of a citizen of London; the wife and daughter of a rich citizen; and 'a country-woman as they go nowadays'. The first three are probably in what were known as Flanders gowns. Elizabeth I in the 1560s and 1570s had several Flanders gowns, which were 'guarded' (trimmed with bands of contrasting fabric), like the gowns here.
(*Beschrijving der Britische Eilanden*, Lucas de Heere, 1570–7?: British Library, Add. MS 28330, f. 33r)

120

Lucas de Heere tries to depict Englishwomen in the year 1400. On the left the rich burgher's wife belongs around 1440, to judge by her sleeves; in the middle the next burgher's wife is almost impossible to date; and the third woman, described as noble, may have her origin in a badly understood image of around 1430, when English women wore massive horned headdresses.
(*Beschrijving der Britische Eilanden*, Lucas de Heere, 1570–7?: British Library, Add. MS 28330, f. 32r)

In fig. 118, the opening of Psalm 53, 'The fool hath said in his heart, there is no God', is given a new twist, with the psalmist, King David, being Henry VIII, and the fool that of his court, Will Somer, in the *Psalter of Henry VIII* of 1542. The king's outfit has retained many of the elements of the previous decade's fashions, and shows that a certain degree of matching up colours within the outfit is taking place. The outermost layer is still a gown with puffed upper sleeves and pendant lower sleeves, worn over a scoop-fronted coat, which in turn is worn over a slashed and puffed doublet and stomacher (or placard). However, the coat skirts have lost their tubular folds, and lie flat on his upper stocks.

Even in the 1540s a man of fashion would have been likely still to have his codpiece protruding from the skirts of his coat; that the fool's now rather old-fashioned bases with their still-tubular folds and velvet guards (bands of trimming) do not open may be part of the joke against him. Green (not particularly fashionable at the time) seems to have been the colour of his livery clothing: in 1535 he was given a 'coote' (coat) and a 'cappe' of green cloth fringed with red wool, and two coats of green cloth and a hood to go with them. Hoods were now definitely old-fashioned.

Until this point the clothing of the past was something that artists had reconstructed by using long-established elements, such as short sleeves and, more recently, dagging. There is a limited sense that specific earlier artefacts were looked at in a spirit of antiquarianism. In fact, antiquarianism had a long history in Italy, but even there no systematic attempts were made to record the monuments of the past until the second half of the sixteenth century. In England in 1549 Henry VIII's official antiquarian, John Leland, published a book called *The Laboryouse Journey and Serche of John Leylande for Englandes Antiquities*. When this meshed together with the growing interest in the clothing styles of other countries, a market developed for images that recorded both present and past styles. The final images in this chapter come from a manuscript illuminated by the Fleming Lucas de Heere, and are related to a manuscript now in Ghent. Their purpose is not entirely clear, but the British Library manuscript seems to have been produced as a simple history of the English people. The Ghent manuscript was possibly created during de Heere's time in England (1567–77) as an aid to designing interior decoration for Edward Clinton, the Lord High Admiral, with images of the peoples of the world.

Fig. 119 shows a group of English women of various classes. Three of the four women wear gowns that are put on like modern coats, closed tightly across the bodice and left open at the skirt to reveal the kirtle (under-skirt). Gowns like these are common in Flemish portraits; for once, English women are not imitating French styles. These gowns seem to have started life as loose garments, sometimes to be seen on pregnant women, but by the early 1560s they were often as tight in the bodice as the more traditional French gowns had been. The fourth figure is a countrywoman wearing an underdress in the colour so coveted by the lower classes, red. She has kept the linen shoulder cloth only hinted at as a vestige in fig. 112, and protects her face from dust and dirt by a chin-clout. Her hat would also help protect her against the sun, allowing her to maintain the pallor considered so desirable until the twentieth century.

Manuscript illumination was dying as a major form of book production. The great Simon Bening died in 1561. In 1562 François Deserps published in Paris his *Recueil de la diversité des habits* (*Collection of the Diversity of Clothing*), a series of woodcuts and poems, illustrating and explaining the clothing in various parts of the world, for the education of the future Henry IV of France. Fashionable clothing had long been a moral issue for preachers; in books like that of Deserps, national styles of clothing were sometimes discussed as an aspect of the moral qualities (or lack of them) in the peoples portrayed. Costume books were to become best-sellers, and de Heere's countrywoman was to have a long life in them.

The Italian Cesare Vecellio is usually credited with being the first to include the costumes of the past with those of the present in his 1590 *De gli Habiti antichi et moderni di Diverse Parti del Mondo* (*Of the Ancient and Modern Clothing of Various Parts of the World*), but in a sense de Heere had already beaten him to it, even if all he was doing was providing interior decoration for one house and a one-off history book. The final illustration (fig. 120) shows his Englishwomen of the year 1400 – though a look back through this book will show how wide of the mark his dating is. What his sources were is unclear, though tombs are an obvious possibility. How he arrived at his dating is even less clear – the first of these women reappears in the Ghent version of this manuscript as another English burgher's wife, but of around 1200! During de Heere's time in England, a short-lived society of antiquaries was founded in 1572. De Heere was thus part of a growing trend; although his work as a dress historian would hardly merit more than an amused glance today, he nonetheless stands at the start of a new study of dress, of the present and the past, at a time when conventional illuminated manuscripts were starting to disappear.

Bibliography

Abbreviations

CT
David Jenkins, ed., *The Cambridge History of Western Textiles*, 2 vols (Cambridge, 2003)

PL
Jacques-Paul Migne, ed., *Patrologiae Cursus Completus. Series Latina*, 221 vols (Paris, 1844–1903)

RS
Rolls Series: *Rerum britannicarum medii aevi scriptores: The Chronicles and Memorials of Great Britain and Ireland during the Middle Ages*, 244 vols (London, 1858–96)

General reading

Baldwin, Frances Elizabeth, *Sumptuary Legislation and Personal Regulation in England*, Johns Hopkins University Studies in Historical and Political Science, ser. 44, no. 1 (Baltimore, 1926)

Bartlett, Robert, *The Making of Europe. Conquest, Colonization and Cultural Change 950–1350* (London, 1993)

Gay, Victor, and Henri Stein, *Glossaire archéologique du moyen âge et de la renaissance*, 2 vols (Paris, 1887–1929)

Hunt, Alan, *Governance of the Consuming Passions: A History of Sumptuary Law* (Basingstoke, 1996)

Owst, G.R., *Literature and Pulpit in Medieval England. A Neglected Chapter in the History of English Letters and of the English People* (Cambridge, 1933)

Spufford, Peter, *Power and Profit. The Merchant in Medieval Europe* (London, 2002)

van Uytven, Raymond, *Production and Consumption in the Low Countries, 13th–16th Centuries* (Aldershot and Burlington, VT, 2001)

Woodward, John, and George Burnett, *A Treatise on Heraldry British and Foreign*, 2 vols (Edinburgh, 1892)

General works on manuscripts and visual material

Alexander, Jonathan J.G., et al., *A Survey of Manuscripts Illuminated in the British Isles*, 6 parts (London, 1975–96)

Alexander, J.J.G., *Medieval Illuminators and Their Methods of Work* (New Haven and London, 1992)

Backhouse, Janet, 'Manuscript sources for the history of mediaeval costume', *Costume*, 2 (1968), 9–14

Backhouse, Janet, *The Illuminated Manuscript* (London, 1979)

Backhouse, Janet, *The Illuminated Page. Ten Centuries of Manuscript Painting in the British Library* (London, 1997)

Basing, Patricia, *Trades and Crafts in Medieval Manuscripts* (London, 1990)

Brown, Michelle P., *Understanding Illuminated Manuscripts. A Guide to Technical Terms* (London, 1994)

de Hamel, Christopher, *A History of Illuminated Manuscripts*, 2nd edn (London, 1994)

de Hamel, Christopher, *The British Library Guide to Manuscript Illumination: History and Techniques* (London, 2001)

Jones, Peter Murray, *Medieval Medicine in Illuminated Manuscripts*, rev. edn. (London, 1998)

Meesterlijke Middeleeuwen. Miniaturen van Karel de Grote tot Karel de Stoute 800–1475, exh. cat., Stedelijk Museum Vander Kelen-Mertens, Leuven (Zwolle and Leuven, 2002)

Rodley, Lyn, *Byzantine Art and Architecture. An Introduction* (Cambridge, 1994)

Smeyers, Maurits, *Flemish Miniatures from the 8th to the mid-16th Century: The Medieval World on Parchment* (Leuven, 1999)

Ward, H.L.D., *Catalogue of Romances in the Department of Manuscripts in the British Museum*, 3 vols (London, 1892)

Watson, Andrew G., *Dated and Datable Manuscripts c.700–1600 in the Department of Manuscripts, The British Library* (London, 1979)

Watson, Rowan, *Illuminated Manuscripts and Their Makers: An Account Based on the Collection of the Victoria and Albert Museum* (London, 2003)

General works on dress

Bernis Madrazo, Carmen, *Indumentaria medieval española* (Madrid, 1956)

Kazhdan, Alexander P., et al., eds, *The Oxford Dictionary of Byzantium*, 3 vols (New York and Oxford, 1991) under 'Costume' and various garment names

Kovesi Killerby, Catherine, *Sumptuary Law in Italy 1200–1500* (Oxford, 2002)

Levi Pisetzky, Rosita, *Storia del costume in Italia*, vols 1 and 2 (Milan, 1964)

Muzzarelli, Maria Giuseppina, *Gli inganni delle apparenze. Disciplina di vesti e ornamenti alla fine del medioevo* (Turin, 1996)

Vale, Malcolm, *The Princely Court: Medieval Courts and Culture in North-West Europe 1270–1380* (Oxford, 2001): chapter 3, 'Liveries'

Veale, Elspeth M., *The English Fur Trade in the Later Middle Ages* (Oxford, 1966)

General works on textiles

Jenkins, David, ed., *The Cambridge History of Western Textiles*, 2 vols (Cambridge, 2003)

King, Donald, 'Types of silk cloth used in England 1200–1500', in *La seta in Europa sec. XIII–XX, Atti della 'Ventiquattresima Settimana di Studi' 4–9 maggio 1992*, ed. by Simonetta Cavaciocchi (Florence, 1993), 457–64

Munro, John H., 'The medieval scarlet and the economics of sartorial splendour', in *Cloth and Clothing in Medieval Europe. Essays in Memory of Professor E.M. Carus Wilson*, ed. by N.B. Harte and K.G. Ponting, (London, 1983), 13–70

Munro, John H., 'Medieval woollens: textiles, textile technology and industrial organisation, c.800–1500', in CT, I, 181–227

Muthesius, Anna, 'The Byzantine silk industry: Lopez and beyond', *Journal of Medieval History*, 19 (1993), 1–67

Muthesius, Anna, 'The "cult" of imperial and ecclesiastical silks in Byzantium', *Textile History*, 32.1 (2001), 36–47

Muthesius, Anna, 'Silk in the medieval world', in CT, I, 325–54

Pritchard, Frances, 'The uses of textiles, c.1000–1500', in CT, I, 355–77

Chapter 1

BACKGROUND

Barber, Malcolm, *The Two Cities. Medieval Europe, 1050–1320* (London and New York, 1992)

Brown, Giles, 'Introduction: the Carolingian Renaissance', in *Carolingian Culture: Emulation and Innovation*, ed. by Rosamond McKitterick (Cambridge, 1994), 1–51

Devroey, Jean-Pierre, 'The economy', in *The Early Middle Ages. Europe 400–1000*, ed. by Rosamond McKitterick (Oxford, 2001), 97–129

Hyam, Jane, 'Ermentrude and Richildis', in *Charles the Bald: Court and Kingdom*, ed. by Margaret T. Gibson and Janet L. Nelson (Aldershot, 1990), 153–68

Innes, Matthew, and Rosamond McKitterick, 'The writing of history', in *Carolingian Culture: Emulation and Innovation*, ed. by Rosamond McKitterick (Cambridge, 1994), 193–220

Kazhdan, A.P., and Ann Wharton Epstein, eds, *Change in Byzantine Culture in the Eleventh and Twelfth Centuries* (Berkeley, Los Angeles and London, 1985)

McKitterick, Rosamond, 'Politics', in *The Early Middle Ages. Europe 400–1000*, ed. by Rosamond McKitterick (Oxford, 2001), 21–56

Nelson, Janet L., 'Kingship and empire in the Carolingian world', in *Carolingian Culture: Emulation and Innovation*, ed. by Rosamond McKitterick (Cambridge, 1994), 52–87

Pohl, Walter, 'Telling the difference: signs of ethnic identity', in *Strategies of Distinction: The Construction of Ethnic Communities 300–800*, ed. by Walter Pohl, with Helmut Reimitz (Leiden, 1998), 17–70

Reuter, Timothy, ed., *New Cambridge Medieval History*, III (Cambridge, 1999)

Shepard, Jonathan, 'Europe and the wider world', in *The Early Middle Ages. Europe 400–1000*, ed. by Rosamond McKitterick (Oxford, 2001), 201–42

Skinner, Patricia, 'Women, wills and wealth in medieval southern Italy', *Early Medieval Europe*, II (1993), 133–52

Verhulst, Adriaan, *The Carolingian Economy* (Cambridge, 2002)

Wallace-Hadrill, Andrew, 'A Carolingian Renaissance prince: the emperor Charles the Bald', *Proceedings of the British Academy*, LXIV (1978), 155–85

Wood, Ian, 'Culture', in *The Early Middle Ages. Europe 400–1000*, ed. by Rosamond McKitterick (Oxford, 2001), 167–98

MANUSCRIPTS AND OTHER VISUAL MATERIAL

Beckwith, John, *Early Medieval Art*, rev. edn (London, 1969)

Berger, Pamela C., *The Insignia of the Notitia Dignitatum* (New York and London, 1981)

Deshman, Robert, 'The exalted servant: the ruler theology of the Prayerbook of Charles the Bald', *Viator*, 11 (1980), 385–417

Diebold, William J., 'The ruler portrait of Charles the Bald in the S. Paolo bible', *The Art Bulletin*, 76 (1994), 6–18

Dodwell, C.R., *Anglo-Saxon Art. A New Perspective* (Manchester, 1982)

Dodwell, C.R., *The Pictorial Arts of the West 800–1200* (New Haven and London, 1993)

Dumitrescu, C.L., 'Remarques en marge du Coislin 79: les trois eunuques et le problème du donateur', *Byzantion*, 57 (1987), 32–45

Gaehde, Joachim E., 'The Turonian sources of the bible of San Paolo Fuori le Mura in Rome', *Frümittelalterliche Studien*, 5 (1971), 359–400

McGurk, Patricia, and Jane Rosenthal, 'The Anglo-Saxon gospelbooks of Judith, countess of Flanders: their text, make-up and function', *Anglo-Saxon England*, 24 (1995), 251–308

Mayr-Harting, Henry, *Ottonian Book Illumination. An Historical Study*, 2nd rev. edn (London, 1999)

Nees, Lawrence, *Early Medieval Art* (Oxford, 2002)

DOCUMENTARY SOURCES

Annales Fuldenses sive annales regni Francorum orientalis, ed. by Friedrich Kurze after the edition of Georg Heinrich Pertz, in *Monumenta Germaniae historica. Scriptores rerum Germanicarum in usum scholarum separatim editi*, 7 (Hanover, 1978)

Brunwilarensis monasterii fundatio, ed. by Rudolf Koepke, in *Monumenta Germaniae historica. Scriptores rerum Germanicarum*, XIII (Hanover, 1854)

Bury, John Bagnell, *The Imperial Administrative System in the Ninth Century: with a revised text of Kletorologion of Philotheos* (New York, 1958?)

Constantine VII, *Le Livre des cérémonies*, ed. by Albert Vogt, 4 vols (Paris, 1935–40)

De Coussemaker, Ignace, ed., *Cartulaire de l'abbaye de Cysoing* (Lille, 1885)

Ducev, Ivan, intro., *Eparchikon biblion: The Book of the Eparch* (London, 1970)

Dutton, Paul Edward, ed., *Carolingian Civilization. A Reader* (Peterborough, Ontario, 1993)

Glaber, Rodulfus, *Historiarum Libri Quinque: The Five Books of the Histories; Vita Domni Willelmi Abbatis: The Life of St William*, ed. and trans. by John France et al. (Oxford and New York, 1989)

Hildebrandt, Reiner, ed., *Summarium Heinrici*, I (Berlin and New York, 1974)

Lehmann-Brockhaus, Otto, *Schriftquellen zur Kunstgeschichte des 11. und 12. Jahrhunderts für Deutschland, Lothringen und Italien*, 2 vols (Berlin, 1938)

Liutprand of Cremona, *Liudprandi Cremonensis antapodosis; Homelia paschalis; Historia Ottonis; Relatio de legatione Constantinopolitana*, ed. by P. Chiesa (Turnhout, 1998)

Notker the Stammerer, *Monachus Sangallensis de Carlo Magno*, in *Bibliotheca rerum Germanicarum*, 6 vols: IV, *Monumenta Carolina*, ed. by Philipp Jaffé (Berlin, 1867), 628–700

Richer de Saint-Rémy, *Histoire de France (885–995)*, II, ed. and trans. by Robert Latouche, Les classiques de l'histoire de France au moyen âge, XVII (Paris, 1964)

The 'Ruodlieb', ed. by C.W. Grocock (Warminster and Chicago, 1985)

Schramm, Percy Ernst, ed., *Graphia auree urbis Romae*, in *Kaiser, Rom und Renovatio: Studien und Texte zur Geschichte des römischen Erneuerungsgedankens vom Ende des karolingischen Reiches bis zum Investiturstreit*, II (Leipzig and Berlin, 1929)

Tertullian, *De Pallio*, in *Opera*, part 4, ed. by Vincentius Bulhart and Philippus Borleffs (Vienna, 1957), 104–25

Thegan, *Vita Hludowici*, in *Monumenta Germaniae Historica. Scriptores rerum Germanicarum in usum scholarum separatim editi*, 64, ed. by Ernst Tremp (Hanover, 1995)

William of Malmesbury, *Gesta regum Anglorum. The History of the English Kings*, ed. and trans. by R.A.B. Mynors; completed by R.M. Thomson and M. Winterbottom, 2 vols (Oxford, 1998–9)

SECONDARY SOURCES – DRESS

Cameron, Averil, 'A Byzantine imperial coronation of the sixth century A.D.', *Costume*, 7 (1973), 4–9

Grabar, Oleg, 'The shared culture of objects', in *Byzantine Court Culture from 829 to 1214*, ed. by Henry Maguire (Washington, DC, 1997), 115–29

King, Donald, 'Roman and Byzantine dress in Egypt', *Costume*, 30 (1996), 1–15

Kondakov, N.P., 'Les Costumes orientaux à la cour byzantine', *Byzantion*, I (1924), 7–49

Owen-Crocker, Gale R., *Dress in Anglo-Saxon England* (Manchester, 1986)

Bauer, Rotraud, 'Der Mantel Rogers II. und die siculo-normannischen Gewänder aus den königlichen Hofwerkstätten in Palermo', in *Nobiles Officinae. Die königlichen Hofwerkstätten zu Palermo zur Zeit der Normannen und Staufer im 12. und 13. Jahrhundert*, exh. cat., Kunsthistorisches Museum, Vienna, ed. by Wilfried Seipel (Vienna and Milan, 2004), 115–23

Talbot-Rice, Tamara, *Daily Life in Byzantium* (London, 1967)

SECONDARY SOURCES – TEXTILES

Battiscombe, C.F., ed., *The Relics of St Cuthbert* (Oxford, 1956)

Jacoby, David, 'Genoa, silk trade and silk manufacture in the Mediterranean region (ca.1100–1300)', in *Tessuti, oreficerie, miniature in Liguria XIII–XV secolo. Atti del convegno internazionale di studi, Genova, Bordighera, 22–25 maggio 1997*, ed. by Anna R. Calderoni Masetti, C. di Fabio and M. Marcenaro (Bordighera, 1999), 11–40

Sabbe, E., 'Importation des tissus orientaux en Europe au haut moyen âge', *Revue belge de philologie et d'histoire*, 14 (1935), 811–48 and 1261–88

Vogelsang-Eastwood, Gillian, 'The Arabs, AD 600–1000', in *CT*, I, 158–65

Chapter 2

BACKGROUND

Amt, Emelie, *Women's Lives in Medieval Europe. A Source Book* (New York and London, 1993)

Baldwin, John W., *Aristocratic Life in Medieval France: The Romances of Jean Renart and Gerbert de Montreuil, 1190–1230* (Baltimore, 2000)

Barlow, Frank, *William Rufus* (New Haven, 2000)

Bornstein, Diane, *The Lady in the Tower. Medieval Courtesy Literature for Women* (Hamden, CT, 1983)

Borsook, Eve, *Messages in Mosaic. The Royal Programmes of Norman Sicily (1130–1187)*, (Oxford, 1990)

Braswell, Mary Flowers, 'Sin, the lady and the law: the English noblewoman in the late Middle Ages', *Medievalia et Humanistica*, n.s. 14 (1986), 81–101

Bumke, Joachim, *Courtly Culture: Literature and Society in the High Middle Ages*, trans. by Thomas Dunlap (Berkeley, 1991). Originally publ. as *Höfische Kultur: Literatur und Gesellschaft im hohen Mittelalter* (Munich, 1986)

Davies, R.R., 'The failure of the first British Empire? England's relations with Ireland, Scotland and Wales 1066–1500', in *England in Europe 1066–1453*, ed. by Nigel Saul (London, 1994), 121–32

Frugoni, Chiara, 'The imagined woman', in *A History of Women in the West*, II, *Silences of the Middle Ages*, ed. by Christiane Klapisch-Zuber (Cambridge, MA, and London, 1992), 336–422

Fuhrmann, Horst, *Germany in the High Middle Ages c.1050–1200*, trans. by Timothy Reuter (Cambridge, 1986)

Holmes, Urban Tigner, 'Life among the Europeans in Palestine and Syria in the twelfth and thirteenth centuries', in *A History of the Crusades*, 6 vols, gen. ed. Kenneth M. Setton, (Madison, WI, 1969–89): vol 4, *The Art and Architecture of the Crusade States*, ed. by Harry W. Hazard, 3–35

Ibn Jubaïr, *The Travels of Ibn Jubayr: Being the Chronicle of a Medieval Spanish Moor*, trans. by R.J.C. Broadhurst (London, 1952)

Jewell, Helen M., *Women in Medieval England* (Manchester and New York, 1996)

Labarge, Margaret Wade, *Women in Medieval Life* (London, 1986)

La Monte, John Life, *Feudal Monarchy in the Latin Kingdom of Jerusalem 1100 to 1291* (Cambridge, MA, 1932)

Nicholas, David, *The Growth of the Medieval City From Late Antiquity to the Early Fourteenth Century* (London and New York, 1997)

Parsons, John Carmi, *Eleanor of Castile. Queen and Society in Thirteenth-Century England* (Basingstoke and London, 1995)

Phillips, Jonathan, 'The French overseas', in *France in the Central Middle Ages, 900–1200*, ed. by Marcus Bull (Oxford, 2002), 167–96

Prawer, Joshua, *The Crusaders' Kingdom. European Colonialism in the Middle Ages* (New York, 1972)

Rabutaux, Auguste, *De la prostitution en Europe depuis l'antiquité jusqu'à la fin du XVIe siècle* (Paris, 1881)

Runciman, Steven, *A History of the Crusades*, 3 vols (Cambridge, 1951–4): vol. 2, *The Kingdom of Jerusalem and the Frankish East 1100–1187*

White, Lynn, 'Cultural Climates and Technological Advances in the Middle Ages', *Viator*, 2 (1971), 171–201

MANUSCRIPTS AND OTHER VISUAL MATERIAL

Aldobrandino da Siena, *Le Régime du corps de Maître Aldebrandin de Sienne. Texte français du XIIIe siècle*, ed. by Louis Landouzy and Roger Pépin (Paris, 1911)

Alfonso X el Sabio, *Primera partida segun el manuscrito Add. 20.787 del British Museum*, ed. by Juan Antonio Arias Bonet (Valladolid, 1975)

Bible Moralisée. *Codex Vindobonensis 2554, Vienna, Österreichische Nationalbibliothek*, commentary and translation of biblical texts by Gerald B. Guest (London, 1995)

Buchthal, Hugo, *Miniature Painting in the Latin Kingdom of Jerusalem* (Oxford, 1957)

Cahn, Walter, *Romanesque Manuscripts. The Twelfth Century*, 2 vols, in *A Survey of Manuscripts Illuminated in France*, gen. eds François Avril and J.J.G. Alexander (London, 1996)

Folda, Jaroslav, *Crusader Manuscript Illumination at St-Jean d'Acre, 1275–1291* (Princeton, NJ, 1976)

Heslop, T.A., 'Romanesque painting and social distinction: the Magi and the shepherds', in *England in the Twelfth Century. Proceedings of the 5th Harlaxton Symposium, 1988* (Woodbridge, 1990), 137–52

Kauffmann, C.M., 'British Library, Lansdown ms 383: the Shaftesbury Psalter?', in *New Offerings, Ancient Treasures: Studies in Medieval Art for George Henderson*, ed. by Paul Binski and William Noel (Stroud, 2001), 256–79

Lewis, Suzanne, *The Art of Matthew Paris in the 'Chronica Majora'* (Aldershot and Cambridge, 1987)

Lowden, John, 'The royal/imperial book and the image or self-image of the medieval ruler', in *Kings and Kingship in Medieval Europe*, ed. by Anne J. Duggan (London, 1993), 213–40

Oman, C.C., 'The jewels of St Albans Abbey', *The Burlington Magazine*, 57 (1930), 81–2

Rudolph, Conrad, *Violence and Daily Life: Reading, Art and Polemics in the Cîteaux 'Moralia in Job'* (Princeton, NJ, 1997)

Stones, M. Alison, 'Secular manuscript illumination in France', in *Medieval Manuscripts and Textual Criticism*, ed. by Christopher Kleinhenz (Chapel Hill, NC, 1976), 83–102

Stones, M. Alison, 'Sacred and profane art: secular and liturgical book-illumination in the thirteenth century', in *The Epic in Medieval Society: Aesthetic and Moral Values*, ed. by Harald Scholler (Tübingen, 1977), 100–12

Williamson, Paul, *Gothic Sculpture 1140–1300* (New Haven and London, 1995)

Zarnecki, George, Janet Holt and Tristram Holland, eds, *English Romanesque Art*, exh. cat., Hayward Gallery, London (London, 1984)

DOCUMENTARY SOURCES

Aquinas, St Thomas, *The Summa Theologica of St Thomas Aquinas*, trans. by the Fathers of the English Dominican Province (London, n.d.), part II, 2nd part, XIII

Bartholomaeus Anglicus, *John Trevisa's Translation of Bartholomaeus Anglicus 'De proprietatibus rerum': a critical text*, 3 vols, ed. by M.C. Seymour et al. (Oxford, 1975–88)

Bernard of Clairvaux, *De consideratione*, in PL, 182, cols 727–808

Bernard of Clairvaux, *De laude novae militiae ad milites Templi*, ibid, cols 921–40

Boethius, *De Consolatione Philosophiae*, in PL, 63, cols 587–99

Boileau, Etienne, *Réglemens sur les arts et métiers de Paris rédigés au XIIIe siècle*, ed. by G.-B. Depping (Paris, 1837)

Calendar of the Liberate Rolls preserved in the Public Record Office, I, ed. by W.H. Stevenson and J.B.W. Chapman, RS, 156 (London, 1916)

Chrétien de Troyes, *Erec et Enide*, in *Les Romans de Chrétien de Troyes*, I, ed. by Mario Roques, Les Classiques français du moyen âge, 80 (Paris, 1963)

Chrétien de Troyes, *Le Roman de Perceval, ou, le conte du Graal*, ed. by Keith Busby (Tübingen, 1993)

Denifle, Henri, and Emile Chatelain, eds, *Chartularium universitatis Parisiensis*, I (Paris, 1889)

Duplès-Agier, 'Ordonnance somptuaire inédite de Philippe le Hardi', *Bibliothèque de l'école des chartes*, XV (1854), 176–81

Eadmer, *Historia novorum in Anglia*, in RS, 81 (London, 1884)

Fairholt, Frederick W., *Satirical Songs and Poems on Costume: from the 13th to the 19th Century*, Early English Poetry, Ballads and Popular Literature of the Middle Ages, XXVII (London: Percy Society [1849])

Fiero, Gloria K., Wendy Pfeffer and Mathé Allain, trans. and ed., *Three Medieval Views of Women. La Contenance des Fames, Le Bien des Fames, Le Blasme des Fames* (New Haven and London, 1989)

Gerald of Wales (Giraldus Cambrensis), *Topographia Hibernica et expugnatio Hibernica*, in *Opera*, V, in RS 21/5, ed. by James F. Dimock (London, 1867)

Gerbert de Montreuil, *La Continuation de Perceval*, 3 vols, ed. by Mary Williams (Paris, 1922–75)

Guillaume de Lorris and Jean de Meun, *Le Roman de la rose*, 5 vols, ed. by Ernest Langlois, Société des anciens textes français (Paris, 1914–24)

Johannes de Hauvilla, *Architrenius*, ed. and trans. by Winthrop Wetherbee (Cambridge, 1994)

John of Garland, *Dictionarius*, in *A Volume of Vocabularies*, ed. by Thomas Wright (London, 1882)

John of Ibelin, *Livre de Jean d'Ibelin*, ed. by Auguste Beugnot, in *Recueil des historiens des croisades; Lois*, 2 vols (Paris 1841–43): I, 1–432

Johnstone, Hilda, 'The wardrobe and household of Henry, son of Edward I', *Bulletin of the John Rylands Library*, VII (1922), 384–420

Little, A.G., and Decima Douie, 'Three sermons of Friar Jordan of Saxony, the Successor of St. Dominic, preached in England, A.D. 1229', *The English Historical Review*, LIV (1939), 1–19

Lamond, Elizabeth, ed., *Walter of Henley's Husbandry: Together with an Anonymous Husbandry, Seneschaucie, and Robert Grosseteste's Rules* (London and New York, 1890)

Lot, Ferdinand and Robert Fawtier, eds, *Le premier budget de la monarchie française: le compte général de 1202–1203*, Bibliothèque de l'Ecole des Hautes Etudes, Sciences historiques et philologiques, fasc. 259 (Paris, 1932)

Map, Walter, *De nugis curialium: Courtiers' Trifles*, ed. and trans. by M.R. James, rev. edn by C.N.L. Brooks and R.A.B. Mynors (Oxford, 1983)

Neckham, Alexander, *De naturis rerum libri duo*, ed. by Thomas Wright, RS, 34 (London, 1863)

Ordericus Vitalis, *Historia Ecclesiastica*, in PL, 188 (Paris, 1890)

Paris, Matthew, *Chronica majora*, 7 vols, ed. by Henry Richards Luard, RS, 57 (London, 1872–83): III

Pierre the Chanter, *Verbum abbreviatum*, in PL, 205; full version in John W. Baldwin, *Aristocratic Life in Medieval France: The Romances of Jean Renart and Gerbert de Montreuil, 1190–1230* (Baltimore, 2000)

Radulfus Niger, *De re militari et triplici via peregrinationis Ierosolimitane*, ed. by Ludwig Schmugge (Berlin and New York, 1977)

Richard, Canon of Holy Trinity, *Itinerarium peregrinorum et gesta Regis Ricardi*, in *Chronicles and Memorials of the Reign of Richard I*, 2 vols, ed. by William Stubbs, RS, 38 (London, 1864): I

Riley, Henry Thomas, ed., *Munimenta Gildhallae Londiniensis*, 3 vols, RS, 12 (London, 1859–62): II

Robert de Clari, *La Conquête de Constantinople*, ed. by Philippe Lauer, Les Classiques français du moyen âge, 40 (Paris, 1924)

Villehardouin, Geoffroy de, *La Conquête de Constantinople*, ed. by Edmond Faral, 2 vols (Paris, 1938–9)

William of Malmesbury, *Historia Novella. The Contemporary History*, ed. by Edmund King and trans. by K.R. Potter (Oxford, 1998)

SECONDARY SOURCES – DRESS

Anderson, Ruth Matilda, 'Pleated Headdresses of Castilla and León (12th and 13th Centuries)', *Notes Hispanic*, II (1942), 51–79

Delort, Robert, *Le commerce des fourrures en occident à la fin du moyen âge (vers 1300–vers 1450)*, 2 vols (Rome, 1978)

Goddard, Eunice Rathbone, *Women's Costume in French Texts of the Eleventh and Twelfth Centuries*, Johns Hopkins Studies in Romance Literatures and Languages, VII (Baltimore and Paris, 1927)

Harris, Jennifer, '"Thieves, Harlots and Stinking Goats": Fashionable Dress and Aesthetic Attitudes in Romanesque Art', *Costume*, 21 (1987), 4–15

Harris, Jennifer, '"Estroit vestu et menu cosu": evidence for the construction of twelfth-century dress', in *Medieval Art: Recent Perspectives. A Memorial Tribute to C.R. Dodwell*, ed. by Gale R. Owen-Crocker and Timothy Graham (Manchester and New York, 1998), 89–103

Harris, Jennifer, '11th–13th centuries', in *The Dictionary of Art*, ed. by Jane Turner, 34 vols (London, 1996): IX, 254–60

Herrero Carretero, Concha, *Museo de Telas Medievales, Monasterio de Santa María la Real de Huelgas* (Madrid, 1988)

Lachaud, Frédérique, 'Les Livrées de textiles et de fourrures à la fin du moyen âge: l'exemple de la cour du roi Edouard 1er Plantagenêt (1272–1307)', in *Cahiers du Léopard d'Or, I, Le Vêtement*, ed. by Michel Pastoureau (Paris, 1989), 169–80

Lachaud, Frédérique, 'Liveries of robes in England, c.1200–c.1330', *English Historical Review*, 111 (1996), 279–98

Lecoy de La Marche, Richard Albert, *La Chaire française au moyen âge*, 2nd edn (Paris, 1886)

Müller, Mechthild, *Die Kleidung nach Quellen des frühen Mittelalters* (Berlin and New York, 2003)

Platelle, Henri, 'Le Problème du scandale: les nouvelles modes masculines aux XIe et XIIe siècles', *Revue belge de philologie et d'histoire*, 53 (1975), 1071–96

Ritgen, Lore, 'Die Kleidung der Isle de France in der 2. Hälfte des 13. Jahrhunderts', *Waffen- und Kostümkunde*, 4 (1962), 87–111

Staniland, Kay, 'The medieval "corset"', *Costume*, 3 (1969) 10–13

Staniland, Kay, 'Clothing provision and the Great Wardrobe in the mid-thirteenth century', *Textile History*, 22 (1991), 239–52

Trichet, Louis, *Le Costume du clergé. Ses origines et son évolution en France d'après les règlements de l'église* (Paris, 1986)

Vestiduras Ricas. El monasterio de Las Huelgas y su época, exh. cat., Palacio Real de Madrid (Madrid, 2005)

Waugh, Christina Frieder, '"Well-cut through the body": fitted clothing in twelfth-century Europe', *Dress*, 26 (1999), 3–16

SECONDARY SOURCES – TEXTILES

Chorley, Patrick, 'The cloth export of Flanders and northern France during the thirteenth century: a luxury trade?', *Economic History Review*, 2nd ser., XL (1987), 349–79

Constable, Olivia Remie, *Trade and Traders in Muslim Spain: The Commercial Realignment of the Iberian Peninsula, 900–1500* (Cambridge, 1994)

King, Donald, 'Sur la signification de "Diasprum"', *Bulletin du C.I.E.T.A.*, 11 (1960), 42–7

Monnas, Lisa, 'The cloth of gold of the pourpoint of the Blessed Charles de Blois; a Pannus Tartaricus?', *Bulletin du C.I.E.T.A.*, 70 (1992), 117–29

Falcandus, Hugo, *La Historia o Liber de regno Sicilie e la Epistola ad Petrum Panormitane ecclesie thesaurarium di Ugo Falcando*, 2 parts, ed. by Giovanni Battista Siragusa, Fonti per la storia d'Italia, 22 (Rome, 1897, 1904)

Van Uytven, Raymond, 'Cloth in medieval literature of western Europe', in *Cloth and Clothing in Medieval Europe. Essays in Memory of Professor E.M. Carus Wilson*, ed. by N.B. Harte and K.G. Ponting (London, 1983), 151–83

Wyatt, James C.Y., and Anne E. Wardwell, *When Silk Was Gold. Central Asian and Chinese Textiles*, exh. cat., Metropolitan Museum of Art, New York, and Cleveland Museum of Art (New York, 1997)

Chapter 3

BACKGROUND

Abulafia, David, *The Western Mediterranean Kingdoms 1200–1500. The Struggle for Dominion* (London and New York, 1997)

Backman, Clifford R., *The Decline and Fall of Medieval Sicily: Politics, Religion and Economy in the Reign of Frederick III, 1296–1337* (Cambridge, 1995) ·

Belgrano, Luigi Tommaso, *Della vita privata dei Genovesi*, 2nd edn (Genoa, 1875)

Boulton D'Arcy, J.D., 'Insignia of power: the use of heraldic and paraheraldic devices by Italian princes, c.1350–c.1500', in *Art and Politics in Late Medieval and Early Renaissance Italy: 1250–1500*, ed. by Charles M. Rosenberg (Notre Dame and London, 1990), 103–27

Braswell, Mary Flowers, 'Sin, the lady and the law. The English noblewoman in the late Middle Ages', *Medievalia et Humanistica*, n. s., 14 (1986), 81–101

Bratianu, Gheorghe Ioan, *Recherches sur le commerce génois dans la Mer Noire au XIIIe siècle* (Paris, 1929)

Caggese, Romolo, *Roberto d'Angiò e i suoi tempi*, 2 vols (Florence, 1922–30)

Dyer, Christopher, *Standards of Living in the Later Middle Ages. Social Change in England c.1200–1500* (Cambridge, 1989)

Gray, H.L., 'Incomes from land in England in 1436', *English Historical Review*, 49 (1934), 607–39

Langlois, Charles Victor, *La Vie en France au moyen âge d'après quelques moralistes du temps* (Paris, 1908)

Larner, John, *Italy in the Age of Dante and Petrarch 1216–1380* (London and New York, 1980)

Rashdall, Hastings, *The Universities of Europe in the Middle Ages*, rev. edn by F.M. Powicke and A.B. Emden, 3 vols (Oxford, 1936)

Waugh, Scott L., *England in the Reign of Edward III* (Cambridge and New York, 1991)

MANUSCRIPTS AND OTHER VISUAL MATERIAL

Age of Chivalry. Art in Plantagenet England 1200–1400, exh. cat., Royal Academy of Arts, London (London, 1987)

Alexander, Jonathan J.G., *Studies in Italian Manuscript Illumination* (London, 2002)

Avril, François, *Manuscript Painting at the Court of France. The Fourteenth Century (1310–1380)*, trans. by Ursule Molinaro and Bruce Benderson (London, 1978)

Backhouse, Janet, *Books of Hours* (London, 1985)

Backhouse, Janet, 'Devotions and delights. The illuminated books of Gothic England', in *Age of Chivalry. Art and Society in Late Medieval England*, ed. by Nigel Saul (London, 1992), 79–89

Backhouse, Janet, *Medieval Rural Life in the Luttrell Psalter* (London, 2000)

Backhouse, Janet, James D. Marrow and Gerhard Schmidt, *Biblia Pauperum: Kings ms 5, British Library, London* (Lucerne, 1994)

Camille, Michael, *Mirror in Parchment. The Luttrell Psalter and the Making of Medieval England* (London, 1998)

Cogliati Arano, Luisa, *The Medieval Health Handbook*, trans. by Oscar Ratti and Adele Westbrook (London, 1970)

Convenevole da Prato, *Regia Carmina dedicati a Roberto d'Angiò re di Sicilia e di Gerusalemme*. 2 vols, ed. and trans. by Cesare Grassi et al. (Milan, 1982)

Crinelli, Lorenzo, ed., *Treasures from the Italian Libraries*, trans. by Eleanor Daunt Puccioni (London, 1997, first publ. as *Grandi tesori delle biblioteche italiane*, 1997)

Fabri, Francesca, 'Il "cocharelli": osservazione e ipotesi per un manoscritto genovese del XIV secolo', in *Tessuti, oreficerie, miniature in Liguria XIII–XV secolo. Atti del convegno internazionale di studi, Genova, Bordighera, 22–25 maggio 1997*, ed. by Anna R. Calderoni Masetti, C. di Fabio and M. Marcenaro (Bordighera, 1999), 305–20

Gardner, Arthur, *Alabaster Tombs of the Pre-reformation Period in England* (London, 1924)

Gibbs, Robert, 'Antifonario N: A Bolognese choirbook in the context of Genoese illumination between 1285 and 1385', in *Tessuti, oreficerie, miniature in Liguria XIII–XV secolo. Atti del convegno internazionale di studi, Genova, Bordighera, 22–25 maggio 1997*, ed. by Anna R. Calderoni Masetti, C. di Fabio and M. Marcenaro (Bordighera, 1999), 247–78

Hedeman, Anne D., *The Royal Image: Illustrations of the 'Grandes Chroniques de France,' 1274–1422* (Berkeley and Los Angeles, 1991)

Hunt, Tony, *The Medieval Surgery* (Woodbridge and Rochester, NY, 1992)

Kirsch, Edith W., *Five Illuminated Manuscripts of Giangaleazzo Visconti* (University Park, PA, and London, 1991)

Morgan, Nigel, 'The Coronation of the Virgin by the Trinity and other texts and images of the Glorification of Mary in fifteenth-century England', in *England in the Fifteenth Century: Proceedings of the 1992 Harlaxton Symposium*, ed. by Nicholas Rogers (Stamford, 1994), 223–41

Narkiss, Bezalel, *The Golden Haggadah* (London, 1997)

O'Meara, Carra Ferguson, *Monarchy and Consent: The Coronation Book of Charles V of France. British Library MS Cotton Tiberius B. VIII* (London and Turnhout, 2001)

Scott, Kathleen L., *Later Gothic Manuscripts 1390–1490*, in *Survey of Manuscripts Illuminated in the British Isles*, VI (London, 1996)

Sherman, Claire Richter, 'Representations of Charles V of France (1338–1380) as a wise ruler', *Medievalia et Humanistica*, n.s., no. 2 (1971), 83–96

Smith, Kathryn A., 'The Neville of Hornby Hours and the design of literate devotion', *The Art Bulletin*, 81 (1999), 72–92

Thomas, Marcel, *The Golden Age. Manuscript Painting at the Time of Jean, Duc de Berry*, trans. by Ursule Molinaro and Bruce Benderson (London, 1979)

Walther, Ingo F., *Codex Manesse. Die Miniaturen der Großen Heidelberger Liederhandschrift* (Frankurt am Main, 1988)

Welch, Evelyn S., *Art and Authority in Renaisance Milan* (New Haven and London, 1995)

DOCUMENTARY SOURCES

Anstey, Henry, ed., *Munimenta academica: or, Documents Illustrative of Academical Life and Studies at Oxford*, 2 vols, RS, 50 (London, 1868)

Baildon, W. Paley, 'A wardrobe account of 16–17 Richard II, 1393–4', *Archaeologia*, LXII (1911), 497–514

Boccaccio, Giovanni, *Decameron*, new edn by Vittore Branca, 2 vols (Turin, 1980)

Dean, Trevor, trans., *The Towns of Italy in the Later Middle Ages* (Manchester and New York, 2000)

Douët-d'Arcq, L., *Nouveau Recueil de comptes de l'argenterie des rois de France*, Société de l'histoire de France (Paris, 1874)

Fairholt, Frederick W., *Satirical Songs and Poems on Costume: from the 13th to the 19th Century*, Early English Poetry, Ballads and Popular Literature of the Middle Ages, XXVII (London: Percy Society [1849])

Félibien, Michel, *Histoire de la ville de Paris*, 5 vols (Paris, 1725): III

Gessler, Jean, ed., *Le Livre des Mestiers de Bruges et ses dérivés* (Bruges, 1931)

Gratian, *Decretum*, PL, 187 (Paris, 1891)

Graves, Frances Marjorie, *Deux Inventaires de la maison d'Orléans (1389 et 1408)* (Paris, 1926) (Some of the Orléans papers are in the British Library as Additional Charters.)

Jackson, Richard A., 'The Traité du sacre of Jean Golein', *Proceedings of the American Philosophical Society*, 113 (1969), 305–24

Jones, P.J., 'Travel notes of an apprentice Florentine statesman, Giovanni di Tommaso Ridolfi', in *Florence and Italy. Renaissance Studies in Honour of Nicolai Rubinstein*, ed. by Peter Denley and Caroline Elam (London, 1988), 263–80

La Tour Landry, Geoffroy de, *Le livre du Chevalier de la Tour Landry pour l'enseignement de ses filles*, ed. by A. de Montaiglon (Paris, 1854)

Mussis, Joannes de, *Chronicon Placentium ab anno 222 usque ad annum 1402*, in *Rerum Italicarum Scriptores*, ed. by L.A. Muratori, 16 (1723)

Petit, Ernest, 'Inventaire et testament de Jeanne de Chalon, comtesse de Tonnerre, 1360', *Bulletin de la société des sciences historiques et naturelles de l'Yonne*, 66 (1912), 653–77

Pisan, Christine de, *Le Livre des fais et bonnes meurs du sage roy Charles V*, 2 vols, ed. by S. Solente, Société de l'histoire de France (Paris, 1936–40)

Polo, Marco, *Il Milione*, ed. by Luigi Foscolo Benedetto (Florence, 1928)

Pseudo-Codinus, *Traité des offices*, ed. by Jean Verpeaux (Paris, 1966)

Rhodes, W.E., 'The inventory of the jewels and wardrobe of Queen Isabella (1307–8)', *English Historical Review*, 12 (1897), 517–21

Sacchetti, Franco, *Il trecentonovelle*, ed. by Davide Puccini (Turin, 2004)

Venette, Jean de, *The Chronicle of Jean de Venette*, trans. by Jean Birdsall and ed. by Richard A. Newhall (New York, 1953)

Verga, Ettore, 'Le legge suntuarie milanesi. Gli statuti del 1396 e del 1498', *Archivio storico lombardo*, 25 (1898), ser. 3, vol. IX, 5–79

Ward, Jennifer, *Women of the English Nobility and Gentry 1066–1500* (Manchester and New York, 1995)

SECONDARY SOURCES – DRESS

D'Ancona, Paolo, *Le vesti delle donne fiorentine nel secolo XIV* (Perugia, 1906)

Boucher, François, *A History of Costume in the West*, new enlarged edn (London, 1987)

Evans, Joan, *Dress in Mediaeval France* (Oxford, 1952)

Hargreaves-Mawdsley, W.N., *A History of Legal Dress in Europe until the End of the Eighteenth Century* (Oxford, 1963)

Laver, James, *A Concise History of Costume* (London, 1969)

Nevinson, John, 'Buttons and buttonholes in the fourteenth century', *Costume*, 11 (1977), 38–44

Newton, Stella Mary, *Fashion in the Age of the Black Prince: A Study of the Years 1340–1365* (Woodbridge, 1980)

Newton, Stella Mary, 'Queen Philippa's squirrel suit', in *Documenta Textilia: Festschrift für Sigrid Müller-Christensen*, ed. by Mechthild Flury-Lemberg and Karen Stolleis (Munich, 1981), 342–8

Scott, Margaret, *Late Gothic Europe, 1400–1500* (London and Atlantic Highlands, NJ, 1980)

Scott, Margaret, *A Visual History of Costume: The Fourteenth and Fifteenth Centuries* (London, 1986)

Staniland, Kay, 'Clothing and textiles at the court of Edward III 1342–1352', *Collectanea Londiniensia: Studies in London Archaeology and History Presented to Ralph Merrifield*, London and Middlesex Archaeological Society Special Paper, 2 (1978), 223–34

Staniland, Kay, 'The Great Wardrobe accounts as a source for historians of fourteenth-century clothing and textiles', *Textile History*, 20 (1989), 275–81

Staniland, Kay, 'Extravagance or regal necessity?: the clothing of Richard II', in *The Regal Image of Richard II and the Wilton Diptych*, ed. by Dillian Gordon, Lisa Monnas and Caroline Elam (London, 1997), 85–93

SECONDARY SOURCES – EXTANT DRESS

Blanc, Odile, 'Le pourpoint de Charles de Blois: une relique de la fin du moyen âge', *Bulletin du C.I.E.T.A.*, 74 (1997), 65–82

Crowfoot, Elisabeth, Frances Pritchard and Kay Staniland, *Textiles and Clothing c.1150–c.1450*, Medieval Finds from Excavations in London, 4 (London, 1992)

Grew, Francis, and Margrethe de Neergaard, *Shoes and Pattens*, Medieval Finds from Excavations in London, 2 (London, 1988)

Tarrant, Naomi, *The Development of Costume* (London, New York and Edinburgh, 1994)

Wilson, Verity, *Chinese Dress* (London, 1986)

See also Monnas (1992) in Secondary sources – textiles

SECONDARY SOURCES – TEXTILES

Cardon, Dominique, 'Echantillons de draps de laine des archives Datini (fin XIVe – début XVe siècle). Analyses techniques, importance historique', *Mélanges de l'école de Rome*, 103.1 (1991), 359–72

Monnas, Lisa, 'The cloth of gold of the pourpoint of the Blessed Charles de Blois; a Pannus Tartaricus?', *Bulletin du C.I.E.T.A.*, 70 (1992), 117–29

Monnas, Lisa, 'Dress and textiles in the St Louis Altarpiece: new light on Simone Martini's working practice', *Apollo*, CXXXVII (1993), 166–74

Monnas, Lisa, 'Textiles for the coronation of Edward III', *Textile History*, 32 (2001), 2–35

Newton, Stella Mary, and Mary M. Giza, 'Frilled edges', *Textile History*, 14 (1983), 141–52

Yver, Georges, *Le Commerce et les marchands dans l'Italie méridionale au XIIIe et au XIVe siècle* (Paris, 1903)

Chapter 4

BACKGROUND

Abulafia, David, ed., *The French Descent into Italy 1494–95. Antecedents and Effects* (Aldershot and Brookfield, VT, 1995)

Cole, Alison, *Art of the Italian Renaissance Courts: Virtue and Magnificence* (London, 1995)

Davis, Robert C., 'The geography of gender in the Renaissance', in *Gender and Society in Renaissance Italy*, ed. by Judith C. Brown and Robert C. Davis (London and New York, 1998), 19–38

Frati, Ludovico, *La vita privata di Bologna* (Bologna, 1900)

Gage, John, *Colour and Culture. Practice and Meaning from Antiquity to Abstraction* (London, 1993)

King, Margaret L., *The Death of the Child Valerio Marcello* (Chicago, 1994)

Mestre i Campi, Jesús, ed., *Diccionari d'historia de Catalunya* (Barcelona, 1992)

Molmenti, Pompeo, *La storia di Venezia nella vita privata dalle origini alla caduta della repubblica*, IV, *La Grandezza* (Bergamo, 1905)

Mosto, Andrea da, *I dogi di Venezia con particolare riguardo alle loro tombe* (Venice, 1939)

Nicholas, David, *Medieval Flanders* (London and New York, 1992)

Pavan, Elizabeth, 'Police des moeurs, société et politique à Venise à la fin du moyen âge', *Revue historique*, 264 (1980), 241–66

Pullan, Brian, '"Three Orders of Inhabitants": social hierarchies in the republic of Venice', in *Orders and Hierarchies in Late Medieval and Renaissance Europe*, ed. by Jeffrey Denton (Basingstoke and London, 1999), 147–68

Rainey, Ronald Eugene, 'Sumptuary legislation in Renaissance Florence', PhD thesis, Columbia University, 1985

Ruiz, Teofilo F., *Spanish Society, 1400–1600* (Harlow, London and New York, 2001)

Ryder, Alan, *The Kingdom of Naples under Alfonso the Magnanimous* (Oxford, 1976)

Shell, Jane, and Grazioso Sironi, 'Ceclia Gallerani: Leonardo's Lady with an Ermine', *Artibus et historiae*, XXV (1992), 47–66

Thompson, Guy Llewelyn, *Paris and its People under English Rule. The Anglo-Burgundian Regime 1420–1436* (Oxford, 1991)

Vale, M.G.A., *Charles VII* (London, 1974)

MANUSCRIPTS AND OTHER VISUAL MATERIAL

Andrea Mantegna, exh. cat., Royal Academy of Arts, London, and Metropolitan Museum of Art, New York, ed. by Jane Martineau (London, 1992)

Backhouse, Janet, 'Founders of the Royal Library: Edward IV and Henry VII as collectors of illuminated manuscripts', in *England in the Fifteenth Century. Proceedings of the 1986 Harlaxton Symposium*, ed. by Daniel Williams (Woodbridge and Wolfeboro, NH, 1987), 23–41

Backhouse, Janet, *The Bedford Hours* (London, 1990)

Baxandall, Michael, *Painting and Experience in Fifteenth-century Italy. A Primer in the Social History of Pictorial Style*, 2nd edn (Oxford and New York, 1988)

Brown, Patricia Fortini, *Venetian Narrative Painting in the Age of Carpaccio* (New Haven and London, 1988)

Brown, Patricia Fortini, *The Renaissance in Venice* (London, 1997)

Campbell, Lorne, *Renaissance Portraits* (New Haven and London, 1990)

Costanje, Charles van, Yves Cazan et al., *Vita sanctae Coletae (1381–1447)* (Tielt and Leiden, 1982)

Evans, Mark L., 'Jean Fouquet and Italy "...buono maestro, maxime a ritrarre del naturale"', in *Illuminating the Book. Makers and Interpreters. Essays in Honour of Janet Backhouse*, ed. by Michelle P. Brown and Scot McKendrick (London, Toronto and Buffalo, 1998), 163–89

Filangieri, Riccardo, ed., *Una cronaca napoletana figurata del Quattrocento* (Naples [1956])

Gothic. Art for England 1400–1547, exh. cat., Victoria and Albert Museum, London, ed. by Richard Marks and Paul Williamson (London, 2003)

Hedeman, Anne D., *The Royal Image: Illustrations of the 'Grandes Chroniques de France,' 1274–1422* (Berkeley and Los Angeles, 1991)

Hindman, Sandra, 'The composition of the manuscript of Christine de Pizan's collected works in the British Library: a reassessment', *The British Library Journal*, 9 (1983), 93–123

Illuminating the Renaissance: The Triumph of Flemish Manuscript Painting in Europe, exh cat., J. Paul Getty Museum, Los Angeles, and Royal Academy of Arts, London, 2003, ed. by Thomas Kren and Scot McKendrick (London, 2003)

Kren, Thomas, ed., *Margaret of York, Simon Marmion, and 'The Visions of Tondal'* (Malibu, 1992)

Meiss, Millard, *French Painting in the Time of Jean de Berry: The Limbourgs and Their Contemporaries*, 2 vols (London, 1974)

Mulas, Pier Luigi, 'Cum aparatu ac triumpho quo pagina in hac licet aspicere. L'investitura ducale di Ludovico Sforza, il messale Arcimboldi e alcuni problemi di miniatura lombarda', in *Artes*, II (1994), 5–38

The Painted Page. Italian Renaissance Book Illumination 1450–1550, exh. cat., Royal Academy of Arts, London, and Pierpont Morgan Library, New York, ed. by Jonathan J.G. Alexander (New York and Munich, 1994)

Paris 1400. Les Arts sous Charles VI, exh. cat., Musée du Louvre, Paris (Paris, 2004)

Penketh, Sandra, 'Women and books of hours', in *Women and the Book: Assessing the Visual Evidence*, ed. by Lesley Smith and Jane H.M. Taylor (London and Toronto, 1997), 266–81

Renaissance Painting in Manuscripts. Treasures from the British Library, exh. cat., British Library, London, J. Paul Getty Museum, Malibu, and Pierpont Morgan Library, New York, ed. by Thomas Kren (New York, 1983)

Splendours of the Gonzaga, exh. cat., Victoria and Albert Museum, London, ed. by David Chambers and Jane Martineau (London, 1981)

Sutton, Anne F., and Livia Visser-Fuchs, 'Choosing a Book in Late Fifteenth-century England and Burgundy', in *England and the Low Countries in the Late Middle Ages*, ed. by Caroline Barron and Nigel Saul (Stroud, 1995), 61–98

Trecanni, Giovanni, and Adolfo Venturi, *La bibbia di Borso d'Este* (Milan, 1937)

Welch, Evelyn, *Art and Society in Italy 1350–1500* (Oxford and New York, 1997)

DOCUMENTARY SOURCES

Anon, 'Racconti di storia napoletana', *Archivio storico per le provinc napoletane*, XXXIII (1908), 474–544

Baildon, W. Paley, 'The trousseau of Princess Philippa, wife of Eric, king of Denmark, Norway, and Sweden', *Archaeologia*, 67, 2nd series, 17 (1916) 163–88

Barclay, Alexander, *The Ships of Fools* (Edinburgh and London, 1874)

Barone, Nicola, 'Le cedole di tesoreria dell'archivio di stato di Napoli', *Archivio storico per le provinc napoletane*, IX (1884), 387–429

Beccadelli el Panormita, Antonio, *Dels fets e dits del gran rey Alfonso. Versio catalana del segle XV de Jordi de Centelles*, ed. by Eulàlia Duran (Barcelona, 1990)

Bellezza Rosina, Margherita, 'Tre corredi inediti della seconda metà del Quattrocento', in *Tessuti serici italiani 1450–1530*, exh. cat., Castello Sforzesco, Milan (Milan, 1983), 64–8

Bernardino of Siena, San, *Le prediche volgari...dette nella Piazza del Campo l'anno MCCCCXXVII*, 3 vols, ed. by Luciano Banchi (Siena, 1880–8)

Bisticci, Vespasiano da, *Vite di uomini illustri*, ed. by Paolo d'Ancona and Erhard Aeschliman (Milan, 1951)

De Blasiis, G., 'Tre scritture napoletane del secolo XV', *Archivio storico per le provinc napoletane*, IV (1879), 411–67

Brouwers, D.D., ed., *Mémoires de Jean, Sire de Haynin et de Louvignies 1465–1477*, 2 vols (Liège, 1905–6): I

Calzona, Arturo, 'L'abito alla corte dei Gonzaga', in *Il costume nell'età del Rinascimento*, ed. by Dora Liscia Bemporad (Florence, c.1988), 225–52

Chaucer, Geoffrey, *The Romaunt of the Rose, and Le Roman de la Rose. A parallel-text edition*, ed. by Ronald Sutherland (Oxford, 1967)

Du Clercq, Jacques, *Mémoires de Jacques du Clercq (1448–1467)*, ed. by Jean Alexandre Buchon, vols 37–40 of *Collection des chroniques nationales françaises*, 47 vols (Paris, 1826–8)

Corvisieri, C., 'Il trionfo romano di Eleonora d'Aragona nel giugno del 1473', *Archivio della reale società romana di storia patria*, X (1887), 629–87

Dallari, Umberto, and Luigi Alberto Gandini, 'Lo statuto suntuario bolognese del 1401 e il registro delle vesti bollate', *Atti e memorie della R. deputazione di storia patria per le provinc di Romagna*, ser. 3, VII (1889), 1–44

Diario ferrarese dall'anno 1409 sino al 1502 di autori incerti, ed. by Giuseppe Pardi. With Appendix *Diario ferrarese di Bernardino Zambotti (aa. 1476–1504)* (Bologna, 1933)

Laborde, Léon de, *Les Ducs de Bourgogne*, part II: *Preuves*, 3 vols (Paris, 1849–52)

The Lawes and Actes Maid be King Iames the First and His Successours of Scotland (Edinburgh, 1597)

Lecoy de La Marche, A., *Extraits des comptes et mémoriaux du roi René* (Paris, 1873)

Liber feudorum maior: cartulario real que se conserva en el Archivo de la Corona de Aragón, ed. by Francisco Miquel Rosell (Barcelona, 1945)

Luzio, Alessandro, and Rodolfo Renier, 'Delle relazioni di Isabella d'Este Gonzaga con Ludovico e Beatrice Sforza', *Archivio storico lombardo*, ser. 2, VII (1890), 346–99

Luzio, Alessandro, and Rodolfo Renier, 'Il lusso di Isabella d'Este marchesa di Mantova', *Nuova antologia*, ser. IV, LXIII (1896), 441–69

Madurell Marimón, José Ma., *Mensajeros barceloneses en la corte de Nápoles de Alfonso V de Aragón, 1435–1458* (Barcelona, 1963)

Minieri Riccio, Camillo, 'Alcuni fatti di Alfonso I di Aragona dal 15 aprile 1437 – 31 di maggio 1458', *Archivio storico per le provinc napoletane*, VI (1881), pp. 1–36, 231–58, 411–61

Natale, Alfio Rosario, 'Il diario di Cicco Simonetta', *Archivio storico lombardo*, ser. 8, V (1954–5), 292–318

Newett, M. Margaret, *Canon Pietro Casola's Pilgrimage to Jerusalem in the Year 1494* (Manchester, 1907)

Nicolas, Nicholas Harris, *Privy Purse Expenses of Elizabeth of York: Wardrobe Accounts of Edward the Fourth. With a Memoir of Elizabeth of York, and Notes* (London, 1830)

de Pisan, Christine, *The Treasure of the City of Ladies or the Book of the Three Virtues*, trans. by Sarah Lawson (Harmondsworth, 1985)

Pocquet du Haut-Jussé, B.-A., 'Anne de Bourgogne et le testament de Bedford (1429)', *Bibliothèque de l'école des chartes*, XCV (1934), 296–306

De Rosa, Loise, *Napoli aragonese nei ricordi di Loise de Rosa*, ed. by Antonio Altamura (Naples, 1971)

Santoro, Caterina, 'Un registro di doti sforzesche', *Archivio storico lombardo*, ser. 8, vol. III (1953), 133–85

Sicily Herald, *Le Blason des couleurs, en armes, livrées et devises par Sicile, hérault d'Alphonse V, roi d'Aragon*, ed. by Hippolyte Cocheris (Paris, 1860)

Strozzi, Alessandra, *A. Macinghi negli Strozzi. Lettere di una gentildonna fiorentina del secolo XV ai figliuoli esuli (1446–70)*, ed. by C. Guasti (Florence, 1877)

Sutton, Anne F. and P.W. Hammond, eds, *The Coronation of Richard III: the Extant Documents* (Gloucester and New York, 1983)

Toledo Girau, José, *Inventarios del Palacio Real de Valencia a la muerte de doña María, esposa de Alfonso el magnánimo* (Valencia, 1961)

Verga, Ettore, 'Le leggi suntuarie milanesi. Gli statuti del 1396 e del 1498', *Archivio storico lombardo*, ser. 3, IX (1898), 5–79

Viard, Jules, ed., *Les Grandes Chroniques de France*, 10 vols, Société de l'histoire de France (Paris, 1920–53)

DRESS – SECONDARY SOURCES

Anderson, Ruth Matilda, *Hispanic Costume 1480–1530* (New York, 1979)

Bernis, Carmen, *Trajes y modas en la España de los Reyes Católicos*, 2 vols (Madrid, 1978–9)

Bernis, Carmen, 'Modas españolas medievales en el renacimiento europeo', *Waffen- und Kostümkunde*, I (1959), 94–110; and II (1960), 27–40

Bridgeman, Jane, '"Pagare le pompe": why Quattrocento sumptuary laws did not work', in *Women in Italian Renaissance Culture and Society*, ed. by Letizia Panizza (Oxford, 2000), 209–26

Chabot, Isabelle, '"La sposa in nero": la ritualizzazione del lutto delle vedove fiorentine (secoli xiv–xv)', *Quaderni storici*, 86 (1994), 421–62

Dufresne, Laura Rinaldi, 'A woman of excellent character: a case study of dress, reputation and the changing costume of Christine de Pizan in the fifteenth century', Dress, 17 (1990), 104–17

Izbicki, Thomas M., 'Pyres of vanities: mendicant preaching on the vanities of women and its lay audience', in De Ore Domini. Preacher and Word in the Middle Ages, ed. by Thomas L. Amos, Eugene A. Green and Beverly Mayne Kienzle (Kalamazoo, MI, 1989), 211–34

Krueger, Roberta L., '"Nouvelles choses": social instability and the problem of fashion in the Livre du Chevalier de la Tour Landry, the Ménagier de Paris, and Christine de Pizan's Livre des Trois Vertus', in Medieval Conduct, ed. by Kathleen Ashley and Robert L. Clark, Medieval Cultures, 29 (Minneapolis and London, 2001), 49–85

Harvey, John, Men in Black (London, 1995)

Herald, Jacqueline, Renaissance Dress in Italy, 1400–1500 (London and Atlantic Highlands, NJ, 1981)

Montalto, Lina, La corte di Alfonso I di Aragona: vesti e gale (Naples, 1922)

Muzzarelli, Maria Giuseppina, Guardaroba medievale. Vesti e società dal XIII al XVI secolo (Bologna, 1999)

Newton, Stella Mary, The Dress of the Venetians, 1495–1525 (Aldershot, 1988)

Newton, Stella Mary, 'Gli abiti negli affreschi di Palazzo Schifanoia', in Atlante di Schifanoia, ed. by Ranieri Varese (Modena [1989]), 229–33

Pearce, Stella Mary, 'Classical dress and the Italian Renaissance', History Today, III (1952), 386–93

Piponnier, Françoise, Costume et vie sociale. La cour d'Anjou, XIVe–XVe siècle (Paris and The Hague, 1970)

Piponnier, Françoise, 'Le Costume nobiliaire en France au bas moyen âge d'après les inventaires bourguignons', in Adelige Sachkultur des Spätmittelalters: International Kongress Krems an der Donau 22. bis 25. September 1980 (Vienna, 1982), 343–63

Polidori Calamandrei, E., Le vesti delle donne fiorentine nel quattrocento (Florence, 1924)

Scott, Margaret, Late Gothic Europe, 1400–1500 (London, 1980)

Scott, Margaret, 'Dress in van Eyck's paintings', in Investigating Jan van Eyck, ed. by Susan Foister, Sue Jones and Delphine Cool (Turnhout, 2000), 133–45

Scott, Margaret, 'The role of dress in the image of Charles the Bold, Duke of Burgundy', in Flemish Manuscript Painting in Context: Selected Papers Presented in Conjunction with the Exhibition 'Illuminating the Renaissance', ed. by Thomas Kren and Elizabeth Morrison (forthcoming)

Vale, M.G.A., 'The livery colours of Charles VII of France in two works by Fouquet', Gazette des Beaux-Arts, LXXI (1969), 243–48

SECONDARY SOURCES – TEXTILES

Monnas, Lisa, 'The artists and the weavers: the design of woven silks in Italy 1350–1550', Apollo, vol. 125 (1987), 416–24

Monnas, Lisa, 'Italian silks (1300–1500)', in 5000 Years of Textiles, ed. by Jennifer Harris (London, 1993), 167–71

Monnas, Lisa, '"Tissues" in England during the fifteenth and sixteenth centuries', Bulletin du C.I.E.T.A., 75 (1998), 62–80

Thirsk, Joan, 'Knitting and Knitware [sic], c.1500–1780', in CT, I, 562–84

Chapter 5

BACKGROUND

Bryant, Lawrence M., 'The medieval entry ceremony at Paris', in Coronations: Medieval and Early Modern Monarchic Ritual, ed. by János M. Bak (Berkeley, 1990), 88–118

Giesey, Ralph E., 'The presidents of Parlement at the royal funeral', The Sixteenth Century Journal, VII (1976), 25–34

Goodman, Anthony, John of Gaunt. The Exercise of Princely Power in Fourteenth-Century Europe (Harlow, 1992)

Hutchison, Jane Campbell, Albrecht Dürer. A Biography (Princeton, NJ, 1990)

Kamen, Henry, Philip of Spain (New Haven, 1997)

Knecht, R.J., Renaissance Warrior and Patron: The Reign of Francis I (Cambridge, 1994)

Matarasso, Pauline, Queen's Mate. Three Women of Power in France on the Eve of the Renaissance (Aldershot and Burlington, VT, 2001)

Richardson, Glenn, Renaissance Monarchy. The Reigns of Henry VIII, Francis I and Charles V (London, 2002)

Russell, Joycelyne Gledhill, The Field of Cloth of Gold. Men and Manners in 1520 (London, 1969)

Schnapp, Alain, The Discovery of the Past (New York, 1997), trans. by Ian Kinnes and Gillian Varndell (Conquête du passé, Paris, 1993)

Sherman, Michael, 'Pomp and circumstances: pageantry, politics, and propaganda in France during the reign of Louis XII, 1498–1515', The Sixteenth Century Journal, IX (1978), 13–32

Starkey, David, ed., Henry VIII: A European Court in England (London, 1991)

MANUSCRIPTS AND OTHER VISUAL MATERIAL

Albuquerque, Martim de, and João Paulo de Areu e Lima, António de Holanda e Simão Bening: La genealogia do Infante Dom Fernando de Portugal. Facsímile do MS. da British Library, Add. 12531 (Oporto and Lisbon, 1984)

Anglo, Sydney, The Great Tournament Roll of Westminster: A Collotype Reproduction of the Manuscript (Oxford, 1968)

Bloem, Hélène M., 'The processions and decorations at the royal funeral of Anne of Brittany', Bibliothèque d'Humanisme et Renaissance, LIV (1992), 131–60

Buck, Stephanie, and Jochen Sander, Hans Holbein at the Court of Henry VIII (London, 2003)

Carley, James P., The Books of Henry VIII and His Wives (London, 2004)

Chotzen, Th. M., and A.M.E. Draak, Beschrijving der Britische eilanden door Lucas de Heere (Antwerp, 1937)

Deserps, François, A Collection of the Various Styles of Clothing which are presently worn in countries of Europe, Asia, Africa, and the savage islands, all realistically depicted 1562, ed. and trans. by Sara Shannon (Minneapolis, 2001)

Dynasties. Painting in Tudor and Jacobean England 1530–1630, exh. cat., Tate Gallery, London, ed. by Karen Hearn (London, 1995)

Fink, August, Die Schwarzen Trachtenbücher (Berlin, 1963)

Gardner, Arthur, Alabaster Tombs of the Pre-reformation Period in England (London, 1924)

Illuminating the Renaissance. The Triumph of Flemish Manuscript Painting in Europe, exh. cat., J. Paul Getty Museum, Los Angeles, and Royal Academy of Arts, London, ed. by Thomas Kren and Scot McKendrick (Los Angeles and London, 2003)

Jones, Michael, 'Les manuscrits d'Anne de Bretaigne', Mémoires de la société d'histoire et d'archéologie de Bretagne, LV (1978), 43–81

Pächt, Otto, and J.J.G. Alexander, Illuminated Manuscripts in the Bodleian Library, I, German, Dutch, Flemish, French and Spanish Schools (Oxford, 1966)

Renaissance Painting in Manuscripts. Treasures from the British Library, exh. cat., British Library, London, J. Paul Getty Museum, Malibu, and Pierpont Morgan Library, New York, ed. by Thomas Kren (New York, 1983)

Rowlands, John, Drawings by German Artists and Artists from German-speaking Regions of Europe in the Department of Prints and Drawings in the British Museum: The Fifteenth Century, and the Sixteenth Century by Artists born before 1530, 2 vols (London, 1993)

Scailliérez, Cécile, 'Un portrait méconnu de François Ier peint par Jean Clouet: le frontispice des Histoires de Diodore de Sicile au musée Condé de Chantilly', Revue du Louvre, XLVI (1996), 47–52

Scailliérez, Cécile, François Ier par Clouet (Paris, 1996)

Sherman, Claire R. 'The queen in Charles V's Coronation Book: Jeanne de Bourbon and the Ordo ad Reginam Benedicendam', Viator, 8 (1977), 255–98

Strong, Roy, The English Icon: Elizabethan and Jacobean Portraiture (London, 1969)

Weiditz, Christoph, Das Trachtenbuch des Christoph Weiditz von seinen Reisen nach Spanien, 1529, und den Niederlanden, 1531–32, ed. by Theodor Hampe et al. (Berlin and Leipzig, 1925)

Vecellio, Cesare, De gli Habiti antichi et moderni di Diverse Parti del Mondo (Venice, 1590)

DOCUMENTARY SOURCES

Borde, Andrew, *The fyrst boke of the introduction of knowledge*, ed. by James Hogg, Analecta Cartusiana, 92 (Salzburg, 1979)

Byrne, Muriel St Clare, ed., *The Lisle Letters*, 6 vols (Chicago, 1981)

Calendar of state papers and manuscripts, relating to English affairs, existing in the archives and collections of Venice, and in other libraries of northern Italy, vol. 2, 1509–1519, ed. by Rawdon Brown (London, 1867)

Castiglione, Baldassare, *Il libro del cortegiano* (Rome, 1986), reprint of edn of 1528 (Venice)

Choque, Pierre, dit Bretaigne, 'Discours des cérémonies du mariage d'Anne de Foix, de la maison de France, avec Ladislas VI, roi de Bohème, de Pologne et de Hongrie', ed. by Antoine Jean Victor Le Roux de Lincy, *Bibliothèque de l'école des chartes*, 5e série, II (1861), 156–85 and 422–39

Cocheris, Hippolyte, ed., *Entrées de Marie d'Angleterre femme de Louis XII à Abbeville et à Paris* (Paris, 1859)

Compota Thesauriarorum Regum Scotorum. Accounts of the Lord High Treasurer of Scotland, VI, A.D. 1531–1538, ed. by James Balfour Paul (Edinburgh, 1905)

Elyot, Thomas, *The Boke named the Governour* (London and New York, 1907)

Hall, Edward, *The Triumphant Reigne of Kyng Henry the VIII*, ed. by Charles Whibley (London, 1904)

Lalaing, Antoine de, Seigneur de Montigny, *Voyage de Philippe le Beau en Espagne, en 1501*, in *Collection des voyages des souverains des Pays-Bas*, I (Brussels, 1876), 121–340

Le Glay, André, et al., eds, *Inventaire-sommaire des archives départementales antérieures à 1790…Nord. Répertoire numérique série B*, 10 vols (Lille, 1863–1908), VII

Letters and Papers, Foreign and Domestic, of the Reign of Henry VIII, Preserved in the Public Record Office, the British Museum and Elsewhere, ed. by J.S. Brewer et al., 21 vols and addenda (London, 1826–1932), I, part II, and V

Luzio, Alessandro, and Rodolfo Renier, 'Il lusso di Isabella d'Este marchesa di Mantova', *Nuova antologia*, ser. IV, LXIII (1896), 441–69

More, Thomas, *Utopia*, ed. by J. Churton Collins (Oxford, 1904)

Rabelais, François, *Gargantua*, ed. by Ruth Calder, M.A. Screech and V.L. Saulnier (Geneva, 1970)

Starkey, David, ed., *The Inventory of King Henry VIII: Society of Antiquaries MS 129 and British Library MS Harley 1419* (London, 1998)

Vives, Juan Luis de, *De Institutione Feminae Christianae: The Education of a Christian Woman. A Sixteenth-century Manual*, ed. by Charles Fantazzi (Chicago and London, c.2000)

SECONDARY SOURCES – DRESS

Anderson, Ruth Matilda, *Hispanic Costume, 1480–1530* (New York, 1979)

Anderson, Ruth Matilda, 'Spanish dress worn by a queen of France', *Gazette des Beaux-Arts*, 98 (1981), 215–22

Arnold, Janet, *Queen Elizabeth's Wardrobe Unlock'd* (Leeds, 1990)

Ashelford, Jane, *A Visual History of Costume. The Sixteenth Century* (London, 1983)

Currie, Elizabeth, 'Prescribing fashion: dress, politics and gender in sixteenth-century Italian conduct literature', *Fashion Theory*, 4 (2000), 157–78

Dihle, Helene, 'Nachklänge der spanischen Tracht', *Waffen- und Kostümkunde*, 16 (1974), 1–20

Doege, Heinrich, 'Die Trachtenbücher des 16. Jahrhunderts', in *Beiträge zur Bücherkunde und Philologie*, ed. by August Wilmanns (Leipzig, 1903), 429–44

Hayward, Maria, '"The sign of some degree"?: the financial, social and sartorial significance of male headwear at the courts of Henry VIII and Edward VI', *Costume*, 36 (2002), 1–17

Nevinson, John, 'The dress of the citizens of London 1540–1640', *Collectanea Londiniensia: Studies in London Archaeology and History Presented to Ralph Merrifield*, London and Middlesex Archaeological Society Special Paper No. 2 (1978), 265–80

Newton, Stella Mary, *Renaissance Theatre Costume and the Sense of the Historic Past* (London, 1975)

Olian, Jo Anne, 'Sixteenth-century costume books', *Dress*, 3 (1977), 20–45

Petrascheck-Heim, Ingeborg, 'Tailors' Masterpiece-books', *Costume*, 3 (1969), 6–9

Post, Paul, 'Das Kostüm der deutschen Renaissance 1480–1550', *Anzeiger des Germanischen Nationalmuseums* (1954–9), 21–42

Reade, Brian, *Costume of the Western World. The Dominance of Spain 1550–1660* (London, 1951)

Venturelli, Paola, *Vestire e apparire. Il sistema vestimentario femminile nella Milano spagnola (1539–1679)* (Rome, 1999)

Zander-Seidel, Jutta, *Textiler Hausrat: Kleidung und Haustextilien in Nürnberg von 1500–1650* (Munich, 1990)

Glossary

Bareta and variants thereof (It) Man's cap or bonnet.

Base coat (Eng M) Garment with gored skirts, worn on its own or between doublet and gown in late fifteenth and early sixteenth centuries.

Beccho/ becchetto (It) Strip of cloth that formed the tail of a hood, like the French *cornette* and English liripipe. Retained in Venice as a strip of cloth about 10 inches (25 cm) wide, worn over the shoulder by noble and citizen men.

Bliaut (Fr) Seems to have been a word for a very rich silk, often with gold thread in it, deriving from the German word *Plialt* for such a silk. In Germany the original meaning was kept; in France the meaning was extended to describe a sleeved garment made from such a silk. The word also sometimes meant a sleeved garment, whatever it was made of.

Bogy shanks (Eng) Sheepskin; 'bogy' derives from the port of Bougie in North Africa, which used to export sheepskins.

Bourrelet (Fr) Padded roll worn by women as headdress, in various shapes, in the first half of the fifteenth century. Also, the padded face-opening of men's hoods in the same period. From French *bourrer*, to stuff.

Braccio (It) Measurement of length, varying between 23 and 25 inches (58–64 cm).

Brial (Sp F) Upper-class Spanish woman's gown, made of expensive fabrics. Usually decorated with horizontal bands of contrasting fabric, which were stuffed to create early form of farthingale. Highly fashionable in 1480s; less so thereafter. In Naples called *briale*.

Brocade (Eng) Fabric in which variously coloured threads used to make a pattern are confined to the area of the pattern, as opposed to being carried across the entire width of the fabric at the back.

Brunette (Fr) Type of woollen fabric, possibly a very dark brown-purple, though sometimes specified as being black *brunette*. Probably served as an acceptable alternative for black.

Camora/gamurra (It) Woman's under-tunic, made of expensive fabric, worn in summer. At the end of the fifteenth century becomes word for 'gown'.

Cendal (Eng) Lightweight silk, used as lining for clothes in summer, eleventh to fourteenth centuries.

Chainse (Fr) Under-tunic in French romances. Usually white.

Chlamys (Gk) Cloak with curved lower edge, worn with opening at the side. In Byzantine dress the side edges were decorated with panels called *tablia*.

Codpiece (Eng M) Junction of men's stockings at the crotch. Frequently padded and decorated in sixteenth century.

Cornettes (Fr) Tails on sleeves in fourteenth century and on hoods in fourteenth and fifteenth centuries.

Coote (coat) (Eng M) Open-fronted garment worn on its own or between doublet and gown in sixteenth century.

Cote (Fr) Under-tunic.

Cote hardie (Fr) Lterally 'daring *cote*'. Worn in fourteenth and early fifteenth centuries. Women's versions were tight-fitting outer garments.

Cotta (It) Under-tunic. In fifteenth century, women's under-dress worn in winter.

Cottardita (It) Deriving from *cote hardie*?

Dagging (Eng) Slashed edges, cut in various patterns, on clothing in the fourteenth and early fifteenth centuries. Pieces survive in the Museum of London.

Dalmatic (from Lat M) Short-sleeved, open-sided garment worn by priests, especially by deacons.

Included in some coronation robes as mark of quasi-clerical status of rulers.

Diapre (Fr) or diaspryn (Eng) A silk widely used between the eleventh and fourteenth centuries. Its earliest forms had white-on-white patterns of birds and animals.

Divetesion (Gk M) Most formal of tunics worn at the Byzantine court. Decorated with gold bands at the arms and hem. Only the emperor could wear a purple *divetesion*.

Doublet (Eng M) Short, jacket-like garment, often padded, worn over shirt and under gown, from latter part of fourteenth century.

Ermine (Eng) White winter fur of a member of the weasel family, with black spots, each spot supposedly the tail of one animal.

Flanders gown (Eng F) Name given to a coat-like gown, fastening on the bodice only, with short puffed sleeves, worn especially in the 1550s, 1560s and 1570s. Often black, with trimming (guards) in contrasting fabric or colour.

French hood (Eng F) Name used in English sources for a head-covering worn by upper-class French and Netherlandish women from about 1490 until about 1550, and by Englishwomen increasingly from about 1530. Characterized by, at first, black frontlets on a small cap behind.

French gown (Eng F) Name used in English sources in sixteenth century for a gown with a square front neckline and wide sleeves, turned back on themselves to reveal contrasting linings.

Frontlet (Eng F) Name conventionally given to the strip of black fabric worn at the front of Franco-Flemish steeple-shaped headdresses in the 1460s and 1470s, and the early versions of the French hood.

Gamurra (see *Camora*)

Giornea (It) Sleeveless outer garment, joined only on the shoulders; short on men, full-length on women, who wore it in the summer. Common in fifteenth century.

Goun, gown (Eng) Word for garment resembling *houppelande*, and then for sleeved outer garments that followed it.

Guard (Eng) Trimming in contrasting fabric or colour at edges of garments in sixteenth century.

Heuque (Fr M) Sleeveless outer garment, joined only on the shoulders; frequently issued to bodyguards. Similar to the Italian *giornea*, though apparently, unlike the *giornea*, rarely worn belted; rare references to *heuques* for women.

Himation (Gk) Rectangular cloak, slung under the right arm and over the left shoulder.

Houce (Fr) Long outer garment with cape-sleeves to elbow level and 'tongues' (of fur) on chest. Worn late thirteenth to late fourteenth centuries.

Houppelande (Fr) Sleeved, front-closing outer garment worn by both sexes, introduced *c.*1360 and disappearing from fashion around 1430. Always full-length on women; sometimes short on men. Characterized *c.*1400 and later by huge sleeves.

Kabbadion (Gk M) Apparently a narrow, sleeved, centre-front closing garment. Described in 899 by Philotheos in the *Kletorologion* as the dress of the *ethnikoi* (foreigners). Over the centuries it was absorbed into the wardrobe of the imperial court.

Kermes (Eng) The fastest and most expensive red dye available. Derived from the dried pregnant bodies of an insect, the *coccus ilicis*, found in Mediterranean regions. Root of the word 'crimson'.

Lampas silks (Eng) Patterned silks produced by a technique introduced around 1000 in the eastern Mediterranean. Identifiable accurately only by examination of the fabrics themselves; but patterns involved include pairs of animals or birds.

Lettice (Eng) A white fur, from animal of weasel family, that could substitute for ermine.

Liripipe (Eng) The tail of a hood.

Loros (Gk) Jewelled band worn by high-ranking members of Byzantine court, and representing a vestigial survival of the ancient Roman *toga*. Word implies it was made of leather (*lorion* means 'strip of leather').

Maniple (Eng) A strip of fabric, hung on the priest's left arm during the celebration of the Eucharist.

Marten (Eng) fur of member of the weasel family, dark in colour; fashionable from middle of fifteenth century.

Miniver (Eng) The side and belly fur of the European squirrel, caught in winter. Identifiable by characteristic shield-shape of white centre (belly), edged in grey (sides).

Mi-parti (Fr) Dividing of clothes vertically into two different colours and/or patterns. Fashionable at end of twelfth century and again from 1320s. Remained in use, especially in Italy, for livery stockings, into fifteenth century.

Pallium (Lat) Roman name for the rectangular cloak worn by the Greeks, which many Romans adopted because it was comparatively easy to wear.

Peliçon, pellison or pliçon, and variants thereof (Fr). *Pel* means 'skin' or 'fur'. In twelfth century the term refers to a garment on which the most important feature is the fur that it contains, presumably because it was worn on the outside.

Pellanda (It) Garment equivalent to the northern *houppelande*.

Pellote (Sp) Sleeveless over-tunic with, in thirteenth century, scooped-out sides and fur lining. Presumably linked to the Latin word for 'fur' (*pellis*).

Peplum (Lat) Can mean 'cloak', but seems more frequently to mean 'veil'.

Purpura (Lat) Could originally have meant 'purple cloth', but the term seems to have changed gradually to mean some type of high-quality silk cloth, possibly shiny, and not necessarily purple in colour.

Riccio sopra riccio (It, 'loop over loop') Type of cloth of gold probably invented in 1420s, with areas of pattern in velvet, through which gold loops of varying heights protrude. The most expensive type of cloth of gold. Known in English as 'tissue'.

Roba (Lat), *robe* (Fr) Initially a set of garments, often made from the same fabric. Around 1430 changed to refer to a sleeved outer garment.

Rock (Ger) In twelfth century, a richly patterned over-tunic. Word survives into later periods as outer layer, such as a gown.

Sable (Eng) Fur of marten-like animal, highly prized when it was black. Fashionable from middle of fifteenth century. There are references to *martres sebellines*, suggesting that the furs were confused, or that one was treated to resemble the other.

Samite (Eng, from Gk meaning 'six threads') Slightly shiny silk with pronounced diagonal rib in the weave; fashionable until fourteenth century.

Samitum rotatum (Lat, singular), *samita rotata* (plural) Samite with pattern of roundels containing animals, birds, flowers.

Saya encordada (Sp) Garment laced at the side.

Sayon (Fr M) Probably akin to the English base coat.

Sbernia (It F) Cloak, worn under one arm and over the other shoulder, at end of fifteenth century in northern Italy.

Scarlet (Eng) Literally 'shorn cloth'; highest-quality woollen cloth, usually dyed in kermes.

Skaramangion (Gk) Byzantine silk tunic of Persian origin. Apparently, like a *divetesion*, trimmed with gold bands, but unlike it, never worn on most formal occasions.

Strandling (Eng) The fur of the European squirrel taken in autumn; has a reddish tinge around the white belly-fur.

Stomacher (Eng) Piece of fabric that was placed at front of male doublet, at end of fifteenth and start of sixteenth centuries; and at front of women's bodices.

Supertunica (Lat) Anglicized as 'super-tunic'. Possibly synonymous with *surcot(e)*.

Surcot(e) (Fr) General term used from end of twelfth century into fourteenth century to describe outer garment. Also called *sourcos, sorcot(e)*; in Italian, *surcotto*.

Surcot(e) ouverte (Fr F) Woman's sleeveless *surcote*, with armholes that deepened towards the hips in the middle of the fourteenth century. Retained as symbol of rank for aristocratic women into sixteenth century.

Tablion (Gk M) A decorative panel on the vertical edge of the *chlamys*.

Tartar silk (Eng) Silk originally from the East, with small, not necessarily representational, patterns in metal threads. Much sought after in Europe at end of thirteenth century, and imitated by various weaving centres after that time. Remained popular into the fourteenth century.

Tippet (Eng) The 'tail' that hung from the sleeves of outer garments in the fourteenth century.

Tissue (Eng) See *Riccio sopra riccio*.

Tranzado (Sp F) Upper-class female headdress, in which the hair was drawn to the back of the head and wrapped in a long scarf attached to a small coif. Often made of fine linen and embroidered. Found in later fifteenth and early sixteenth centuries.

Toga (Lat) Cloak, possibly semi-circular, of Roman citizens; extremely cumbersome to wear. Also, gown of citizens of Venice; and generic term for gown in texts written in Latin.

Tunic (Eng) From Latin *tunica*. Strictly speaking, a T-shaped garment, worn between the undershirt and the outer layer, such as the *toga*. Convenient term for simply shaped, sleeved garments.

Upper stocks (Eng M) Sixteenth century, stockings for the upper legs.

Index

Page numbers in *italics* refer to illustrations and their captions.

First published 2007 by
The British Library
96 Euston Road
London NW1 2DB

Text copyright © Margaret Scott
Pictures copyright © The British Library Board
and other named copyright holders

British Library Cataloguing-in-Publication
Data
A CIP record for this volume is available from
The British Library

ISBN 0 7123 0675 7
ISBN 978 0 7123 0675 1

Designed and typeset by
Andrew Barron @ thextension
Printed in Hong Kong by
South Sea International Press

The British Library would like to thank all
copyright holders for permission to reproduce
material and illustrations. While every effort
has been made to trace and acknowledge
copyright holders, we would like to apologize
for any errors or omissions.

Front jacket illustration: Louis of Orléans
receiving a book from Christine de Pisan
(Collected Works of Christine de Pisan, Paris,
Cité des dames Master and shop, c.1415:
British Library, Harley MS 4431, f. 95r, detail)

Back jacket illustration: Figure in Spanish
secular dress (Gratian, Decretals, Spain:
Barcelona?, mid-1300s: British Library, Add.
MS 15274, f. 185, initial)

Page 3 illustration: Two youths in doublet and
hose, one pair in mi-parti (Spiegel der Weisheit,
Austria, c.1415: British Library, Egerton MS
1121, f. 51v)